A Synthesis of Research on What Works in High-Performing, High-Poverty Schools

The Kids Left Behind

Catching Up the Underachieving Children of Poverty

ROBERT D. BARR
WILLIAM H. PARRETT

Foreword by Kati Haycock

Solution Tree | Press

a division of
Solution Tree

555 North Morton Street
Bloomington, IN 47404
800.733.6786 (toll free) / 812.336.7700
FAX: 812.336.7790

email: info@solution-tree.com
solution-tree.com

Cover Design by Grannan Graphic Design, Ltd.
Text Design and Composition by Steve French

Printed in the United States of America

ISBN 978-1-935542-35-3

Table of Contents

About the Authors

Robert D. Barr, Ph.D., is a nationally recognized scholar, speaker, and author who has been quoted in the *New York Times* and has appeared on national television programs such as *Firing Line* with William Buckley, *ABC Evening News With Peter Jennings,* and the *O'Reilly Factor.* Dr. Barr has served as an expert witness at many state and federal trials and has presented testimony to subcommittees of the U.S. Congress. His work in teacher education has earned three national awards for excellence in teacher education: the AACTE Distinguished Achievement Award, the AASA Showcase of Excellence Award, and the Theodore Mitou Award. Dr. Barr has had extensive international experience as well.

Dr. Barr is the former director of teacher education at Indiana University and dean of the College of Education at Oregon State University. He is currently senior analyst for the Center for School Improvement and Policy Studies, where he directs a project funded by the J. A. and Kathryn Albertson Foundation on the National Board for Professional Teaching Standards. Dr. Barr has authored or coauthored eight books.

William H. Parrett, Ph.D., is the director of the Center for School Improvement and Policy Studies, where he coordinates funded projects and reform initiatives that exceed $1.2 million annually. He has received international recognition for his work in school improvement, small schools, and alternative education, and for his efforts to help youth at risk. He consults with state departments, boards of education, state and regional service providers, and school districts in 35 states and 8 nations. His professional experiences include public school and university teaching, curriculum design, principalships, college leadership, and media production. Dr. Parrett holds a Ph.D. in secondary education from Indiana University and is currently a professor of education at Boise State University.

Dr. Parrett is the author or coauthor of eight books and numerous contributions to national publications and international and national conferences. His documentary, *Heart of the Country* (1998), was nominated for the Pare Lorentz Award at the 1999 International Documentary Awards and has won the Award of Commendation from the American Anthropological Association, a Gold Apple Award from the National Education Media Network Festival, a National CINE Golden Eagle Award, and a Judges' Award at the 24th Northwest Film Festival. In addition, *Heart of the Country* was an invited feature and screened at the Cinema du Reel festival in Paris (1998) and the Margaret Mead Film Festival (1998) in New York City.

Drs. Parrett and Barr are also the coauthors of *Saving Our Students, Saving Our Schools* (2003, Corwin), *Hope Fulfilled for At-Risk and Violent Youth: K–12 Programs That Work* (2001, Allyn & Bacon), and *How To Create Alternative, Magnet, and Charter Schools That Work* (1997, Solution Tree).

Preface

The Kids Left Behind could not have happened without the assistance and support of many groups and individuals. First, we are deeply indebted to the scholars, educators, evaluators, and authors who were responsible for the 18 studies, reports, and data analyses of high-poverty, high-performing schools that are the foundation of this work. Collectively, these pioneering efforts to identify how schools and districts have closed the achievement gap for underachieving poor students provide a blueprint for America's districts and schools.

We offer our heartfelt respect and gratitude to Kati Haycock, executive director of the Education Trust, one of the leading organizations committed to advocacy for students of poverty. In addition to writing the foreword, she found time to review our early manuscripts and provided insight and suggestions that helped shape this book.

We also extend our appreciation to the authors and supporting organizations of each of the included studies, reports and data analyses. They include: G. Borman, G. Hewes, L. Overman, and S. Brown (Center for Research on the Education of Students Placed at Risk); S. Carter (Heritage Foundation); B. Goodwin (Mid-continent Research for Education and Learning); J. Greene and G. Forster (Manhattan Institute, Center for Civic Innovation); C. Jerald (Education Trust); P. Kannapel and S. Clements (Prichard Committee for Academic Excellence); R. Kitchen, J. DePree, S. Celedon-Pattichis, and J. Brinkerhoff (University of New Mexico); G. Manset, D. Gordon, M. Richie, E. St. John (North Central Regional Educational Laboratory); D. Massell (Center for Policy Research); G. McGee (Northern Illinois University Center for Governmental Studies); D. Reeves (Center for Performance Assessment); J. Richardson (National Staff Development Council); J. Rutherford (Just for the Kids / National Center for Educational Accountability); C. Teddlie and S. Stringfield (Teachers College Press); W. Togneri and S. Anderson (Learning First Alliance); T. Williams, M. Kirst, and E. Haertel (EdSource); the Iowa Association of School Boards; and the U.S. Department of Education.

We also humbly thank the thousands of educators in the remarkable schools studied by the above listed authors and organizations. Indeed, their work, dedication, and successes made these among the first schools in the nation to demonstrate that underachieving poor and minority students can indeed achieve high standards.

We hope that our efforts to compile and represent their achievements do justice to the daily work in each of their districts, schools, and classrooms, and we hope that this book will lead to similar student achievement and successes in all schools.

The preparation and writing of this book initially began with the identification and analysis of 11 studies, and over the next year, 6 more were added as they became available. The last study was analyzed and inserted in the spring of 2006, as the book was being formatted for publication. We believe these studies represent a most timely resource for educators struggling to close achievement gaps for poor and minority students across the United States. Again, we extend our deepest professional appreciation to the scholars and organizations who are responsible for these important studies.

As in each of our earlier books, we have supplemented our research and analysis with interviews, discussions, and observations from our recent work in schools and districts in 41 states. While this manuscript was in development, we presented at over two dozen national conferences and met with scholars at Boise State University, George Washington University, Ohio State University, Oregon State University, UCLA, the University of Alaska, the University of Iowa, the University of Toronto, and the University of Washington. We have worked with advocacy organizations including the Texas Public Policy Foundation, the Mercatus Center at George Mason University, the Idaho Association of Commerce and Industry, the Alaska Council on Economic Education, the National Dropout Prevention Center/ Network, the National Alternative Education Association, the California Education Alliance, the National School Boards Association, the National Staff Development Council, the Association for Supervision and Curriculum Development, and the American Association of School Administrators. Interaction with each of these organizations gave us unique opportunities to share our preliminary conclusions, discuss public policy issues, and gain valuable information.

We owe a particular word of thanks to the J. A. and Kathryn Albertson Foundation, in particular Joe Scott, chairman; Jamie Skillern, director; Tom Wilford, chief executive officer; Lori Fisher, executive director; and their colleagues and other board members for the Foundation's unprecedented support of school improvement in the state of Idaho. Through Foundation partnerships, many Idaho schools, like nationally recognized Lapwai Elementary, have emerged as beacons of improvement for any school or district committed to ensuring proficiency and success for every child.

We have also been welcomed, assisted, supported, and occasionally corrected by several most knowledgeable individuals. Harold Ott, superintendent, and Teri Wagner, elementary principal of the Lapwai School District helped us envision one school's dramatic improvement and challenged us to share the lessons learned there. Lapwai's successes represent collaboration throughout the district's certified and classified staff, the parents, and community. Our thanks also go to school board representatives Julie Kane and Brenna Terry and all of the other members who have worked diligently to support and guide the Lapwai District. Our friends and colleagues Rick Stiggins and Michael Fullan carefully reviewed our manuscript and provided invaluable insight and recommendations. Finally, Jay Goldman, editor of the American Association of School Administrator's *School Administrator* and his staff helped us craft and share the Lapwai story.

Throughout the book, we have included quotes from our interviews and practical, firsthand examples of practices and innovations that work. For these, we have many state leaders to acknowledge and thank. Special appreciation goes out to our many friends and colleagues at a number of state departments of education. In Oregon, we thank Susan Castillo, superintendent of public instruction; Pat Burke, deputy superintendent for policy; Vickie Fleming, assistant state superintendent; and Donna Bolt, director of special projects. In Idaho, we thank Marybeth Flachbart, bureau chief of special population services; Margo Healy, director of student achievement and school accountability; and Rose Rettig, director of Reading First. In Iowa, we thank Ray Morley, director of at-risk programs, and in Oklahoma, Sandy Garrett, superintendent of education.

Other colleagues opened the doors to their districts, schools, and classrooms and allowed us to observe and converse. We express our gratitude to the following and apologize to any we may have failed to acknowledge: Harry Martin and Linda Hardin in Ketchikan, Alaska; Darrell Smith in Wynn, Arkansas; Stan Olsen, Ann Farris, and Susan Williamson in Boise, Idaho; Clemmye Jackson in Ames, Iowa; Eric Smith in Annapolis, Maryland; Barb Mukenhirn in Redwing, Minnesota; Rick Harris, Juanita Jeanney, and Denise Galluos in Reno, Nevada; Patricia Cloud in Santa Fe, New Mexico; Dawn Tarzian in Corvallis, Oregon; George Russell in Eugene, Oregon; Jannine Weeks in Nyssa, Oregon; Nancy Golden and Paul Weill in Springfield, Oregon; John Metcalfe and Tom Martin in Lander, Wyoming; and the educators of Norfolk, Virginia; Charlotte-Mecklenburg, North Carolina; and Aldine and Brazosport, Texas.

We also sincerely appreciate the support of a number of individuals affiliated with national and state organizations who invited us to share our ongoing work.

They include Debbie Brown and Ann Cunningham-Morris of the Association for Supervision and Curriculum Development; Gina Van Horn of the California Education Alliance; Sybil Fickle, Georgia Southern University; Linda Shirley, John Peters, and Jay Smink of the National Dropout Prevention Center/Network; Kanisha Williams-Jones of the National School Boards Association; Hae Yung Kim and Cheryl Williams of Teachscape; Marc Levin of the Texas Public Policy Foundation; and Barb McClure-Lukens of the University of Wisconsin–Green Bay.

We also express our appreciation to Steve and Jan Chappuis at the ETS Assessment Training Institute; Dennis White at George Washington University; Dan Rea at Georgia Southern University; George Jackson at Iowa State University; Diana Leigh at Ohio State University; Sam Stern at Oregon State University; Steve Jackstadt at the University of Alaska–Anchorage; Fritz Erickson at University of Wisconsin–Green Bay; Jim Stigler at UCLA and the LessonLab; Diane Boothe, Kathleen Budge, Ken Coll, Jonathan Brendefur, Phil Kelly, Roger Stewart, Ross Vaughn, and Scott Willison at Boise State University; and Boise State University doctoral students Marybeth Flachbart, Margo Healy, Celia King, Lisa Kinnaman, Sheila Scott, and Jane Walther, who each read early drafts and provided timely feedback. We are especially indebted to Deb Yates, assistant professor at Albertson College of Idaho. Deb first heard Bob Barr speaking in Indianapolis 10 years ago, later came to Boise State to study with us, and became Barr's last doctoral student. She not only coauthored his last book, *Welcome to Middletown* (Solution Tree, 2006), but constantly "trolled" the Internet, finding late-breaking research that was used throughout this book.

Our heartfelt thanks go to the Center for School Improvement and Policy Studies staff; Diana Esbensen, Jenny Newhouse, and Kerri Pickett provided much-needed assistance throughout this project. We couldn't have done this without your support.

Our thanks also go out to the many folks at Solution Tree who have made this possible: Jeff Jones, Rhonda Rieseberg, Jane St. John, and the rest of the crew; and our editors extraordinaire, Sue Kraszewski and Gretchen Knapp. You have shaped this book in so many ways. It's great to be back home.

And to Bev Moss, the "glue" of our production team, who stuck with us through another 18 months of late night and weekend drops, frantic emails and unreasonable requests, your word processing and research assistance allowed this book to happen. . . . We can't thank you enough.

Bob Barr: Thanks to a number of friends in Newport on the Oregon Coast who shared their music, support, encouragement, and even an occasional dinner while I wrote portions of this book. Special thanks to Dick Schwartz, Beth Mallory, Maggie Bortz, Clay Foster, Jill Pridgeon, Renae and Sky Richmond, DeEtt Brault, Sandy Wieneke, Howard Shippey, Scott Paterson, Gus Willemin, and, of course, my pals, Tami, Rick, Peggy, Barry, Burt, and Duane.

Special thanks are in order to my entire family: to my wife, Beryl Barr; to my daughter, Bonny Barr, and her family, Jerry Williams, Sadie, and Sam; and to my son, Brady Barr, and his family, Mei Len and little Isabella—all of whom, once again, rallied around to help me struggle through yet another major research and writing project.

William Parrett: Thanks to Tom, Therese, Jessie, Carey, Danielle, Christina, Patti, Tim, Jeannie, Holly, Dad, and Jan. Each of you in some way helped me make it through another book. Finally, to the Parrett-Dehner family, Ann, Mia, and Jonathan—words could never express how much your patience, encouragement and support have meant to me throughout this work. I could never have completed this without the three of you.

Foreword

For many years, most Americans—including most American educators—have believed that schools can't make much of a difference in the lives of the children they serve. Especially if those children are poor or members of minority groups, their destiny was thought to be low achievement, no matter what their schools did. Sure, maybe one or two could be saved. But surely not all or even most. Why? Because, in the end, "socioeconomic factors" like poverty, low levels of parent education, and the like would always win out.

The view that schools can't make a difference has covered up a multitude of sins. While many Americans believe that the underachievement of minority or low-income students is largely about them and their families—that is, that all kids are taught the same things, but some simply manage to learn less—the truth is actually quite different. Certainly, these students often enter school behind. But instead of organizing our educational system to ameliorate that problem, we organize it to exacerbate the problem. How do we do that? By giving less to these kids who come to us with less. Indeed, we give these students less of everything that both research and experience tell us make a difference.

Thus, instead of helping to close gaps between groups, what we do in schools often has exactly the opposite effect. Children who come to us a little behind leave a lot behind. African-American and Latino students leave high school with skills in math and reading that white students have when they leave middle school. And the gaps between poor and rich are also cavernous.

What's so devastating about all of this is that we now know that it doesn't have to be this way. For around the country, there are schools that are proving every single day of the school year that poor and minority children *can* achieve at high levels—if we teach them at high levels and provide them and their teachers with the support they need to get there. Demography is not, in other words, destiny—or at least it doesn't have to be.

It is hugely important for both educators and the general public to know how powerful schools can be. And indeed, the stories of schools that serve very poor children, yet produce very high results provide exactly the tonic of hope and inspiration that can help restore the luster of a public education system that has lost considerable public confidence over the last two decades.

But these schools are important for far more than inspiration. The educators in these schools have unlocked some of the mysteries that still plague schools more generally. How, indeed, do we enable all of our students—including those who seem disaffected and disengaged—to master the high-level skills and knowledge they need to secure a foothold in our increasingly complex economy and society?

There have, of course, been some studies of these high-performing, high-poverty schools. But these are often small and idiosyncratic. And until now, nobody has tried to look *across* these studies and distill some of the key lessons that can provide a foundation for improvement efforts in other communities.

With this book, Bob Barr and Bill Parrett have done an enormous service to educators who want to jump-start improvement efforts in their own schools or communities. In one volume, they've looked across all of the many studies and distilled the major findings in a highly readable fashion.

There's a lot here. But then again, real improvement never follows from just one new program. Indeed, in our own studies of high-performing schools, what's immediately obvious is that the educators in those schools think differently about almost everything.

The Kids Left Behind will give you plenty of food for thought.

—Kati Haycock, Director of the Education Trust
Washington, DC

Chapter 1

A New American Revolution

*"What does it mean to be an American?
Well, to me, it means that no matter who you are or how many
problems you have, in America, everybody has a chance."*

—*Fourth-Grade African-American Student*

A revolution is occurring in public education, and it has generated dramatic changes in our nation's schools and classrooms. This revolution is shattering attitudes and beliefs that have existed for decades and focusing national attention on the need to educate all students effectively. With a high-quality education, almost anyone, regardless of race, gender, social class, or national origin, can gain access to economic prosperity and security. Without an adequate education, the promise of prosperity and security that is the foundation of a democratic society is out of reach. Without a high-quality education, a person can live in the richest nation on earth yet lack adequate job opportunities, housing, and health benefits, and he or she can too easily fall victim to crime, addiction, abuse, and other dangerous behavior. A high-quality education has become so vital that it is now viewed as an essential and guaranteed civil right.

The culture of K–12 public education established long ago is changing in remarkable ways. Local control of schools is being transformed through federal and state policies and sanctions. The old process of sorting students into general education, college preparatory, and vocational tracks—the standard in most of the world's developed nations—has been supplemented by policy-driven mandates for minimal student achievement proficiencies and is giving way to a system designed to provide a single rigorous curriculum for all students. "Slow-learning" tracks and "acceptable dropout rates" are being replaced with the goal of all students meeting proficiency standards and graduating. Bell-curve evaluations are being replaced with mastery learning. Freelance teaching based on textbooks, teacher interest, and personal prerogative is being set aside by a system of carefully planned, aligned, and prescribed instruction. However, as the traditional philosophies that have governed public education for so long have begun to change, remnants of their failed policies will likely linger for some time. While more blatant school sorting practices are being challenged and increasingly eliminated, others, like assigning each student a "class rank," still reflect the bell-curve mentality and are not likely to vanish anytime soon. We are rapidly leaving the old world of education behind and being swept into a new world driven by an emerging science of teaching and learning, dramatic changes in the economic marketplace and technology, and new state and federal legislation and policies. This educational revolution is unprecedented in the history of our civilization. Has any nation, anywhere and at any time, truly been determined to *leave no child behind*?

Education's transformation into an essential and guaranteed civil right has not happened by chance. It has emerged through a long and turbulent history of social protests and educational policy, from the denial of education to a variety of under-represented and disadvantaged groups, to segregated and "separate but equal" education, to equal opportunity and education for all, and finally to the goal of academic proficiency for all children and youth. The American Association of School Administrators has illustrated this journey to academic proficiency for every student by identifying key milestones of the past two centuries (figure 1.1).

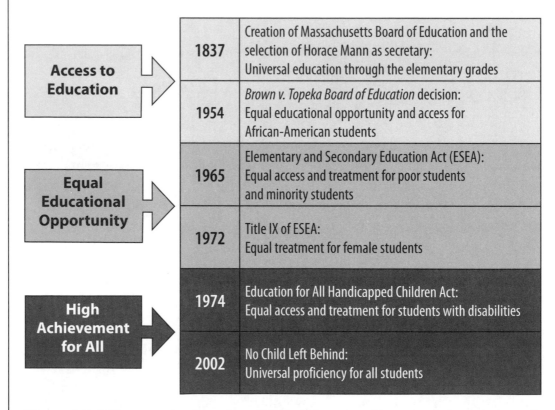

Figure 1.1: Milestones in American Public Education (American Association of School Administrators, 2004)

The Struggle for Education

The recognition of education as a civil right essential for economic opportunity did not happen overnight. For close to 200 years, policymakers and educators have slowly taken significant steps in the often tortuous struggle toward educational freedom for all citizens. This journey has progressed from access to education for only the advantaged, where many groups were denied educational opportunities, to the expectation of proficiency for all. Those denied the right to an education included African Americans, Latinos, and other minorities; the poor; women; the handicapped; people living in isolated, rural areas; and many others. These transformations in public education have been accomplished through a long history of social strife.

From Exclusion to Access

Beginning in the mid-1800s, states began to enact legislation and policies designed to provide access to "universal" public education. Access to elementary education for all was slowly enacted in the United States, first in Massachusetts, and then in scattered locations along the East Coast. But even in states where policies were established for educational access, the vast majority of children were too often unable to participate. Even into the early 1900s, few students attended school beyond the elementary level. At that time, more than 9 out of 10 children failed to graduate from high school. By the late 1950s, the dropout rate was still at least 50% (Education Commission of the States, 1998).

Segregated and Separate but Equal

Although the end of the Civil War marked the freeing of slaves in the United States, southern states continued to deny civil rights to African Americans—including the right to effective education—though the creation of Jim Crow laws. Among other things, these laws established a poll tax and literacy tests for voting. In addition, they denied African Americans the right to participate in a fully integrated society by denying them open housing, by segregating them in poor neighborhoods, and by restricting their access to public transportation, city parks, swimming pools, restaurants, many forms of entertainment, and other services.

In 1954, the court case of *Brown v. Topeka Board of Education* seemed to finally make the dream of equal education for all a reality; however, 2 years later, federal troops were required to protect nine African-American students in Little Rock, Arkansas, as they enrolled in all-white Central High School. In the early 1960s, James Meredith became the first African American to enroll at the University of Mississippi, and civil rights demonstrations continued to sweep across the South. By the early 1970s, federal courts increasingly ordered school desegregation in the major cities of America.

Equal Opportunity and Education for All

Soon after Lyndon Johnson became president in 1963, he launched his War on Poverty. A significant portion of this legislation was the Elementary and Secondary Education Act (ESEA). This landmark legislation established the goal of equal access and treatment for poor and minority students and supported these students with a variety of compensatory programs such as Title I.

By the mid-1970s, separate but equal was finally giving way to a national policy of equal education for all, and new legislation began to ensure the equal treatment of female students in public education. The Title IX section regarding female students was added to ESEA and began a massive realignment of educational programs and funding for young women that continues today. Following the legislation and court decisions that opened access and opportunity to females was the Education for All Handicapped Children Act passed by Congress in 1974, which sought to end the segregation of handicapped students by providing them with equal access and opportunity.

Despite this long struggle to provide equal educational access and opportunity for the poor, minorities, female students, and the handicapped, even into the year 2000, researchers have continued to document schools that still use the destructive practices of segregation and isolation of poor and minority students. School districts have redrawn boundaries to establish school attendance zones that isolate poor and minority neighborhoods; ability grouping and tracking programs have been used to segregate poor and minority students within schools. "White flight"— when middle-class and affluent families sell their homes in cities and relocate to suburbia—exacerbates this problem. Poor children have been isolated into second-class facilities with insufficient and outdated instructional materials, where they are far more likely to be taught by inexperienced, inadequately prepared, or misassigned teachers. Inner-city schools have thus been largely abandoned to poor and minority students, leaving our nation's schools more segregated by race and socioeconomic status today than before federal desegregation policies went into effect.

Sadly, educational research in the mid-1960s provided an intellectual rationale for the continued use of these destructive school practices. James Coleman of the University of Chicago conducted the largest educational study to date, gathering data from 600,000 students, 60,000 teachers, and 6,000 schools. He concluded that teachers could only impact about 10% of the effects of poverty (Coleman et al.,

1966). Although Coleman's conclusion was later disproved, the flawed research led to more than 3 decades of destructive school practices that stigmatized the neediest of our children and youth and created a growing underclass of Americans who are undereducated, illiterate, underemployed, or, even worse, unemployable.

A New Standard of Excellence: Academic Proficiency for All

In the late 1990s, as state and federal legislators began to recognize the relationship between education, civil rights, and economic justice, they began to transform the policy of equal opportunity in education into the new expectation of academic proficiency for all students. Pressure from state and federal agencies coupled with a growing realization that all children and youth can achieve high academic excellence have fostered this unprecedented change in public education. Starting in Kentucky, Texas, Colorado, and North Carolina, state legislatures began establishing policies about learning standards, achievement proficiency, and consequences for failure. With the enactment of the No Child Left Behind (NCLB) federal legislation in 2002, the United States became the first nation to establish a national goal of all students attaining proficiency in reading, math, and science. This elevation of education from something available to only a few to a civil right that is absolutely essential has been fueled by two powerful and relatively new forces: changes in the economic marketplace and the emerging science of teaching and learning.

The Changing Economic Marketplace

The first development driving the new American revolution has been the changing economic marketplace. The economic marketplace has changed in four significant ways:

1. The world of work has given way to the "age of the mind."
2. There is an ever-growing demand for new skills.
3. New technology continues to develop.
4. The relationship between education and income is becoming increasingly significant.

From the World of Work to the Age of the Mind

In today's world, there is only one door of opportunity to the good life: education. The old concept of hard work and perseverance has been transformed by the technological revolution. The world of work is transforming into the "age of the mind." Jobs that previously employed millions of upwardly mobile but largely uneducated men and women in the United States have all but disappeared. Industrial robots and other forms of technology have replaced many of these laborers. Those jobs that are available typically pay only minimum wage, provide little or no health benefits, and are often filled by new immigrants to the country. Many other manufacturing jobs have been transferred to foreign countries where labor, insurance, and litigation costs are far lower.

The Demand for New Skills

Even jobs traditionally seen as requiring less-specialized skills and training, such as jobs in construction, food services, and retail industries, now usually require detailed, often expensive training and licensure. Almost all jobs require a working knowledge of computer technology. More and more jobs require a high school education and postsecondary training programs. Most branches of the American military will not accept young men and women recruits with a GED. In community colleges, many vocational/technical associate degree programs require calculus as an admission requirement. Associate degree programs in sheet metal and tool and die training now require algebra and trigonometry. Today, business, industry, and the armed forces have no opportunities for dropouts.

New Jobs Require Greater Education and Skills

- Eighty percent of the 30 fastest growing jobs will require an education beyond high school.

- Thirty-six percent of all new jobs will require at least a bachelor's degree.

(Hecker, 2005)

Continuing Technological Development

The evolution of increasingly sophisticated job skills demands higher student competencies, and the only technological certainty is that we will experience more change. Public school students must not only master high levels of academic proficiency and complex technological skills, but must also build a sufficiently strong educational foundation for *ongoing* development so that they can continue to explore and learn for the rest of their lives.

The Relationship Between Education and Income

In recent decades, there has been a growing understanding of the relationship between salary and education that further supports the role of education as an individual's civil right. The best way to predict lifetime income levels—to predict those who will live their lives in poverty and those who will enjoy the benefits of the middle class—is education level. Without sufficient education, there is little or no hope for a stable economic life (figure 1.2, p. 7).

	No High School Diploma	High School Diploma	Some College	4 Years of College or More
Males	$19,225	$26,339	$31,336	$42,292
Females	$11,583	$16,573	$21,597	$32,238

Figure 1.2: Predicted Yearly Income Based on Educational Level (National Center for Education Statistics, 2002, p. 163)

American workers without an adequate education are underemployed, work for minimum wage, often hold two or three part-time jobs, or are unemployed or unemployable. Many of these poverty-level adults may decline into depression and despair and fall victim to drug and alcohol abuse, dysfunctional family life, and socially unacceptable behavior. Large numbers turn to crime and end up in jails and prisons. The number of men and women in prison in the United States has doubled in the past 20 years. For decades, over 80% of prison inmates in the United States have been dropouts; well over 50% are illiterate (U.S. Department of Commerce, 1999). In addition, the cost of public education's failures is high:

- The cost of retaining one child is $6,500 per grade (Shepard & Smith, 1990).
- The cost of special education services per child is $9,369 per year (National Education Association, 2006).
- The cost of lost taxes, lost wages, and lost productivity over their lifetimes will "cost our nation more than $260 billion" (Spellings, 2005).

As the economic marketplace of the world has changed in both developed and developing nations, there is an ever-growing disparity between those who have high-quality education and those who do not. Today the differences that characterize and separate the various social classes are more and more dramatic. Simultaneously, the wealth of the most affluent nations has soared to unparalleled heights while a growing "underclass" of citizens living in poverty has suffered declining economic opportunities. The rich have become richer and the poor poorer. The result is an "apartheid of ignorance" where education is the key factor that separates the rich from the poor, economic opportunity from economic despair, and the good life from the tragic world of the "other America." Those who are well-educated have access to the richest economic system that the world has ever known. For those who lack education, the door of opportunity is slammed shut. The apartheid of ignorance has become an unavoidable reality in the United States.

An Emerging Science of Teaching and Learning

The second development driving the new American revolution in education is the emergence of a sophisticated research base for teaching and learning. After hundreds of years with little more than philosophy and theory as the foundation for teaching and learning, research has suddenly provided a strong and growing structure to guide the field of education. Perhaps the most important of these insights are the conclusions of research on schools where poor and minority students have been learning effectively. This research provides new understanding about how schools can effectively address the most challenging task in public education: teaching the vast numbers of our nation's children who live in poverty. There is a growing consensus that underachieving poor children of any ethnic background can achieve high standards of academic excellence and break the cycle of poverty.

This research base includes a variety of specific areas of inquiry. Perhaps most important is the neuroscience research and research on human growth and development. Neuroscience research has provided an understanding of the conditions that encourage and support learning, as well as those conditions that make learning next to impossible. Neuroscience research has helped to identify everything from infant bonding and conditioning, to parenting techniques, to personality development, to effective classroom strategies.

There has also been important longitudinal research that has followed preschool and elementary children for more than 30 years. These longitudinal studies, particularly in the fields of early childhood education and learning disabilities, have helped to identify the long-term impacts of effective and ineffective school practices, permitting long-term analysis of the cost effectiveness of various educational programs and practices. In addition, there is a growing database of knowledge emerging from the research on resilient youth, violent youth, the relationship between teen risk behavior and health costs, and factors in the home, community, and schools that can predict both positive and negative attitudes and school success. There has also been substantial research on instructional and classroom management strategies, effective reform models, leadership, and ways that high-poverty schools reverse trends of low performance. The compelling conclusions from this research give us the ability to make long- and short-range predictions with a high degree of accuracy regarding teaching, learning, and the influence of educational policy on underachieving students of poverty.

As a result of the unprecedented educational research of the last decade, a number of major conclusions have emerged:

All Children Will Learn

We know with absolute certainty that all children and youth will learn and achieve acceptable standards of academic excellence and school success, even children who are poor, non–English speaking, and learning disabled.

Schools Make a Difference

Recent research has disproved Coleman's conclusions that poverty has such a negative, pervasive impact on children and youth that schools can have little or no positive effect on these students' education. Today, thousands of schools serving poor, at-risk students report academic levels similar to those of middle-class and upper-class students. It is now evident that a good school can overcome the debilitating effects of poverty and dysfunctional family life.

Teachers Make a Difference

Research has shown that teacher quality is the single most influential factor in student achievement. It is not surprising that some teachers can significantly raise student achievement while other teachers have little or no positive impact on student success. This is a crucial finding because many students actually show a decline in achievement over the course of the school year. It takes 2 years for these students with ineffective teachers to regain the resulting loss in achievement. If a student has an ineffective teacher for 2 years in a row, she or he is unlikely to ever catch up (Sanders & Rivers, 1996).

Immediate Gains Are Possible

Research has clearly identified instructional strategies, targeted programs, interventions, and exemplary models that ensure that low-performing students accelerate their learning and achievement. With appropriate action, schools and classrooms can expect immediate, dramatic results.

Best Practices Work for At-Risk Students

There is growing evidence that poor and minority students can learn effectively when research-based best practices are used in schools and in the classroom (Barr & Parrett, 2003). When schools replace the failed practices of the "pedagogy of poverty" (drills, worksheets, and lectures) with research-based strategies, learning increases significantly, especially for the children of poverty. Research has identified very specific classroom strategies that will significantly increase student achievement when used correctly.

Low-Performing Schools Can Become High-Performing Schools

Throughout the United States, a growing number of high-poverty, low-performing schools have become high-performing schools. By employing research on effective schools and best practices for low-performing and other at-risk students, and by monitoring student performance, these schools have transformed student learning in dramatic ways.

These proven strategies identified by researchers give educators the ability to make accurate long-term predictions about student learning. Today, we know, without a shadow of doubt, that all kids can and will learn; however, this knowledge must be put into action, or children will be left behind.

The Continuing Battle in Education

The changes in the economic marketplace and the emerging education research have motivated policymakers and lawmakers to conclude that all children and youth must be taught effectively and achieve high academic proficiency. This does not, however, mean that social and political battles have ceased. Rather, the new educational policy of No Child Left Behind has catapulted the nation into the next great battle for civil rights in America. The No Child Left Behind Act has suddenly focused the spotlight on the effectiveness of America's schools in teaching the children of poverty. New requirements for student subgroups, data reporting, adequate yearly progress, and teacher quality have refocused the efforts of every school and school district in the United States and generated an effort toward school improvement and reform that is unparalleled in America's history.

Challenges of the Educational Revolution: Policy Change, Pressure, and Reactions

> *"I am sick of all the spin doctors' jargon and the weak policymakers' sleight-of-hand concoction that is being called 'Leave No Child Behind.' It doesn't take a rocket scientist to understand that what they are talking about is 'dumbing down' public education."*
>
> —*Parent, California*

Like any revolution, the transition occurring in public education is charged with conflict, confusion, confrontation, and in some cases, chaos. The good news is that in schools, districts, and communities across the country, many parents, policymakers, and educators have embraced this dramatic new educational challenge and are working diligently to ensure that all students, especially poor and minority students, are learning effectively. Unfortunately, despite the overwhelming support of this policy, some believe the No Child Left Behind Act will blaze for a while and then burn out and disappear. The first impulse of many educators is to be patient and simply wait out this new intrusion into their schools and classrooms. It is no surprise that a policy shift of this magnitude has spawned a firestorm of critique and dissent and led to a variety of reactions—some positive and many negative.

Teachers

"I love my students, and I want all of them to succeed; but there is only so much a teacher can give. I have other responsibilities to my own family, my church, and my community. . . . Teachers do all of the work and get all of the blame."

—*Elementary School Teacher, Indiana*

State and federal legislation has significantly altered the lives of teachers and the expectations for student performance in their classrooms. While many teachers enthusiastically support the concept of all students attaining proficiency, many are objecting to these new demands because of the lack of accompanying funding and support. Some teachers seem to have concluded that No Child Left Behind actually means, "No Teacher Left Standing." Many others have welcomed the Act as long overdue and eminently necessary. For teachers and administrators who have served as advocates of poor and minority students, the federal legislation has provided a way to document school funding inequalities and failed practices, programs, and policies, and provided powerful new incentives and penalties that have focused school and community attention on teaching all students effectively.

Teacher Organizations

"The No Child Left Behind legislation sounds pretty good unless you are working in a dilapidated building with insufficient instructional materials, in classes with more than 30 kids, surrounded with a lot of tired, burned-out teachers, and little or no funding to achieve the awesome job of remediation. Is there any doubt in anyone's mind that this is an unfunded federal mandate being carried squarely on the backs of teachers?"

—*School District President, Oregon Education Association*

The National Education Association and the American Federation of Teachers have been forceful in their critique of No Child Left Behind. These organizations have criticized the legislation for putting the focus on teachers and targeting them for all the problems in schools. Former Education Secretary Rod Paige angered teachers when, during a White House meeting with governors, he called the nation's largest teachers union a "terrorist organization." Paige later said he was joking but stood by his claim that the 2.7 million–member National Education Association uses "obstructionist scare tactics" to oppose education reforms (King, 2004). While steadfast in their critique of NCLB, these organizations continue to offer informed recommendations for statutory changes and amendments to improve the act.

State Departments

"Too many children begin life disadvantaged, attend poor schools, learn little, drop out in school or in college, and wind up at the margins in low-skill, low-paying jobs. We have made progress in closing the gap, but not enough. . . . Both research and our progress so far show that people can achieve at much higher levels."

—New York State Commissioner of Education (Hoff, 2005, p. 23)

"Here comes No Child Left Behind . . . and there go states' rights."

—State Department Official, Utah

Several state department of education leaders have criticized the legislation as yet another unfunded federal mandate and are calling for significant changes. Others are unhappy that the federal come-lately legislation interferes with the standards and assessment policies that they have been implementing and perfecting for years. States like Texas, North Carolina, and Colorado began requiring districts to test all students and report results by ethnicity, socioeconomic status, and disability years before the federal government established the No Child Left Behind policy (Chaddock, 2004). While some states' policies and practices were far ahead of the new federal policies, more than 20 other states have requested relief from and exceptions to the legislation; yet today, most of that early opposition has dissipated. As of early 2005, only the governors of Maine, Utah, and Vermont signed bills critical of the act.

School Boards

"I am absolutely infuriated. Whatever happened to local control of public education? Whatever happened to our elected politicians resisting this encroaching federalism? What on earth is going on?"

—School Board Member, Utah

Many school board members have been shocked and angered by the federal government imposing this mandate on their district policies and practices. School boards and administrators often see No Child Left Behind as an intrusive federal effort designed to erode the authority of local boards—a directive that requires significant new accountability without adequate fiscal support. Despite these widespread concerns, most board members tend to agree with the Act's purpose of closing achievement gaps and holding high expectations for all students.

School Districts

"This NCLB law is untenable for our small district. Who is going to do all of this accounting and paperwork? Where is the money for more staff and technology?"

—*Superintendent of a Rural School District, Nebraska*

Most school districts in the United States are diligently working to meet the requirements of No Child Left Behind; however, it has not been easy. Early resistance and disbelief have given way to a growing resolve that the law is here to stay, that all students can indeed succeed and reach proficiency, and perhaps most important, that change must occur if we are to make required progress.

Parents

"I know we need to help our school with the kids that are furthest behind, but I don't want to see it coming out of the resources going to my child."

—*Parent, Michigan*

Parents and parent groups, especially those from middle-class and affluent families, have expressed concern with the No Child Left Behind legislation. They fear that the resources for their children will be redirected toward underachieving poor and minority students, and that closing the achievement gap means lowering expectations and standards for the most successful students. More recently, news stories have focused not only on the lack of attention provided to high-achieving students, but also on the lack of attention to average students ("Class Focus," 2005).

When Kati Haycock, executive director of the Education Trust, meets with parents and educators around the country and challenges them to replace their schools' inferior curriculum for underachieving, poor, and minority students with a rigorous educational program and to start assigning experienced and qualified teachers to poor schools and classrooms, she often hears the same troubling response:

> If schools eliminate the general education or vocational tracks, then who will become the next generation of plumbers, electricians, maintenance personnel, chefs, customer service employees, landscape technicians, and builders? . . . We could probably do what you are suggesting. We could put these kids in tougher classes. We could beef up the rigor of their assignments. We could assign them some of our strongest teachers, instead of novices. But I'm thinking about the black lady who served my room service breakfast this morning [at my hotel]. She seemed so

very happy. And I am only thinking, if she had gone to college for even a little while, she probably wouldn't be so happy. (Haycock, 2003, p. 2)

Analysis of Parent Perception Shows Encouraging Results

The 36th Annual Phi Delta Kappa/Gallup Poll showed that public school parents believe (by a margin of 2 to 1) that the No Child Left Behind legislation will improve student achievement. These findings show that No Child Left Behind is gaining support and momentum.

According to Susan L. Traiman, a proponent of No Child Left Behind and the director of Education and Workforce Policy for the Business Roundtable, "It is also encouraging that the more people know about the law, the more likely they are to favor it" (Rose & Gallup, 2004, p. 43). However, the poll found that two-thirds of the respondents still knew little about the law. As Traiman notes, their views may depend on whether they receive accurate facts or misinformation about the legislation. The language used in the poll's questions, she believes, also has an impact and can lead to negative results; other polls have produced more positive responses, especially among African-American and Hispanic parents. Traiman notes, "I would have expected more favorable attitudes in this poll had respondents been given the facts about testing, including the percentages of students who cannot perform at even the basic level in reading and math" (p. 43).

Traiman believes that as the legislation moves all students toward proficiency, support will continue to grow from the public because No Child Left Behind supports learning in reading and math—the gateways to all other learning.

Fortunately, these reactions do not characterize the majority of parent voices in our public schools. Many other parents take exception to this thinking and suggest that class prejudice, bigotry, and institutional racism are the driving forces behind opposition to the legislation and it is about time that our schools focus on the most in-need students. Yet negative reactions do consistently appear, often providing opposition to efforts to increase educational equality and to demonstrate high academic proficiency for all students, the central purpose of No Child Left Behind.

Unfortunately, more challenges and troubling implications of the educational revolution beyond public opinion have emerged as No Child Left Behind has been implemented across the country.

Data, Dropouts, and Funding

"There is no denying that NCLB has brought some long overdue attention to the problem of educational inequality. . . . The problem is that what NCLB proposes to do about this inequality is woefully inadequate to the task and, in some cases, will make things worse."

—Stan Karp (Meier & Wood, 2004, p. 64)

Attaining reliable data on the number of students who drop out of school, especially the number of poor and minority students, is a persistent challenge with No Child Left Behind. A recent report by the Urban Institute found that contrary to published reports of a national graduation rate of 85%, minority students (many of whom are poor) have little more than a 50/50 chance of earning a diploma (Swanson, 2004). The Institute also reported that nearly one-third of all students fail to graduate. "Beleaguered school officials might feel so pressured to raise test scores that pushing low-performing students out of school would seem like the best way to boost their numbers," explained Christopher Swanson of the Urban Institute. Unfortunately, he goes on to say, "the reasons that dropouts go uncounted range from deliberate falsification of data to the genuine difficulties in tracking a student who leaves a school" (Swanson, 2004, p. 36).

Arguably one of the most insidious actions of school districts is encouraging students to drop out or altering school dropout data and reports. Suddenly, large groups of students are "transferring" to other school districts or choosing home-schooling. In some school districts, low-achieving students have been pushed to enroll in GED programs, charter schools, or other programs in an effort to remove these students from the assessment pool. Some states and school districts have established barrier tests at the fifth-, ninth-, and eleventh-grade levels. Students who fail these tests are held back. In one urban district, some students have failed the fifth-grade test three times and have consequently been retained in elementary school. Since the district's policy prevents teenagers from attending elementary school, after 3 years in the fifth grade, the students are reassigned to the eighth grade. Inevitably, almost all of these students drop out of school. It has been estimated that as of 2004 in one of the nation's largest urban districts, more than 50,000 students have been retained because of barrier testing policies. Most of these students will likely drop out of school and join the growing numbers of uneducated, hopeless urban American youth.

There also seems to be a growing conviction among many that if educators cannot defeat the policies of No Child Left Behind, they can obscure and distort data to protect their districts' reputations. There have been news reports throughout the country chronicling district employees who have reputedly "massaged" data on standardized tests or employed relaxed test security to make assessment results look better. Copies of standardized tests have been secretly distributed to teachers and students, some students have been encouraged to stay home on test days, and test participation and results have been tampered with. Some leading critics of the act have actually called upon teachers and educators to practice civil disobedience and refuse to participate in the state assessments (Kohn, 2000). There have been isolated incidents where high school students have done just that.

The requirements of No Child Left Behind have significantly changed the way school districts report data, especially data regarding student achievement. For many districts that have used aggregate achievement data in the past to hide the failings of poor and minority students, the disaggregation requirements of No Child Left Behind (for various subgroups of poor, minority, and exceptional students) have shocked communities that thought their schools were the very best. "Suburban school districts didn't expect to have schools on the watch list," says Jack Jennings, director of the Center on Education Policy in Washington, DC. "[No Child Left Behind] made them realize they are accountable for all groups" (Chaddock, 2004, p. 2). In Illinois, over 694 schools, more than half of them in affluent suburban communities, were facing No Child Left Behind sanctions in 2004, underscoring the changing economic and racial demographics throughout the United States (Chaddock, 2004).

Top Suburban Schools Hit by No Child Left Behind Sanctions

A 2004 article in the *Chicago Tribune* reported that many suburban schools found themselves labeled as failures for the first time when they were judged not only on school-wide scores, but also on the performance of different racial, economic, and special-education subgroups. Those schools that had one or more subgroups fail to meet state standards would be subject to penalties. Many of the suburban schools identified were associated with affluent bedroom communities, which educators say underscores the growing economic and racial diversity of their student bodies (Cohen & Banchero, 2004).

Another significant concern about No Child Left Behind is its potential to punish the nation's weakest and most vulnerable students. Writing with emotion in *Many Children Left Behind*, Deborah Meier and George Wood (2004) raise serious concerns regarding the long-range impact of No Child Left Behind on poor and minority students. The authors, joined by Linda Darling-Hammond and Ted Sizer, raise legitimate concerns over historical challenges that continue to exist today: the level of funding between poor and affluent school districts, the quality of teachers in poor and affluent school districts, the lack of federal funding to support the mandates of No Child Left Behind, and the legion of complex technicalities that create obstacles to learning instead of support for improvement.

Other educators argue that without No Child Left Behind, in schools and school districts where racism and class prejudice are still rampant, no one would really care whether or not poor and minority students learned. It can be argued that the intent of No Child Left Behind—to close achievement gaps between "high- and low-performing children, especially . . . between minority and non-minority students . . . and disadvantaged children and their more advantaged peers" (No Child Left Behind Act, 2002)—has drawn widespread support. Like most public policies, increased attention and refinement will undoubtedly improve the legislation over time. Key issues that must be addressed in the immediate future include:

- **The equitable funding of public schools.** The No Child Left Behind legislation did nothing to equalize funding between school districts or between schools in a district. Funding inequalities have led to a growing number of court cases and legislation that have transformed funding formulas in some states. Unfortunately, the problem continues to exist in far too many states.
- **Fiscal support for new requirements.** No Child Left Behind is an underfunded federal mandate that has caused many school districts to divert their already stretched resources in order to meet the new requirements of the law.
- **Accountability methods and balanced assessment.** Almost everyone worries about using a single standardized test to determine the success or failure of K–12 students. Fortunately, a growing number of states are supplementing standardized testing with an array of more authentic assessments.
- **Differing state expectations and discrepant scores.** While each state has implemented its own accountability plan and assessments, comparisons with National Assessment of Educational Progress (NAEP) annual results reveals significant discrepancies between individual state results and NAEP state data, as well as performance discrepancies among states.
- **High school graduation requirements.** In order to achieve the goals of No Child Left Behind, many states have had to upgrade their high school graduation requirements to include a stronger emphasis on science, math, and language arts.
- **The pushing-out of students.** No Child Left Behind has little or no accountability or standard reporting requirements regarding the number of dropouts in a school or school district. This has led to both overt and subtle efforts by some schools and districts to persuade students to leave school; when these marginal students drop out, the test score averages go up and look better for the rest.
- **Alternative routes to competency and proficiency.** Addressing these challenges will strengthen public support for both the intent and outcomes of the No Child Left Behind legislation.

Growing Support for the Revolution

"We can choose to renounce NCLB, look outside our districts for excuses, wring our hands, ignore the successes around us, and shift our focus every- where but upon ourselves and what we are or are not doing. . . . Every child, including every disadvantaged child, is waiting for us to make our choice."
—Anne Loring *(Haycock & Chenoweth, 2005, p. 28)*

In spite of the opposition, the concepts that form the foundation of No Child Left Behind are surely here to stay. The No Child Left Behind legislation passed the House of Representatives with a 381 to 41 vote and an 87 to 10 vote in the Senate. This bipartisan support is especially unique in this day of strict party-line voting patterns in Congress. Both major political parties continue to support the concept of the legislation. And while many state departments of education and state legislators may be less than excited about federal intervention in their state educational policies, No Child Left Behind is consistent with most of the standards and assessment policies that have been established by states in recent years.

In late 2004, more than 100 African-American and Latino superintendents of major urban districts signed an open letter to President George W. Bush urging the administration to "not turn back the clock" as they voiced their support of the accountability provision of Title I: "We recognize that the goal of educating all students presents a tremendous challenge. We believe that American public education is up to the task. We add our voices to those who have stepped up to the challenge" (Education Trust, 2003a, p. 1). Stephanie Robinson, former superintendent of the Kansas City, Missouri, public schools, spoke in support of the Act:

> The politicians and talking heads of the education establishment in Washington need to understand that this law is actually helping to get public education more focused on raising achievement for all students and on closing achievement gaps between groups. These superintendents thought Washington needed to hear from educa- tors in the field who are using the accountability provisions to ad- vance the mission of public education. (Education Trust, 2003a, p. 1)

In fact, there are thousands of schools and school districts across the country that not only have implemented the policies of the state and federal legislation, but have also established a remarkable track record of success in teaching the vast majority of their students, even underachieving poor and minority students. A growing number of low-performing schools have become high-performing schools, or "turn-around schools." The Education Trust continues to identify thousands of elementary, middle, and high schools where poor and minority students are out-achieving 75% of their state's more advantaged peers (2003a).

Even more encouraging is that educators in virtually every school district in the country, from the largest urban setting to the smallest rural district, have a new sense of urgency to implement effective strategies to ensure that their poor and minority students learn effectively. For the first time in the history of the United States, the vast majority of schools and districts are seriously attempting to raise the performance of students who were previously assigned to slow-learning tracks and special education and to raise the performance of so many other students who arrived at school academically behind, too often failed, and subsequently dropped out of school. This new focus represents the dramatic American revolution in education.

Realizing the Revolution for the Children of Poverty

> *"I have a dream that one day this nation will rise up and live out the true meaning of its creed: 'We hold these truths to be self-evident: that all men are created equal.'"*
>
> —*Reverend Martin Luther King, Jr. (1963)*

The battle for educational civil rights is alive with enthusiasm, hope, conflict, and contradiction. For the first time, poor and minority students have become the focus of public education; from the boardrooms to our living rooms, we are watching the learning curve of our most neglected children and underachieving students advance as achievement gaps close. The educational revolution in America is unfolding in dramatic and powerful new ways, as the tragedies of the past give way to the attainable goal of high-quality education for all students. The cycle of poverty and despair that has characterized our American underclass can be halted once and for all. It is only through a high-quality education that poor and minority students can break out of the debilitating cycle of poverty and gain access to the social, political, and economic freedoms promised by our country's most sacred documents.

It is with this goal in mind—the goal of a high-quality education for all students—that we have crafted this book for teachers, administrators, policymakers, and parents. In the pages that follow, we will identify, summarize, and analyze how schools have failed the children of poverty. Most importantly, we will identify an abundance of research-based strategies that have emerged through years of educational research. These strategies form a pattern of improvement with eight specific components that have proven successful in increasing the achievement of children of poverty in a growing number of high-performing, high-poverty schools and school districts across the United States.

Chapter 2

How Schools Have Failed the Children of Poverty

"It took me a while, but I figured it out. It's all about poverty. All of our challenges and problems center on making our system and schools work for all kids."

—*School District Professional Development Director, Oregon*

The greatest challenge facing public education in the United States today is educating all students to proficiency and truly leaving no child behind. The most difficult aspect of this challenge is teaching the underachieving children of poverty. These students live on the other side of the apartheid of despair and represent a huge and growing underclass of Americans who have been locked out of the world of abundance and opportunity that characterizes America.

These students are the children of the "other America." They live in conditions far more typical of a third world nation than what is typical of the vast majority of children and youth living in the richest nation on earth. These are the "forgotten kids"—the disadvantaged, disconnected, and dislocated. Their parents have little education and often work several low-paying jobs, still unable to make ends meet. They are often without adequate health care, nutrition, housing, and clothing. They experience little educational stimulation outside of school. They do not have computers, calculators, encyclopedias, books, and magazines; most do not have even pencils and paper. Many arrive at school with significant deficiencies in their vocabulary and reading readiness and are far behind their more advantaged classmates. Without enormous attention and intervention, they fall even further behind. Few will ever catch up, and most will drop out of school. The children of poverty often comprise a significant portion of a school's enrollment, and their only hope for escaping the cycle of poverty is a high-quality education.

The great promise to all U.S. citizens has always been freedom and justice for all and the right to a free public education. Unfortunately, vast numbers of poor and disadvantaged minority students in our nation have not realized this promise. The reality for them is freedom and justice for *some* and the right to an inferior public school education. Far too often, schools have blamed poor families for their children's deficiencies and have in effect waged war against our neediest students.

Poverty in the United States

"My high school had over 4,000 students. I couldn't dress like most of the other students, couldn't afford to go out to lunch every day . . . just didn't fit in very well. I wasn't just lost in the mob. . . . I was invisible. No one knew my name. No one cared if I came to school. So I didn't."

—Student, Miami, Florida

The number of poor students attending public school in the United States is staggering. Poverty exists in all ethnic groups and in every geographic region; it often plagues many generations in a family and thus perpetuates a vicious cycle of despair for the neediest children. Unfortunately, in recent years, the economic conditions for the nation's children have further disintegrated. As of 1999, more than 12 million children were living in poverty in America (Payne, 2001). By 2003, the number of children living in poverty had risen to over 18% of all children in the United States—or over 13 million children (U.S. Census Bureau, 2005). In 2003, it was reported that 23% of America's families lived at or below the federal poverty level of $18,400 for a family of four (Cauthen, 2006). Yet according to the National Center for Children in Poverty, it would take twice that amount to provide food and housing in most parts of the United States (Cauthen, 2006). Of the millions of America's children residing in low-income families, 64% are Latino, 37% are African-American, and 34% are white (Cauthen, 2006).

In 1990, it was estimated that at least 40% of the children in the United States were minority, poor, and imminently at risk of school failure. These numbers continued to increase into the new century. There has also been a significant increase in enrollment of African-American, Hispanic, and Asian children in public schools: Between 1976 and 1996, the percentages of minority students in U.S. public and private schools increased from 24% to 36% (Goodwin, 2000). By the year 2010, that number could increase to 42%. From 1978 to 1998, enrollment of Latino elementary students increased over 150% (*Latinos in Schools,* 2001). Most states are projecting 20% to 40% increases in Hispanic student enrollment in public schools during the next 20 years (Land & Legters, 2002). A significant percentage of these minority students are poor (Land & Legters, 2002). Educating these at-risk students to proficiency presents a significant challenge for public schools.

Who Are the Students at Risk?

The children of poverty come from homes with few books and little or no technology other than a television. They too often suffer from poor nutrition, poor health care, and little educational stimulation. Research has documented that they come to school with a limited vocabulary and few reading readiness skills. In recent years, researchers have identified a number of specific factors that place students at risk of failing in school. By the late 1990s, more than 45% of our students were characterized by one or more of these factors:

- Being culturally diverse and living in poverty
- Having limited English proficiency
- Having parents with less than a high school education
- Living with a single parent (Land & Legters, 2002)

It is no surprise that being a minority, living in poverty, and speaking a language other than English top this list of critical factors. In 2004, researchers at the Center for Civic Innovation at the Manhattan Institute identified a more complex set of student factors that influence a child's well-being and capacity to learn (Greene & Forster, 2004):

- Readiness
- Community
- Race
- Economics
- Health
- Family

The researchers used these factors as benchmarks of "teachability" to compare state efforts to teach children who possess these factors. The authors of this study analyzed state data on the factors and then created a "Teachability Index" that compared school achievement with the factors. The Teachability Index provides a far more comprehensive set of variables that may influence student achievement than earlier efforts to analyze the challenges in identifying at-risk learners. The 16 factors each have a documented relationship to student achievement. Since each variable contributes to the challenge of teaching a particular student, the Teachability Index provides a unique approach to developing an individualized profile for each student (Greene & Forster, 2004).

While each factor in the Teachability Index has a stand-alone impact on student achievement, the more factors that a particular student has, the more confounding the challenges of effective teaching and learning will be. For example, a student at the poverty level living in a single-parent family with a mother who is a Spanish-speaking high school dropout and is using a drug will often have a significantly greater challenge in learning than a student from a two-parent, English-speaking family living at the poverty level. Schools are using the Teachability Index to identify as early as possible students who have the greatest learning challenges. The personalized profiles developed for each student can be used as a basis for individualized learning plans. The Teachability Index factors are listed in figure 2.1.

Teachability Index			
Readiness		**Economics**	
■ Preschool enrollment ■ Language other than English ■ Parents' education		■ Income ■ Poverty	
Community		**Health**	
■ Crime victimization ■ Drug use ■ Religious observance ■ Residential mobility		■ Disabilities ■ Mortality ■ Low birth-weight survival ■ Suicide	
Race		**Family**	
■ Non-Hispanic white		■ Teenage birth ■ Single parenthood	

Figure 2.1: The Teachability Index (Greene & Forster, 2004, p. 4)

Researchers have helped schools throughout the United States understand the life conditions that adversely affect student achievement. To ensure that all students learn effectively, schools must stop blaming students for their deficiencies and must develop programs and practices designed to address their needs. This is precisely what high-performing, high-poverty schools have been doing. Unfortunately, many school policies, practices, and programs continue to damage students and "manufacture" low achievement. Often it is not the students who are failing, but the schools who have failed the students.

"Poor Underachieving Children Can't Catch Up"

The American public school system's lack of effectiveness in teaching children and youth with low socioeconomic status is our nation's single greatest educational failure. While there have always been isolated, but remarkable, examples of schools and classrooms with high-poverty, high-achieving students, they unfortunately stand in stark exception to a national tradition of failure and humiliation. The statistics of the failures of our public educational system are sobering:

- One-fourth of all American youth drop out of high school. The vast majority of these students are poor or disadvantaged minorities. Few of these students ever achieve middle-class status during their lifetimes, thus perpetuating the cycle of poverty. Most of these students face lives of unemployment, or at best underemployment.

- There is a direct relationship between students who are illiterate and those who drop out of school. More than 50% of the 1.8 million men and women in prison in the United States today are illiterate high school dropouts.

- One fourth of all high school graduates who progress to higher education drop out of college.

- One-third of all college freshmen take remedial classes. (National Commission on the High School Senior Year, 2001)

In addition, a recent study funded by the Bill & Melinda Gates Foundation concluded that only two of every three students who enter high school will graduate (Bridgeland, Dilulio, & Morison, 2006).

A main reason for the failure of public education to educate poor children and youth is the serious misconception regarding poverty that was reinforced by the Coleman study of 1966, which concluded that even a good school will have little effect on the achievement of poor children. This flawed conclusion reinforced the racism and class prejudice of educators and provided a faulty motivation and rationale for decades of disastrous school policies, practices, and programs that helped to impede generation after generation of poor or minority students. Since it was believed that underachieving, poor children could not catch up, few if any were surprised when these students failed, were retained, or were placed in slow-learning or special education classes and ultimately dropped out of school.

Because of the belief that many poor children could not catch up to the level of their advantaged peers, federal, state, and district policies, programs, and practices evolved that have subsequently failed generations of poverty-level youth. Several decades of research have documented the disastrous effects of these ineffective educational approaches. The vast majority of poor children have traditionally been assigned to poor schools and school districts where the per-pupil funding is dramatically lower than in affluent communities. They have often been subjected to less-qualified teachers in less-challenging courses. They have been disproportionately retained, tracked, and assigned to special education or have frequently been assigned to in-school suspension or detention when they act out in frustration or anger. They have been excluded and expelled. In many states, poor, underachieving students have been removed from regular classrooms and placed in pseudo-alternative schools and programs where the goal is behavior modification rather than academic acceleration. The majority of students segregated in these flawed interventions have been poor, male, and minority (Barr & Parrett, 2003; Levin, 2006). Many poor children in the U.S. receive Title I or other pull-out reading support, but until very recently, the majority of these students never learned to read effectively. They have been victims of an insidious bell-curve mentality and, along with their families, have been blamed for frequent mobility, lack of motivation, and low performance.

Scholars have continued to document the disastrous effects these practices have had on low-socioeconomic-status and minority students. The belief that poor children could not catch up has not helped poor students; rather, it has stigmatized, isolated, and abandoned the very students who are in the most desperate need of our help.

Destructive Policies, Programs, and Practices

Many destructive school policies, programs, and practices used for decades in this country have resulted in long-term negative effects on low-performing minority and poor students. These approaches exacerbate and complicate the problems of poor and minority students, and seriously affect their ability to learn effectively, succeed in school, and achieve economic success in later life. Many of these approaches are still used widely in public schools throughout the United States—in spite of research documenting their tragic effects on students (Barr & Parrett, 2001, 2003). Everyone who is committed to ensuring that all students reach proficiency and achieve success in school should be aware of these approaches and work to eliminate them.

- Lack of choice
- Inequitable school funding
- Inexperienced, poorly prepared teachers
- Ineffective teaching practices
- Retention and tracking
- Misassignment to special education
- Over-reliance on medication to modify behavior
- Pullout programs
- Schools that are too big
- Suspension and expulsion
- Educational neglect

Lack of Choice

Poor students and parents have traditionally been denied choice in the vast majority of public schools. Most students, even today, are assigned to schools, teachers, programs, and educational tracks based on a street address. Many affluent and middle-class parents choose their place of residence based on school performance, or they choose private schools. Poor families are often trapped in underfunded, failing schools (Nathan, 1989, 1996).

Inequitable School Funding

Distressed neighborhoods or communities are usually served by schools with significantly fewer financial resources. Analysis by the Education Trust and others show that many states provide the lowest levels of financial support to their highest-poverty school districts. Students who depend the most on public education for their academic development are often getting the least (Carey, 2003).

Twenty-two states continue to fund high-poverty schools and districts at a lower rate than affluent school districts (Haycock, 2003). Most recently, California has committed $188 million as the result of a class-action lawsuit that contended that the state neglected its low-income students. The money will repair buildings and purchase textbooks for 2,400 low-performing schools (Asimov, 2004). More experienced, better-trained teachers with higher salaries and graduate degrees are more likely to be found in more affluent schools. Funding public education with property tax revenue creates a tragic economic "funding gap" that continues to dramatically separate public schools into the rich and the poor (Kozol, 2005).

Inexperienced, Poorly Prepared Teachers

Low-socioeconomic-status students are five times more likely than affluent students to have inexperienced teachers. In every subject area in high-poverty schools, students are more likely to be taught by less well-prepared teachers. In math and science, only about half of the teachers in schools with 90% or greater minority enrollment meet their state's minimum requirements for certification (Fenwick, 2001). In Florida, teachers at poor schools were 44% more likely to have failed the basic skills test than those at rich schools. The gap in teacher scores is even more pronounced in predominantly minority schools (Associated Press, 2004). Unfortunately, these patterns can be found in poverty-level and minority schools regardless of the measure of teacher qualification, experience, certification, academic preparedness, or performance on licensing tests. Kati Haycock concludes, "We take the students who most depend on their teachers for subject-matter learning and assign them to teachers with the weakest academic foundation" (Jerald, 2001, p. 1).

Ineffective Teaching Practices

Many schools fail to effectively teach poor and minority students the essential skills necessary for success in school. Many poor and minority students arrive at school unprepared to learn, and without intensive remediation, they fall further and further behind. If students do not learn to read by the end of the third grade, they face a number of unfortunate consequences (Barr & Parrett, 2001, 2003; Karoly et al., 1998). If students do not learn to read—and read well—in their early school years, they cannot do their homework or school work. Many will ultimately drop out of school. Few of these students are any more successful outside of school than they were at school, and far too many will live out their lives unemployed or unemployable.

Retention and Tracking

In too many schools, students who do not master basic skills are required to repeat the grade level again, or they are tracked into basic classes with low expectations. Students who are retained and tracked almost never catch up to their age-group peers, and many fail to ever advance from the slow-learning track (Fager & Richen, 1999; Loveless, 1998). Many children of poverty are also assigned to in-school suspension or expelled. In many states, poor, underachieving students have been removed from regular school and placed in low-performing or failing alternative schools and programs where the goal is behavior modification rather than acceleration. Most of the students segregated into these interventions have been poor, male, and minority, and the results have been tragic. A recent review of a Texas program (Alternative Disciplinary Schools) serving over 100,000 predominantly African-American, Hispanic, and poor male K–12 students found these students were:

- Assigned to schools where instruction occurred only 2 hours per day
- Undiagnosed for reading levels
- Left without basic knowledge
- Provided instruction in a multi-grade-level class
- Limited to working with textbooks and worksheets

The students were removed from regular classes, assigned to special programs for as little as 10 days, and then returned to their regular classroom. As a result of this educational disruption, the students fell further behind, and large numbers ultimately dropped out of school. This practice, in effect, constitutes a type of racial cleansing of public education in the state of Texas.

Misassignment to Special Education

Far too many teachers and schools are quick to order special education assessments for students who "just don't fit in." Unfortunately, the reasons for this poor fit may have more to do with learning environment than with students' learning deficiencies. Research over the last two decades has documented the unfortunate effects of mismatching students' learning styles with teachers' instructional styles. Overused and ineffective strategies that contribute to this mismatch include the drills, worksheets, and lectures that are used so often with poor students (Barr & Parrett, 2003; Haberman, 1991). For the underachieving students of poverty, misassignment to special education can deny them the opportunities and high expectations awarded to regular education students (Barr & Parrett, 2001).

Over-Reliance on Medication to Modify Behavior

During the last two decades, millions of children have been prescribed medication intended to improve their school behavior and achievement. Today, as many as 1 in 10 students in the United States are medicated. Boys are medicated five times more often than girls. While such medication does indeed render many students more passive, less active, and more obedient, questions abound regarding the scope of its effectiveness relating to achievement and the long-term effects of this over-reliance on medication (Barr & Parrett, 2001).

Pullout Programs

Historically, many intervention programs have pulled students out from their regular classrooms to provide instruction in reading. For decades, Title I reading programs used a pullout approach as a primary strategy. But when students are pulled out of their regular classrooms, they miss regular classroom instruction and interaction with higher-performing peers. Decades of study have documented how little success these programs have had with poor children (Barr & Parrett, 2001).

Schools That Are Too Big

The United States has far too many schools that have lost the asset of community due to huge enrollments. For many poor and minority students, a small school with a personalized environment is essential for their educational needs. In big schools, these students often feel "isolated, anonymous, and alienated, and they sometimes become disrupters, bullies, or victims of bullies. Others simply underachieve or drop out. The larger the school, the more student disruptions can be expected. For every additional 600 students in a school, there is a corresponding increase in negative student behavior. Conversely, studies demonstrate an almost total lack of violence and considerably higher student academic success in small schools" (Howley & Bickel, 2002, p. 21).

Suspension and Expulsion

Suspension and expulsion do little to help students. Students suspended from school for a few days will only return to school further behind and may become even more disconnected from school. They also tend to become repeat disrupters. Expulsion is perhaps the most disastrous school policy. Too many students who are unable to cope in a school setting have been turned out into the community without supervision and have gone on to participate in antisocial or even criminal behavior. Expelled students often find themselves arrested and incarcerated (Colorado Foundation for Families and Children, 1995).

Educational Neglect

Recent research has identified yet another practice that has had detrimental effects on the children of poverty: educational neglect (Kelly, 2006). A recent study on educational neglect at the Center for School Improvement at Boise State University found that almost two million (1,708,463) school-aged children nationwide were unaccounted for educationally: It is not known where or if they are being educated, if they have dropped out, been expelled, are home-schooled, or have moved to another school. It was found that 15 states do not even know the number of students being educated through home schooling in their state. This leads to the conclusion that many school districts and states do not care whether or not children are being educated—as long as their poor performance is not counted in school, district, and state No Child Left Behind assessment reports. This raises another issue since many students who are unaccounted for have most likely dropped out. The Bill & Melinda Gates Foundation report (Bridgeland, Dilulio, & Morison, 2006) found that few students drop out of school prior to their 16th birthday, which is the end of compulsory schooling in almost every state. The report questions why states have not raised the age for compulsory schooling until high school graduation (Kelly, 2006).

Many of these destructive policies, programs, and practices are still used in spite of decades of research that has documented their ineffectiveness. One explanation of the continued use of these destructive activities is that they are so ingrained into the culture of schools in the United States that they are justified, not by thoughtful research, but through unfortunate and widely believed mythologies about teaching and learning—or worse, through racism and class prejudice.

The Pedagogy of Poverty

In addition to these destructive approaches, there are strong indications that poor and minority students also suffer from ineffective classroom instructional practices. Researchers such as Martin Haberman have concluded that public schools continue to use instructional practices that are not effective for poor and culturally diverse students. Haberman and others have come to describe these ineffective instructional practices as the "pedagogy of poverty" (Haberman, 1991; Padrón, Waxman, & Rivera, 2002). These practices include the overuse of the following:

- **Teacher-controlled discussions and decision-making.** Teacher-centered classrooms have a debilitating effect on poor and minority students. Research has shown that students need hands-on, involved learning in order to learn effectively. In addition, teacher attitudes and prejudices have a powerful influence on learning—both good and bad. If a teacher holds low expectations for poor and minority students, and he or she controls the discussions and decision-making in the classroom, poor and minority students are destined for low achievement.

- **Lecture, drill, and practice techniques.** These strategies have been documented as some of the techniques most frequently used with poor and minority students. They have also been documented as some of the most ineffective strategies used with any student.

- **Worksheets.** These tend to be "upgrades" of questions typically found in textbooks at the end of the chapter. Some ineffective classes use these "worksheets du jour" on a regular basis.

Other researchers (Jagers & Carroll, 2002; Barr & Parrett, 2001, 2003) have identified additional ineffective instructional practices:

- **Cultural aberration.** Many public schools reflect middle-class values, thus creating a "collision of cultures" with the value structures of poor and minority students.

- **Low-quality of education.** Observations in classrooms of predominately poor and minority students have found that the lessons and assignments are significantly less demanding than those found in middle-class classrooms. Poor and minority students spend a remarkable amount of time making collages and posters and coloring pictures under the guise of "hands-on learning." Poor and minority students are often tracked into general education courses in which regular subject matter from the academic disciplines has been replaced with courses like "opportunity math" for students who supposedly cannot learn algebra.

- **Low expectations.** Research has documented that a poor student is five times more likely to have an inexperienced or inadequately trained teacher, and these teachers often focus their instruction on achievement levels that reflect a cultural bias; for example, teachers often do not believe poor and minority students can achieve high academic proficiency, so instruction and assignments are watered down to low levels of expectation.

- **Classroom practices that are unresponsive to students.** Too many classroom teachers focus their energy on what is taught rather than on what is learned. Effective teachers focus their lessons first on the needs of their students.

After visiting urban schools throughout the United States, Kati Haycock and her colleagues were stunned not only by how little was expected of poor students, but also by the low level of classroom assignments that were given to them. Even worse, in high-poverty middle and high schools, Haycock reported a surprising number of coloring assignments, rather than assignments in writing and math: "Even at the high school level, we found coloring assignments. 'Read *To Kill a Mockingbird*,' says the 11th-grade English teacher, 'and when you're finished, color a poster about it'" (Haycock, 2001, p. 8).

Eliminating the Bigotry of Low Expectations

"When I became superintendent, I carefully reviewed data from throughout the school district. I was surprised to see that 800 students in our largest high school had not taken algebra, and they were not scheduled to take algebra in the future. When confronted with the data, [the principal of the school] looked puzzled and shrugged. 'I guess they just kinda fell through the cracks,' he explained. I reacted fairly quickly: 'It must have been a hell of a crack!' Upon further examination, I learned all 800 students were African American. I directed the principal to immediately schedule all of the students in pre-algebra and then algebra. He shook his head and explained, 'I can't do that. The schedule has already been completed.' I responded, 'Today is Friday. You have all weekend to make the necessary adjustments. I want the revised schedule in my office on Monday morning.'"

—*Superintendent, North Carolina*

While the bigotry of low expectations appears to be far less pervasive in recent years, it does linger on. In his closing statement in a recent South Carolina school finance case, an attorney for the state remarked: "The effects [poverty] has are deeply embedded in society and culture in the state. Is altering the effects of poverty something schools can do, or is that something society has to muster? The answer is no, we don't know how to do this. It's not happening anywhere" (Richards, 2005,

p. 19). In fact, it *is* happening—in many schools and districts in South Carolina and across the country. Poor children are indeed achieving at high levels.

Evidence abounds to support an immediate expansion of the successful intervention practices currently being employed with underachieving, poor youth (Barr & Parrett, 2001). Despite decades of research regarding the detrimental approaches used in public education, too many educators have yet to acknowledge the proven consequences of these destructive practices and replace them with more effective approaches to educating poor students.

Educators must address the pedagogy and mythology of the past to create schools that can indeed effectively educate the underachieving children of poverty. Critical to reorganizing schools and classrooms for success is the need to support and enhance the capacity of classroom teachers. Without question, it is the child's teacher who represents hope and promise for our under-performing poor children.

The next chapter provides an overview of the research, evaluation, and data analyses conducted on high-performing, high-poverty schools. It includes a wide variety of classrooms, schools, school districts, and community strategies that have been unusually effective in improving the achievement and school success of the underachieving children of poverty.

Chapter 3

Research on High-Performing, High-Poverty Schools

"We have much more to learn from studying high-poverty schools that are on the path to improvement than we do from studying nominally high-performing schools that are producing a significant portion of their performance through social class rather than instruction."

—*Richard Elmore (2005, p. 45)*

Research has identified a steadily growing number of schools where poor and minority students are learning effectively and achieving high academic standards. In the late 1970s, Ron Edmonds and his colleagues began identifying the traits of effective schools where this phenomenon was occurring. Later, scholars at Louisiana State University analyzed more than 100 separate studies over a 10-year period that identified schools in high-poverty areas where the students were achieving at similar levels as middle-class students. More recently, schools associated with the High Schools That Work (HSTW) program reported that all types of underachieving students, particularly poor and minority high school students, could perform satisfactorily when provided with a rigorous, relevant college-prep curriculum and when better supported in their studies (Bottoms & Anthony, 2005).

Perhaps most significant was a series of reports from the Education Trust that began in 1999 and attracted national attention to schools in every part of the nation where poor and minority students were outperforming their more advantaged peers. *Dispelling the Myth* (Barth et al., 1999) identified 366 schools where more than half of the poor or minority (African-American and Hispanic) students were achieving in the top 25% of the schools in reading and math. *Dispelling the Myth Revisited* (Jerald, 2001) identified more than 4,500 schools where some aspect of students' academic performance placed them above 75% of the schools in their states. More recently, *Dispelling the Myth . . . Over Time* (Education Trust, 2002) reported on this continued trend, focusing on thousands of schools that were maintaining sustained achievement success. The work of the Education Trust has further documented that effective schools can successfully teach poor and minority students and ensure that they are achieving high levels of proficiency.

The fact is that we *can* successfully educate all students when we choose to do so. Hopefully, the flawed conclusions of the past about the lack of influence schools have on the academic achievement of poor children and youth have finally been put to rest. The policies and practices inspired by Coleman's report—and other research of that time—were wrong and destructive. We now possess vivid, powerful evidence to document the tragic errors that have impeded the achievement of generations of children and can begin to correct those errors.

Identifying Strategies for Accelerating the Achievement of Poor Children

Scholars, research organizations, and concerned educators and community members continue their efforts to discover and disseminate information on why and how some schools have been so successful with the children of poverty. By 2005, 18 studies had been published on the policies, programs, and practices that have encouraging results with children of poverty. While our nation has perpetually sought to better our schools, the specific work of improving low-performing schools that enroll a significant number of children of poverty is rooted in the late 1970s when Ron Edmonds and his colleagues began identifying the correlates of effective schools (Edmonds, 1979a, 1979b, 1981, 1982). Soon thereafter, the Louisiana School Effectiveness Study conducted and analyzed a decade of research that explained remarkable school successes with poor and minority students in that state (Teddlie & Stringfield, 1993).

Beginning in the late 1990s and continuing to the present, the number and sophistication of these studies and reports have steadily increased. Joining these efforts are a large number of successful schools and districts that have independently reported the specific strategic actions they have taken that have led to their successes and effectiveness with poor and minority children and youth. This growing body of evidence may well prove to be the most important information ever assembled regarding the effective instruction of the children of poverty.

It is important to note that the accumulation of such specific detail for improving the achievement of students of poverty has been driven by a number of policy changes, including the development of comprehensive state standards and accountability measures, advances in technology that have enabled educators to better understand and use data, state and federal policy changes requiring both comprehensive and disaggregated assessment, as well as required yearly goal-setting and progress reporting. These changes have prompted educators to intensify and accelerate their efforts and resolve to effectively teach the underachieving children of poverty. The framework of research on high-performing, high-poverty schools (figure 3.1, pages 38–39) documents the unprecedented work of many of our schools to better serve the underachieving students of poverty.

A Framework of Research on High-Performing, High-Poverty Schools

> *"What surprises you about high-poverty, high-performing schools is the whole positive attitude, the can-do spirit. . . . They are human bulldozers. They literally roll over obstacles and they believe that no obstacle is too great. When you see this in person, the magnitude of how dramatically different this attitude is from that in high-poverty, low-performing schools really knocks your socks off."*
>
> —*Louisiana Staff Development Council Investigator (Richardson, 2005, p. 1)*

The 18 studies, reports, and data analyses compiled in figure 3.1 document an emerging pattern of school improvement strategies and practices that are being implemented effectively by all types of schools in every area of the country. Analysis of these sources yields eight specific strategies and practices found in successful high-performing, high-poverty schools. According to the studies, these schools:

Ensure effective district and school leadership.

Engage parents, communities, and schools to work as partners.

Understand and hold high expectations for poor and culturally diverse students.

Target low-performing students and schools, particularly in reading.

Align, monitor, and manage the curriculum.

Create a culture of data and assessment literacy.

Build and sustain instructional capacity.

Reorganize time, space, and transitions.

The framework identifies these eight primary recommendations or conclusions of the studies as well as successful strategies and practices from the individual participating schools. These strategies and practices are marked with asterisks.

The findings from these 18 efforts (listed chronologically in the framework) provide a sufficient basis to conclude that this pattern can be successfully applied by other schools and districts attempting to improve their educational programs for underachieving students of poverty.

EIGHT STRATEGIES AND PRACTICES

RESEARCH ON HIGH-PERFORMING, HIGH-POVERTY SCHOOLS	Ensure Effective District and School Leadership	Engage Parents, Communities, and Schools to Work as Partners	Understand and Hold High Expectations for Poor and Culturally Diverse Students	Target Low-Performing Students and Schools, Particularly in Reading	Align, Monitor, and Manage the Curriculum	Create a Culture of Assessment and Data Literacy	Build and Sustain Instructional Capacity	Reorganize Time, Space, and Transitions
Louisiana School Effectiveness Study (LSES): "Schools Make a Difference" (Teddlie & Stringfield, 1993)	✓	*	✓	✓	✓	✓	✓	*
Education Trust: Dispelling the Myth, Revisited, and Over Time (Barth et al., 1999; Jerald, 2001; Education Trust, 2002)	✓	✓	✓	✓	✓	✓	✓	✓
Just for the Kids: Studies of High-Performing School Systems (1999–2006)	✓	✓	✓	✓	✓	✓	✓	✓
Mid-continent Research for Education and Learning: "Raising the Achievement of Low-Performing Students" (Goodwin, 2000)	*	✓	*	✓	✓	✓	✓	✓
North Central Regional Education and Laboratory (NCREL): "Wisconsin's High-Performing/High-Poverty Schools" (Manset et al., 2000)	✓	✓	✓	✓	✓	✓	✓	✓
Consortium for Policy Research in Education (CPRE): "The District Role in Building Capacity" (Massell, 2000)	*	*	*	✓	✓	✓	✓	*
Iowa Association of School Boards: The Lighthouse Inquiry (Iowa Association of School Boards, 2000)	✓	✓	✓	✓	✓	✓	✓	✓
Heritage Foundation: "No Excuses: Lessons From 21 High-Performing, High-Poverty Schools" (Carter, 2001)	✓	✓	✓		*	*	✓	

Figure 3.1 is a matrix table. The row labels (studies) and legend/caption are transcribed below. The column headers for the matrix are not visible/labeled in the image; each cell contains either a ✔ (Primary recommendation or conclusion from the study) or a ✶ (Noted strategy or practice from the participating school(s) or district(s)).

Study									
U.S. Department of Education: "The Longitudinal Evaluation of School Change and Performance (LESCP) in Title I Schools" (U.S. Department of Education, 2001)	✔	✶	✔	✔	✶	✶	✶	✔	✔
Center for Research on the Education of Students Placed at Risk (CRESPAR): "Comprehensive School Reform and Student Achievement: A Meta-Analysis" (Borman et al., 2002)	✶	✶	✶	✶	✶	✶	✶	✶	✶
Northern Illinois University Center for Governmental Studies: "Closing the Achievement Gap: Lessons from Illinois' Golden Spike High-Poverty, High-Performing Schools" (McGee, 2004)	✔	✔	✔	✔	✔	✔	✔	✔	✔
Louisiana Staff Development Council: "The Secrets of 'Can-Do' Schools" (Richardson, 2003)	✔	✔	✔	✔	✔	✔	✔	✔	
Learning First Alliance: "Beyond Islands of Excellence" (Togneri & Anderson, 2003)	✔	✶	✶	✶	✔	✔	✔	✔	✶
Center for Performance Assessment: "High Performance in High-Poverty Schools: 90/90/90 and Beyond" (Reeves, 2003)	✶	✶	✶	✔	✶	✶	✶	✔	✔
Manhattan Institute: "The Teachability Index: Can Disadvantaged Students Learn?" (Greene & Forster, 2004)		✶	✶	✔	✔	✔	✔	✔	
Hewlett-Packard: "High-Achieving Schools Initiative Final Report" (Kitchen et al., 2004)	✶	✶	✔	✶	✶	✔	✔	✔	✶
Prichard Committee for Academic Excellence: "Inside the Black Box of High-Performing, High-Poverty Schools" (Kannapel & Clements, 2005)	✔	✔	✔	✔	✔	✔	✔	✔	✔
EdSource: "Similar Students, Different Results: Why Do Some Schools Do Better?" (Williams, Kirst, & Haertel, et al., 2005)	✔	✶	✔	✔	✔	✔	✔	✔	✔

✔ Primary recommendation or conclusion from the study   ✶ Noted strategy or practice from the participating school(s) or district(s)

Figure 3.1: Framework of Research on High-Performing, High-Poverty Schools

Louisiana School Effectiveness Study (LSES): "Schools Make a Difference" (Teddlie & Stringfield, 1993)

One of the earliest studies occurred in Louisiana and attempted to understand why a number of high-poverty schools were so successful in achieving academic proficiency for their students. The Louisiana School Effectiveness Study (LSES), initiated in 1980, spanned a 10-year period during which its multiple phases explored and compared differences in student achievement that related to student socioeconomic status and school climate. The LSES further identified and studied effective and ineffective schools and sought to understand how students in some of the state's poorest communities were achieving up to and beyond students in the schools in more affluent communities. The study found that effective low-socioeconomic-status schools often possessed:

- Motivating principals and teachers
- Increased instructional time in reading and math
- High principal and teacher expectations for student achievement
- Principals that frequently visited classrooms
- The use of teacher aides
- Younger and less experienced teachers
- Principal autonomy in staff selection (Teddlie & Stringfield, p. 34, 1993)

Leadership was continuously referenced as an essential characteristic of success in this study. The ability to instill in students a belief that they can achieve was identified by the LSES as central to effective teaching of low-socioeconomic-status students. This study concluded that schools indeed do make a difference in student achievement regardless of the socioeconomic status of students. The study also acknowledged the importance of engaging parents, communities, and schools and of reorganizing time and space as characteristics of success in high-performing, high-poverty schools.

Education Trust: Dispelling the Myth, Revisited, and Over Time (Barth et al., 1999; Jerald, 2001; Education Trust, 2002)

Beginning in 1999, staff of the Education Trust, an independent nonprofit organization committed to a "single-minded attention of what is best for students—especially low-income students and students of color" (www2.edtrust. org), attempted to summarize the common characteristics of the high-performing schools they had been analyzing. The Education Trust was one of the first national organizations to study and bring attention to the existence of large numbers of K–12 schools with high-poverty, high-minority enrollments where students were dramatically outperforming schools of far greater economic advantage.

Their *Dispelling the Myth* reports reviewed the growing database of state test results that revealed thousands of high-poverty or high-minority schools that were outperforming over 75% of the schools in their respective states. The Education Trust identified the reasons for these gains:

- Extensive use of state and local standards to design curriculum and instruction, assess student work, and evaluate teachers
- Increased instruction time for reading and mathematics
- Substantial investment in professional development for teachers that focused on instructional practices to help students meet academic standards
- Comprehensive systems to monitor individual student performance and to provide help to struggling students before they fall behind
- Parental involvement in efforts to get students to meet standards
- State or district accountability systems with real consequences for adults in schools
- Use of assessments to help guide instruction and resources and as a healthy part of everyday teaching and learning (Jerald, 2001, p. 3)

Kati Haycock, executive director of the Education Trust, further summarized the characteristics of schools successfully teaching poor and minority students. She indicates that in these schools:

- Standards are the key.
- All students must have a challenging curriculum.
- Students need extra help.
- Teachers matter a lot. (Haycock, 2001)

Four additional elements have emerged as the Education Trust has continued to investigate high-performing, high-poverty schools:

1. They make no excuses. Everybody takes responsibility for student learning.
2. They do not leave anything about teaching and learning to chance. High-performing districts:
    - Have clear and specific goals for what students should learn in every grade, including the order in which they should learn it.
    - Provide teachers with common curriculum assignments.
    - Assess students every 4 to 8 weeks to measure progress.
    - Act immediately on the results of these assessments.

3. They insist on rigor in every respect. Leading districts and states:
   - Align high school exit standards with the skills and knowledge necessary for further education and work.
   - Make college prep the default curriculum for all students.
4. They know that good teachers matter more than anything else.

Just for the Kids: Studies of High-Performing School Systems (1999–2006)

To promote a better understanding of the role of academic standards and data in increasing student achievement, civic leader and public education advocate Tom Luce launched Just for the Kids (JFTK) in 1995. A Texas-based nonprofit organization, JFTK "motivates educators and the public to take action to improve schools by giving them a clear picture of a school's academic condition and identifying the effective practices found in high-performing schools" (Just for the Kids, 2006).

In 1997, the organization began analyzing state test data in search of successful schools and the practices they employed. This work grew into the Just for the Kids School Reports designed to provide educators with a clear and comprehensive picture of a school's academic performance by subject and grade coupled with comparisons of schools with similar demographics that have achieved high levels of academic performance. The comparative aspect of the school reports was assembled through case studies of high-performing schools and the practices they used to acquire their high-performing status. The study resulted in the Best-Practice Framework.

The framework was based on a 4-year analysis of more than 100 high-performing schools through data, observations, and interviews. The framework identified effective district, school, and classroom practices around five organizing themes. It also takes into account four critical areas common to these schools:

1. Mobility
2. Percent of low-income students
3. Percent of limited-English-proficiency students
4. School, grade, and classroom size

Using JFTK data tools, a school can perform a self-audit that adjusts for the four critical areas, compares achievement data from recent tests and current classroom practices in the school, and then applies the framework to locate comparable schools with higher achievement, opening a path for educators to consider in targeting improvements.

The National Center for Educational Accountability (NCEA) was created in 2001 as a partnership between JFTK, the Education Commission of the States, and the University of Texas at Austin to "promote higher student achievement by improving state data collection and identifying practices that distinguish consistently high-performing schools from others and disseminating these findings" (Olsen, 2005, p. 24).

The NCEA, funded through a variety of individual, corporate, government, and private foundation sources, works closely with affiliates in almost half the states to implement NCEA-guided studies of high-performing schools. The Broad Foundation, through a $1.2 million grant, supported this work through 2006 in more than 450 schools located in 17 states. Schools qualifying as study candidates must have demonstrated three consecutive years of high performance on state tests and must make annual yearly progress by No Child Left Behind standards (Olsen, 2005).

To determine key features of high performance, NCEA adapted the Texas Best Practice Framework into its own framework, which focuses on determining evidence of student learning. The framework, presented as a matrix of themes, practices, state and district standards, core beliefs, resources, and local influences, identifies precisely what high-performing schools do to accomplish their success (figure 3.2, page 44). Jean Rutherford, center director, describes the underlying value of this common framework as having "clear and specific goals for students, rooted in state content standards" that have "clearly emerged as the bedrock foundation, . . . which provides a penetrating, deep understanding of what it is children are to know and be able to do and how to connect it across grades" (Olsen, 2005, p. 24).

Mid-continent Research for Education and Learning (McREL): "Raising the Achievement of Low-Performing Students" (Goodwin, 2000)

In 1999, Mid-continent Research for Education and Learning (McREL, formerly the Mid-continent Regional Educational Laboratory) commissioned seven papers from national experts on diversity issues. The goal was to identify causes of the low performance on achievement tests of "marginalized students" (poor and minority), and then to identify research-based strategies for ensuring that these students meet state educational standards. These papers synthesized more than 300 research reports and related documents and focused their recommendations on school district and state policy makers. The summary identified seven

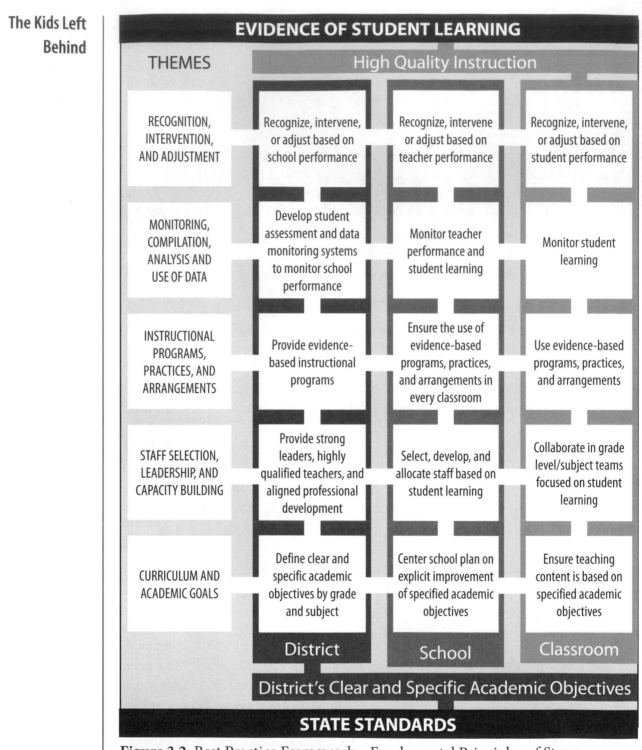

Figure 3.2: Best Practice Framework—Fundamental Principles of Strong
Learning Systems (Used with permission of the National Center for
Educational Accountability and Just for the Kids.)

research-based conclusions for improving the academic performance of poor and minority students:

1. Provide all students with rigorous curriculum.
2. Help teachers improve instruction.
3. Provide support to students.
4. Create smaller classes.
5. Increase parent involvement.
6. Identify the five ways low performance is manufactured.
7. Establish strong, yet fair, accountability. (Goodwin, 2000, p. 1)

The study also acknowledged the importance of understanding and holding high expectations for poor and minority children and the need for sustained support and assistance from instructional leaders.

North Central Regional Educational Laboratory (NCREL): "Wisconsin's High-Performing/High-Poverty Schools" (Manset et al., 2000)

The North Central Regional Educational Laboratory (NCREL) studied high-performing, high-poverty schools in Wisconsin. The study identified 17 features within five prominent characteristics of effective schools.

1. Effective implementation of theory or philosophy
   - Shared leadership
   - Data-based decision-making
   - Student-centered practice
   - High expectations with safety nets
2. Effective professional development opportunities
   - Staff-initiated in-service topics
   - Peer coaching and mentoring
   - Opportunities for collaboration
3. Parent and community involvement
   - Multiple means of communicating with parents
   - Parent advisory committees
   - The school as a community center
4. Effective classroom instruction
   - Emphasis on assessment
   - Project-based instruction
5. Effective classroom structure and organization
   - Small class size
   - Alternative within-school programs

- Integrated curriculum
- Curriculum alignment with state standards
- School-wide discipline system (Manset et al., 2000, pp. iii–iv)

Consortium for Policy Research in Education (CPRE): "The District Role in Building Capacity" (Massell, 2000)

Research has also focused on the effective strategies of school districts in achieving success with low-performing students. The Consortium for Policy Research in Education (CPRE) is composed of scholars from five of the nation's premier research universities: Harvard, Stanford, and the Universities of Michigan, Pennsylvania, and Wisconsin-Madison. Diane Massell led a research team from CPRE that identified four essential capacity-building strategies that were observed in 22 successful school districts in seven reform-active states over a 2-year period. These strategies included:

1. Interpreting and using data
2. Building teacher knowledge and skills
3. Aligning curriculum and instruction
4. Targeting interventions on low-performing students and schools (Massell, 2001, p. 1)

While the study did not specifically identify leadership as an essential capacity-building strategy, the critical importance of effective leadership in successfully implementing these four capacity-building strategies and others found in high-performing, high-poverty schools was implied. Participants in the study also acknowledged the importance of engaging parents, holding high expectations for students, and reorganizing time and space.

Iowa Association of School Boards: The Lighthouse Inquiry (Iowa Association of School Boards, 2000)

In the late 1990s, the Iowa Association of School Boards conducted a study of low-performing and high-performing school districts in the state of Georgia. They studied schools with comparable demographics to Iowa schools that performed very high or very low for 3 consecutive academic years (1995–1996, 1996–1997, and 1997–1998). All of the school districts were small (ranging from 1,395 students to 5,163 students) and rural (Rice et al., 2000, p. 2).

The study identified seven essential conditions for school renewal and described in detail the differences of each of these conditions in high-performing as opposed to low-performing districts. The following describes what was found in the high-performing districts:

- **Shared leadership.** A focus on student learning through a shared vision, high expectations, and dynamic leadership among all levels
- **Continuous improvement.** A continuous focus on improving education with high levels of individual and shared decision-making
- **Ability to create and sustain initiatives.** An understanding of how to organize people and the school environment to start and sustain an improvement effort
- **Supportive workplace for staff.** A supportive workplace that enables all staff to succeed in their roles
- **Staff development.** Regular school-wide staff development that is focused on studying teaching and learning
- **Support for school sites through data and information.** Using data and information on student needs to make decisions and modify actions at the district and building level
- **Community involvement.** A close connection between the school, parents, and community (Rice et al., 2000, pp. 6–10)

The study further acknowledged the importance of connecting instruction to district goals.

Heritage Foundation: "No Excuses: Lessons From 21 High-Performing, High-Poverty Schools" (Carter, 2001)

Another early effort to locate high-performing, high-poverty schools, identify their attributes, and disseminate common elements of their success was sponsored as a part of the Heritage Foundation's "No Excuses" campaign. The purpose of the campaign was to create pressure for better education for the poor: "The No Excuses campaign brings together liberals, centrists, and conservatives who are committed to high academic achievement among children of all races, ethnic groups, and family incomes" (Carter, 2001, p. iv).

The study identified 21 high-performing, high-poverty schools from an initial sample of over 400 prospective schools. The chosen schools (three charter, three private, one rural, one religious, and the rest traditional public schools) each had enrollments of 75% or greater free- and reduced-lunch students and scored at or above the 66 percentile of required achievement tests. The case studies of these 21 schools present an intentionally diverse look at a cross-section of schools that clearly confront the notion that high-poverty schools and students will underachieve.

The common traits of these schools include:

- Principals who are free to spend their resources, hire staff, lead curriculum and instruction, and oversee facilities
- Principals who use measurable goals to establish a culture of achievement
- Master teachers who bring out the best in a faculty
- Rigorous and regular testing that leads to continuous student achievement
- Achievement as the key to discipline
- Principals who work actively with parents to make the home a center of learning
- Effort creates ability (Carter, 2001, pp. 8–11)

U.S. Department of Education: "The Longitudinal Evaluation of School Change and Performance (LESCP) in Title I Schools" (U.S. Department of Education, 2001)

A longitudinal study of 71 high-poverty Title I schools was conducted for the U.S. Department of Education in 2001. The study followed students in these schools as they progressed from the third through the fifth grade. The LESCP claimed to be "the first major study to examine the impact of standards-based reform on student achievement" (U.S. Department of Education, 2001, p. 1). The longitudinal analysis was designed to test the effects of changes in curriculum and instruction called for by advocates of standard-based reforms. The study found that while students in the high-poverty schools did in fact make significant increases in achievement, they *did not* catch up with national norms during the course of the study. Nonetheless, the study identified school practices and standard-based policies that were more likely to result in student achievement gains in reading and math as well as those that were not linked to improving student performance.

According to the study, reading achievement improved more rapidly when:

- Teachers gave high ratings to their professional development in reading. The growth in student test scores between third and fifth grade was approximately 20% greater when teachers rated their professional development high than when they rated it low.
- Third-grade teachers were especially active in outreach to parents of low-achieving students. Growth in test scores between third and fifth grade was 50% higher for those students whose teachers and schools reported high levels of parental outreach early than for students whose teachers and

schools reported low levels of parent outreach activities for the third grade. (U.S. Department of Education, 2001, p. 1)

However, the study found that fifth graders' reading achievement improved less when they spent additional time reading aloud or completing worksheets.

Mathematics achievement gains occurred more frequently when:

- Teachers gave high ratings to their professional development in mathematics. Growth in test scores between grades three and five was 50% higher for those students whose teachers and schools rated their professional development high rather than low.
- There was early teacher outreach to parents of students who initially showed low achievement. Test scores in mathematics grew between the third and fifth grade at a 40% higher rate for students in schools where teachers reported high levels of parental outreach than for students in schools where teachers reported low levels of parental outreach activities.
- Teachers employed instructional practices in upper grades that involved students in more exploration. Growth in test scores between the third and fifth grades was about 17% greater for students whose fifth-grade teachers reported a relatively very high use of exploration in instruction versus students whose fifth grade teachers reported relatively low use. (U.S. Department of Education, 2001, p. 2)

The study further acknowledged the importance of the enactment of standards, accountability for schools, high expectations, and improvement plans aligned to standards.

Center for Research on the Education of Students Placed At Risk (CRESPAR): "Comprehensive School Reform and Student Achievement: A Meta-Analysis" (Borman et al., 2002)

This meta-analysis reviewed the effects of whole-school or comprehensive reforms on student achievement. The study focused on 29 of the more frequently implemented comprehensive school reform (CSR) models, most of which enroll significant numbers of students of poverty. The study concluded that while "the overall effects of CSR . . . appear . . . promising, the combined quantity, quality, and statistical significance of evidence from three of the models, in particular, set them apart" from the other whole-school models (Borman et al., 2002, p. v).

The three programs identified were:

1. Direct Instruction
2. School Development Programs
3. Success for All

The study found that CSR models in use in a school for 5 years or more demonstrated unusually positive effects, both in poverty-level schools as well as in more affluent schools. The study found little evidence to support several of the most widely accepted explanations for raising student achievement, including "staff professional development, measurable goals and benchmarks for student learning, a faculty vote to increase the likelihood of model acceptance and buy-in, and the use of specific and innovative curricular materials and instructional practices assigned to improve teaching and student learning" (Borman et al., 2002, p. 36).

There was strong evidence of the positive influence of school efforts to help parents enrich their children's out-of-school learning opportunities. Unfortunately, efforts to require family participation in school improvement or governance activities, while helping the school grow as an institution, did not appear to improve student achievement (Epstein, 1995).

The key characteristics of the three CSR models recognized as promising in their work with high-poverty students include:

- Leadership
- Engaging parents and families
- High expectations
- Targeting low-performing students
- Curricular alignment
- Data literacy
- Instructional capacity
- Reorganizing time and space

Northern Illinois University Center for Governmental Studies: "Closing the Achievement Gap: Lessons from Illinois' Golden Spike High-Poverty, High-Performing Schools" (McGee, 2004)

Scholars at the Northern Illinois Center for Government Studies conducted a quantitative, qualitative study involving schools in their state with a sustained record of closing the achievement gap between poor and minority students and affluent students. The study identified a number of common characteristics in the effective schools they studied (McGee, 2004).

Characteristics found in over 90% of the effective high-performing, high-poverty schools included:

- Strong, visible leadership advocating high-learning standards, high expectations, and a culture of success for all
- An emphasis on early literacy
- Talented, hard-working teachers who believe that every child can and will learn
- More academic learning time
- Extensive parental involvement

Characteristics found in at least 50% of the schools included:

- An internal capacity for accountability
- Extensive staff use of data to drive instructional decisions
- Attention to the health and safety needs of students
- A strong early childhood education program (McGee, 2004, pp. 115–116)

This study also revealed interesting comparative data between high- and low-performing schools with high poverty levels. Contrary to popular belief, school size, class size, and funding accounted for only minimal differences in student performance between the high- and low-performing schools. On the other hand, the high-performing, high-poverty schools appeared consistently more effective in keeping and teaching transient students as they reported significantly lower rates of student mobility (McGee, 2004).

Louisiana Staff Development Council: "The Secrets of 'Can-Do' Schools" (Richardson, 2003)

The Louisiana Staff Development Council (LSDC) conducted an investigation of 12 schools considered "academically above average" by the Louisiana accountability system. All of the schools had student poverty rates of at least 80%. LSDC investigators documented seven features that characterized each of the schools, which Richardson (2003) summarized as follows:

1. Each school used many types of job-embedded staff development: coaching, mentoring, examination and reflection on student work and instructional practices, visitation to other classrooms and other schools, conferences, workshops, serving on curriculum committees, and so on. Less common was the use of case studies or action research in a formal sense.

2. The principal and staff had a strong sense of efficacy—they believed in the power of teaching and their own ability to ensure that every student learns, regardless of obstacles.

3. In every school, the primary job responsibility of at least one individual (often the principal) was to oversee instruction and know what was going on in classrooms. Although an instructional leader guided the learning process for teachers and provided the necessary resources, each of the 12 schools was a true community of learners where faculty collaboration was considered critical to improved practice.

4. Analyzing student data was the first step and the driving force in the professional learning process. The schools analyzed data, especially looking at test results, to identify areas of broad, common needs and each student's specific strengths and weaknesses.

5. Teachers tried different approaches to meet student needs—grouping and structuring, different materials, a variety of instructional strategies—always with an eye toward continuous assessment.

6. Standards-based instruction was pervasive, and teachers could readily discuss how the lessons matched content standards.

7. All schools had excellent school-wide discipline characterized by a shared sense of responsibility for all students. There was a general understanding that children of poverty often come from homes without a great deal of structure or academic support. Structured classroom procedures and high expectations were considered the foundation for success.

In addition, the study identified school, teacher, and administrator stability as important factors. The investigator found that unlike most high-poverty schools, where teachers move on after 2 or 3 years, the teachers in the studied schools appeared to have the necessary principal and environmental support necessary to performing good work.

Learning First Alliance: "Beyond Islands of Excellence" (Togneri & Anderson, 2003)

The Learning First Alliance, a permanent partnership of 12 professional organizations representing parents, teachers, administrators, curriculum directors, state school officers, school board members, and the Education Commission of the States, works to:

- Ensure that high academic standards are held for all students.

- Ensure a safe and supportive place of learning for all students.
- Engage parents and other community members in helping students achieve high expectations. (www.learningfirst.org/about/goals)

During the 2001–2002 school year, the Alliance conducted an in-depth study of five high-poverty school districts in Texas, California, Maryland, Minnesota, and Rhode Island in which consistent, improved achievement was occurring in reading and/or mathematics. These school districts represented a cross-section of characteristics regarding size, geographic region, urbanicity, and union affiliation. All of the districts had large percentages of poverty-level students. Most importantly, all of the school districts demonstrated achievement across grade levels, subjects, and racial and ethnic groups, although not all were deemed comprehensive, high-achieving districts. The study reported that two districts (Aldine, Texas, and Kent County, Maryland) rose from the lower to the top tier of districts in their states. This remarkable accomplishment took approximately 7 years of sustained effort.

The Alliance's report identified seven strategies the districts used to improve instruction and achievement in all schools (Togneri & Anderson, 2003). All of the school districts exhibited many of the characteristics that were identified with high achievement, and at least three school districts were successfully implementing all of them.

1. Districts had the courage to acknowledge poor performance and the will to seek solutions.
2. Districts put in place a system-wide approach to improving instruction—one that articulated curricular content and provided instructional supports.
3. Districts instilled visions that focused on student learning and guided instructional improvement.
4. Districts made decisions based on data, not instinct.
5. Districts adopted new approaches to professional development that involved a coherent and district-organized set of strategies to improve instruction.
6. Districts redefined leadership roles.
7. Districts committed to sustaining reform over the long haul. (Togneri & Anderson, 2003, p. 3)

The study and its participating districts further acknowledged the value of engaging parents and communities, holding high expectations for all children, and reorganizing time and space to meet the needs of students.

Center for Performance Assessment: "High Performance in High-Poverty Schools: 90/90/90 and Beyond" (Reeves, 2003)

The term "90/90/90 schools" originated from Douglas Reeves' study of Milwaukee, Wisconsin, schools in which 90% or more of the enrollment were minority students, eligible for free and reduced lunch, and performing at or above state or district proficiency levels in reading or other areas. Original analysis was expanded to consider data from 228 schools enrolling in excess of 130,000 students located in a variety of urban, rural, and suburban settings. Using data analysis and site visits, the study determined the five common characteristics of 90/90/90 schools:

1. A focus on academic achievement
2. Clear curriculum choices
3. Frequent assessment of student progress and multiple opportunities for improvement
4. An emphasis on nonfiction writing
5. Collaborative scoring of student work (Reeves, 2003, p. 187)

Reeves and the Center for Performance Assessment emphasize that the 90/90/90 schools achieved long-term sustainable gains without the use of proprietary programs or instructional practices. Reeves concluded his analysis with the reminder of the imperfection associated with any research. In this case, he cautions that the replication of these practices does not guarantee improvement, but suggests that delaying action to continue searching for a perfect intervention is unacceptable when the needs of the current students are of such high priority.

Manhattan Institute: "The Teachability Index: Can Disadvantaged Students Learn?" (Greene & Forster, 2004)

This Manhattan Institute study focused on all 50 states and measured the "teachability of students by examining 16 social factors that researchers agree affect student teachability" (Greene & Forster, 2004, p. 1). The researchers ranked each state on its level of student disadvantagement (teachability) and then compared the state's teachability of students to academic outcomes. The researchers drew two conclusions:

1. Student teachability (or level of disadvantagement) cannot be a valid excuse for the failure of vastly increased spending to produce better results in student academic achievement.
2. What schools do still matters even when students are facing obstacles to learning. (Greene & Forster, 2004, p. 1)

The researchers identified two general conditions that appear to lead to high academic achievement for high-poverty students:

1. More school choice and high performance for poor students was found in states with alternative schools, magnet schools, and vouchers.
2. Stronger accountability testing leads to better school performance for poverty-level students. (Greene & Forster, 2004, p. 1)

The study further acknowledged the value of engaging parents and communities, holding high expectations for students, and targeting low-performing students.

Hewlett-Packard: "High Achieving Schools Initiative Final Report" (Kitchen et al., 2004)

Researchers for the University of New Mexico studied nine schools in low-income neighborhoods throughout the United States that were part of a Hewlett-Packard funded project, the High Achieving Schools Initiative. The study identified seven characteristics common to schools where poor children were succeeding in mathematics:

The initial research findings demonstrate that the nine highly effective schools that serve low-income communities shared some common characteristics. In interviews with mathematics teachers and students across the schools, common themes that emerged included:

- Teaching and learning are prioritized to support high academic expectations.
- Supplemental support is provided for student learning.
- [There is a] strong and well-defined sense of purpose among mathematics faculty.
- Faculty collaborate and support each other.
- [There is an] explicit focus on test preparation.
- Teaching resources are available.
- Teachers have regular access to professional development opportunities. (Kitchen et al., 2004, p. 94)

The study and its participating schools further acknowledged the importance of effective leadership, engaging parents and communities, targeting low-performing students, aligning curriculum, and reorganizing time and space.

Prichard Committee for Academic Excellence: "Inside the Black Box of High-Performing, High-Poverty Schools" (Kannapel & Clements, 2005)

This comparative study contrasting high-performing, high-poverty elementary schools with low-performing, high-poverty elementary schools in Kentucky was commissioned by the Prichard Committee for Academic Excellence to determine the following:

- What common characteristics seem to contribute to high student performance and are shared by a set of high-performing, high-poverty schools?
- What characteristics and practices differentiate a set of high-performing, high-poverty schools with a small achievement gap from similar high-poverty schools that are neither high-performing nor have a small achievement gap? (Kannapel & Clements, 2005, p. 2)

Twenty-six elementary schools were identified as high-performing, high-poverty through a six-factor screening that included a minimum of 50% free- or reduced-lunch enrollments plus a variety of longitudinal student academic performance data. Eight of these schools were selected for further study and compared with eight of Kentucky's low-performing, high-poverty schools. Sixteen schools participated in an on-site audit process that collected and analyzed school data and conducted principal interviews (Kannapel & Clements, 2005).

When compared, the high-performing, high-poverty schools demonstrated significantly higher performance in:

- Review and alignment of curriculum
- Individual student assessment and instruction
- Caring, nurturing environments of high expectations
- Professional development that was driven by student achievement data
- Efficient use of resources and instructional time (p. 3)

Common characteristics of the eight high-poverty, high-performing schools included:

- High expectations for students, faculty, and staff
- Respectful relationships among adults and students
- Strong focus on academics, instruction, and learning
- Systematic focus on instruction
- Positive faculty morale and work ethic
- Intentional processes for recruiting, hiring, and assigning staff (p. 14)

This study concluded that the success of the eight high-performing, high-poverty schools was directly linked to four common factors present in each school:

1. Instruction driven by individual student assessment
2. Careful, intentional selection, placement, and use of personnel
3. Positive attention or treatment of poverty students
4. Authentic alignment of curriculum, instruction, and assessment

EdSource: "Similar Students, Different Results: Why Do Some Schools Do Better?" (Williams, Kirst, & Haertel, et al., 2005)

This California study surveyed 257 principals and 5,500 teachers statewide to determine key factors of higher academic performance in elementary schools serving high populations of low-socioeconomic-status students. The authors of the study examined principal and teacher perceptions of their schools' performance within the following domains:

- Implementing a coherent, standards-based instructional program
- Involving and supporting parents
- Using assessment data to improve student achievement and instruction
- Encouraging teacher collaboration and professional development
- Ensuring instructional resources
- Enforcing high expectations for student behavior
- Prioritizing student achievement (Williams, Kirst, & Haertel, et al., 2005, p. 2)

Analysis of the findings indicated that the following activities and practices were more common at the higher-performing schools as measured by the state's academic performance index (API):

- Prioritizing student achievement
- Implementing a coherent standards-based curriculum and instructional program
- Using assessment data to improve student achievement and instruction
- Ensuring availability of instructional resources
- Redefining principal leadership to focus on effective management of the school improvement process
- District leadership, accountability, and support

The study also acknowledged that providing assistance to struggling students, involving and supporting parents, and encouraging teacher collaboration and professional development were important.

An Emerging Pattern of School Improvement

These 18 studies identify specific strategies and practices for school improvement that have been proven successful in schools across the country. Together, these strategies and practices form a comprehensive pattern for the improvement of low-performing, high-poverty schools. The Framework of Research on High-Performing, High-Poverty Schools can be used by other schools and districts that are attempting to improve their educational programs for their underachieving students of poverty.

Remember, however, that *there is no silver bullet*. The eight components of intervention presented in the framework overlap and occur in no common sequence, yet they consistently appear in successful schools. Taken together, the research provides educators with a comprehensive understanding of the common and critical aspects associated with successfully teaching poor and minority students. What works in your school or district will be as unique as the population you serve. An in-depth examination of the eight critical strategies and practices is presented in chapters 4 through 11. Each chapter concludes with a self-evaluation rubric schools and districts can use to analyze their progress toward implementing, embedding, and sustaining the eight critical strategies in detailed steps. Chapter 12 provides a composite self-evaluation rubric.

Chapter 4

Ensure Effective District and School Leadership

"It had been a great conference. As we returned home, five of us sat at the back of the plane, leaned across the aisle, and actually held hands and committed ourselves to improving the achievement of our low-performing students. We agreed to go over, under, around, or through any barriers placed before us and get the job done!"

—*Five Teachers and a Principal, Idaho*

Effectively leading high-poverty districts and schools may well be the most challenging work in public education today. The clear difference between high-performing, high-poverty schools and their low-performing counterparts is leadership. When effective leadership is present, a district's poor and minority students demonstrate a steady improvement in learning and achievement. When effective leadership is absent, the unfortunate cycle of underachievement for our neediest students continues.

The Old World of Education

Traditionally, school administrators have viewed educational leadership almost exclusively as a management function. Although there has always been talk of the school administrator as instructional leader, the vast majority of school superintendents and building principals have focused their energies on management responsibilities: personnel matters, budgets, building and grounds issues, athletic programs, textbook selection, technology, student discipline, public relations, and so on.

In recent years, concepts and strategies from the world of business have entered into public education. Approaches like W. Edwards Deming's Total Quality Management have been applied in schools and districts throughout the country. Several large city districts also switched to a CEO model of leadership and began experimenting with hiring new superintendents with business or military backgrounds and little or no educational training, experience, or certification. Site-based management has replaced the more traditional top-down management in many districts. Yet site-based management rarely includes shared decision-making on such important issues as personnel and finances.

In the old world of education, school administrators and school boards tended to manage the status quo, emphasizing a cautious, measured approach in dealing with problems and challenges rather than more bold efforts at systemic school and district improvement. School board members and administrators often expressed concern about significant educational reform. This led to slow piecemeal improvement susceptible to every new educational fad, as well as to frequent charges that school improvement is just one new thing after another. Instructional fads have come and gone, as have a wide variety of approaches to classroom teaching and teacher supervision. During the 1960s and 1970s, a curriculum revolution ushered in the "new" social studies, "new" language arts, "modern" math, and whole language; few of these ideas survived the decade. The 1980s brought theme-based education and minimal competency testing; in the 1990s, it was Goals 2000 and standards. Year after year, teachers would gather in a school cafeteria or auditorium, and the hottest new guru would introduce them to the latest new educational fad in what came to be known as "drive-by professional development." Over the past 30 years, school improvement has focused on a wild assortment of innovations, but rarely, if ever, has student achievement been used to evaluate the effectiveness of the new approaches.

In spite of massive efforts with enormous costs, these fads have left teaching and learning all but untouched. In fact, there was a growing conviction that institutions—from neighborhood schools to the federal government—were almost impossible to change. In his influential book, *The Culture of the School and the Problem of Change* (1971), Seymour Sarason argued that the behavioral regularities in any institution make significant change all but impossible. In addition, the combined impact of textbook publishers, union contracts, teacher certification, state laws and educational requirements, college entrance requirements, traditional expectations, and school bus schedules all but paralyzed public education and rendered even modest change next to impossible. Sarason concluded that it was easier to start a new school than change an existing one.

This conclusion prompted all types of reform-minded individuals to start alternative schools, storefront schools, community schools, free schools, experimental schools, magnet schools, and later charter schools. On occasion, teams of university educators from prestigious universities would temporarily take over the leadership of a school or district and experiment with innovations and reform. Most of these experiments lasted only a few years, and then the team of innovators drifted back to more scholarly pursuits at the academy. There were also heroic school administrators who single-handedly created what researchers would later refer to as "islands of excellence." But, as the Ford Foundation discovered (after investing millions of dollars in experimental schools), when the innovative principal moved on to more attractive opportunities, each school slowly reverted back to traditional patterns of education. Until recently, there were precious few examples of a public school district being transformed and only isolated examples of truly innovative schools where teaching and learning were practiced in a significantly different and more effective manner.

In the old world of education, school boards and school administrators measured their success by how many students would go on to college, the percent of high school students in advanced-placement courses, the number of merit scholars, and the success of their athletic teams. Until very recently, student achievement data was reported in aggregated averages that camouflaged the performance of low-achieving students by averaging in the performance of more affluent, higher-performing students.

This old world of educational leadership is now being transformed in the most significant and remarkable manner as our past understandings of institutional school reform are changing. Educators now know schools and school districts can be transformed and that the achievement gaps reflected in ethnicity, socioeconomic status, special education, limited English proficiency, and gender can be narrowed and closed. Schools throughout the nation are demonstrating that when effective leadership is in place, virtually all students can achieve high levels of academic proficiency and school success.

The New World of Education

Every one of the studies that form the basis for the pattern of school improvement presented in this book identifies school leadership as an essential aspect of improving the performance of underachieving poor and minority students. In fact, most of the research identifies leadership as the most important issue. The leadership occurring in these high-performing, high-poverty schools is dramatically different from those used by any previous generation of administrators: It is a distinctly new and different type of leadership.

Essential, Targeted Leadership Characteristics to Improve Student Achievement

> *"We simply had to enact a different approach to the daily business of educating our students. We all had to change. When we collectively looked at the real data on our kids, we knew where to start. A lot of hard work has gotten us closer to where we need to be."*
>
> —*Superintendent, Oregon*

61

The success stories of high-poverty schools are abundant—just check any recent educational journal, newspaper, or book. Visit the web site of the Education Trust (www2.edtrust.org) and others (such as www.greatschools.net or www.schoolstowatch.org) to learn about the thousands of schools that have reversed historic trends of low achievement by poor students. While every example is unique, they all share the common and critical component of effective leadership.

Marzano, Waters, and McNulty's unprecedented meta-analysis of principal leadership in *School Leadership That Works* (2005) ties reliable, valid studies to concrete results in student achievement. Their analysis yielded 21 core practices that yield results for all students; underperforming students will particularly benefit from the practices they describe as "second-order" changes—those changes necessary to significantly improve the operating culture of a school. A principal who wants to improve the performance of underachieving students:

- Communicates and operates from strong ideals and beliefs about schooling
- Is knowledgeable about current curriculum, instruction, and assessment practices
- Ensures faculty and staff are aware of the most current theories and practices and makes discussion of these a regular aspect of the school's culture
- Monitors the effectiveness of school practices and their impact on student learning
- Adapts his or her leadership behavior to the needs of the current situation and is comfortable with dissent
- Is willing to challenge and actively challenges the status quo
- Inspires and leads new and challenging innovations (Marzano, Waters, & McNulty, 2005, p. 42)

These practices reflect those in place in many of the high-performing schools profiles in chapter 3.

The studies that serve as the foundation for this book identified a number of leadership characteristics that must be in place at the district and school level to ensure system-wide improvements to teaching and learning and increased achievement. The Learning First Alliance study (Togneri & Anderson, 2003) provides a blueprint for leading high-poverty districts from low to high performance. The Golden Spike study concluded that having "strong, visible leadership advocating high learning standards, high expectations, and a culture of success for all" is the key component of high-performing, high-poverty schools and districts (McGee, 2004, p. 115).

These and the other studies detailed in chapter 3 provide a compelling confluence of essential targeted district- and school-level leadership characteristics that must be in place if a district and its schools are serious about leading underachieving poor and minority students to proficiency and school success.

Leadership Priorities at the District Level

Nothing in the new educational revolution is more important than enhanced district leadership skills. The traditional management function of superintendents, central office staff, and school boards is giving way to a wide assortment of essential targeted skills, all of which are focused on ensuring that all student subgroups, including poor and minority students, are achieving academic proficiency.

Eight specific actions are essential at the district level:

1. Demonstrate moral and political will.
2. Acknowledge poor performance and seek solutions.
3. Promote a vision of high achievement for all students.
4. Establish measurable goals and monitor progress.
5. Institute accountability and data-driven instructional improvement.
6. Target student needs to prioritize resources and funding.
7. Provide relentless support for teachers and principals.
8. Support focused professional development.

Demonstrate Moral and Political Will

The importance of moral and political will is certainly not a new idea. Asa Hilliard, the impassioned educator from Atlanta, has perhaps said it best:

> The risk for our children in school is not a risk associated with their intelligence. Our failures have nothing to do with I.Q., nothing to do with poverty, nothing to do with race, nothing to do with language, nothing to do with style, nothing to do with the need to discover new pedagogy, nothing to do with the children's families. We have only one problem: do we truly will to see each and every child in this nation develop to the peak of his or her capacities? (Hilliard, 1991, p. 36)

For school systems to become effective in closing achievement gaps and improving the achievement of all students, there must be steadfast determination at the district level. With the help of state and national policies and a growing recognition that all students, even poor and minority students, will achieve proficiency, school administrators must exert rigorous determination to make high-performing, high-poverty schools a reality (Togneri & Anderson, 2003). This understanding has led to the emergence of an ever-growing number of school superintendents, school board members, and community leaders who will not accept any apology, rationalization, or excuse for poor school performance, or permit any blame to be placed on parents and families. These leaders accept responsibility for student failures and use the new state and federal policies to hold classroom teachers and building principals strictly accountable for teaching all students successfully. Often their most powerful tool is public disclosure of student achievement data that is disaggregated by various student subgroups. With public disclosure and data-driven decision-making increasing the pressure for high performance, teachers and school administrators become the lynchpins of improvement and are in a critical position to convey to students, parents, and the community the district's determination to successfully educate all students.

Acknowledge Poor Performance and Seek Solutions

As state and federal policies began demanding the public reporting of student achievement data, many schools and communities were shocked by what they discovered. In almost every case of high-poverty schools that have succeeded in becoming high-performing schools, school and community motivation was generated in part by negative and sometimes shocking news stories about the achievement gap between various student subgroups and the overall poor performance of schools that most thought were performing well. The courage to acknowledge poor school performance is a powerful tool in building the will to change and the determination to improve (Togneri & Anderson, 2003). As Rosa Smith, former superintendent of the Memphis, Tennessee, schools has said, "Leaders cannot be fearful of bad news"; rather, she explains, bad news must be used in a powerful positive manner (Smith, 2005, p. 16).

Bad news must be used continuously to build motivation and determination to improve school performance. Leaders in high-performing, high-poverty schools tell it like it is. They are honest and forthright with their constituencies regarding their student data and pressing challenges. They focus on solutions rather than on making excuses. Focusing on poor student performance enables school district leaders to mobilize school and community support and to use the bad news about student achievement as baseline data to monitor progress, or lack of progress.

**Secrets of Success
in High-Performing, High-Poverty Schools**

Using Bad News

The NCLB legislation's requirement of public disclosure of student achievement for specified subgroups initially shocked communities who had assumed that their schools were excellent. Superintendents and school boards in high-poverty, high-performing schools have since learned to use "bad news" to mobilize school and community support and to monitor progress—or lack of it—against that baseline data. The power of the press has been instrumental in motivating communities to support significant school improvement efforts.

Promote a Vision of High Achievement for All Students

Superintendents and school boards must develop a vision of high expectations for both their school district and their community. The vision should be written into public documents, newsletters, policies, and goals, and even on business cards. It must become a theme for superintendents and school board actions and the criteria for all school decisions. In Aldine, Texas, a school board member reported, "Everything we do is based on what's best for the children, period. Whether you are dealing with an administrative issue or a student issue" (Togneri & Anderson, 2003, p. 5).

Such a vision for a school district is essential in rallying a community to support the goal of all students reaching proficiency. The Iowa Lighthouse Inquiry concluded that without widespread community support, schools will be unable to target their energies to teaching all students, instead of just the sons and daughters of the affluent (Iowa Association of School Boards, 2000). Without strong community support, the achievement gaps between student groups will not be eliminated.

Establish Measurable Goals and Monitor Progress

The vision of a school district must be reflected in a set of carefully developed measurable goals that include specific targets and timelines. For example, figure 4.1 (page 66) shows the 3-year goals established in the Anne Arundel County Public Schools in Annapolis, Maryland.

The school district goals must be used as the focus to allocate funding, provide the basis for professional development, and constantly monitor progress toward goal achievement. Without measurable goals, targets, timelines, and continuous monitoring of progress toward goal attainment, student achievement at the classroom level is not likely to improve (Togneri & Anderson, 2003).

Three-Year Goals for Academic Achievement	
Goal: To accelerate achievement for all students and minimize the achievement disparities among all groups of students.	• Eighty-five percent of students in grades 2–6, 8, and 10 will perform at the proficient level in reading, mathematics, and writing as defined by the Maryland State Department of Education in compliance with No Child Left Behind.
	• Forty-five percent will successfully complete Algebra I by the end of grade 8.
	• Twenty percent of students will compete in regional, state, or national co-curricular competition by the end of grade 11.
	• Forty percent of high school seniors will have completed at least one AP course, and 70% of those students will perform at a level of 3 or better on AP examinations by graduation.
	• Ten percent of high school seniors will have earned one or more international baccalaureate certificates and 70% of these will earn an IB diploma.
	• Seventy-five percent of high school seniors will have taken the SAT by the end of their senior year, and average scores will increase 5% over the baseline (2002–2003).
	• Ninety percent of special education seniors will earn a Maryland high school diploma.
	• Achievement of groups based on race, gender, and socioeconomic status will vary no more than 10 percentage points from the highest performing group on each measured standard.

Figure 4.1: Closing the Achievement Gap: Anne Arundel County Public Schools' 3-Year Goals (Anne Arundel County Public Schools, 2006)

Institute Accountability and Use Data-Driven Instructional Improvement

Eric Smith, superintendent of the year in North Carolina in 2001, firmly believes, "Before anything else, before you provide additional support personnel, specialists, or increase funds, you must hold principals and teachers strictly accountable" (Smith, 2003). With measurable goals, a district-wide accountability system, and data-driven decisions, leadership can continually strive and push when necessary for improved student achievement. The bottom line in all educational decisions must be, "Show me the evidence!"

Target Student Needs to Prioritize Resources and Funding

The funding gap in public education in the United States has been well documented. Schools of poverty almost inevitably have less funding, more inexperienced leaders, and inferior facilities in worse condition than schools in more affluent neighborhoods. Nothing will galvanize a school staff and the community quite like targeting funding to address the most pressing needs in a school district. Leadership must use problems and needs to focus funding and reallocate resources (McGee, 2004). School districts should use existing school district funds to improve instruction; "reliance on external and short-term funding to support improvement efforts puts continued success in jeopardy" (if funds are not renewed), and causes other districts to question how they can follow in the same successful path (Togneri & Anderson, 2003, p. 11).

Provide Relentless Support for Teachers and Principals

Superintendents and school boards need to exercise every possible option to support successful teaching and effective school administration. There are three essential elements critical to succeeding in this effort:

1. **Use student achievement data to identify ineffective or failing teachers and school administrators.** In the era of high expectations for the academic achievement of all students, it is absolutely essential for school leaders to use student achievement data to document teachers and school administrators who are struggling, who need support or assistance, or who are failing. Sanders (1996) and others have documented the tragic impact of ineffective teachers. If struggling and ineffective teachers are unable to improve, they will need intense professional development and additional support personnel. If they remain unable or unwilling to improve their teaching effectiveness, they must be removed from classroom instruction. The same is true for administrators who are unwilling or unable to lead teachers to high student performance. Some states, such as Virginia, are developing "squads" of their most effective principals and teacher leaders to move into failing schools for 2 to 3 years in an effort to turn them around.

2. **Create instructional support teams.** If school leaders and classroom teachers are unable or unwilling to improve, instructional support teams should be made available to assist with instruction, curriculum, assessment, and data analysis (Massell, 2000). The team may include teacher mentors, content specialists, instructional specialists, student tutors, curriculum specialists, assessment experts, and so on.

3. **Develop an effective and stable faculty.** Teacher hiring practices and personnel selection have improved since the passage of No Child Left Behind, and growing pressure is being exerted on colleges and universities to produce more effective teachers and administrators. Novice-teacher support systems are now usually found in schools. School leaders also need to be conscious of

the importance of not just hiring effective teachers and supporting those who are struggling, but also of creating stable school faculties. In the Louisiana "The Secrets of 'Can-Do' Schools" study, 8 of the 12 schools studied had unusually stable school faculties. The study concluded that teachers stayed in these schools because the "working conditions and the environment [were] conducive to doing good professional work" (Richardson, 2003, p. 6).

Support Focused Professional Development

Almost every increase in student achievement can be associated to some degree with effective professional development. This professional development is highly targeted and focused on areas of low achievement. When Idaho's first-grade students lagged behind other grades in the percentage of students reading at grade level, intensive first-grade academies were launched throughout the state for primary teachers. These efforts targeted diagnosis and intervention skill-building and more than 90% of all first-grade teachers participated. The result was an increase of 8% in the number of students reading at grade level.

Student achievement data and careful analysis of teacher and school performance on state and district assessments point to curriculum areas in need of professional development. School district leaders must insist on and plan sequenced professional development to address these areas. One of the most effective approaches to raising student achievement through professional development is to use student achievement data. A quick review of student performance data at the classroom level can identify the teachers who are most effective with poor and minority students. Many schools and districts now use these most effective teachers to help other teachers learn how to become more successful. An increasing number of school districts are also using the teachers identified as most effective to lead study groups and study lessons with other teachers. (See chapter 10 for further information on this topic.)

Leadership Priorities at the School Level

Building principals have always been central to improving a school. Yet the role of the principal has been significantly transformed in recent years. No longer is the principal's primary role solely focused on management, budget, and student discipline. Instructional leadership has now become the predominant trait of high-quality building leaders.

Effective principals of high-performing, high-poverty schools do many things well. Their first focus is on the students. They also listen and communicate effectively. Highly effective principals also visibly demonstrate three additional priorities:

1. Maintain great expectations for student achievement.
2. Understand effective professional development.
3. Develop and support teacher leaders.

The National Staff Development Council has established benchmark standards for staff development. These context, process, and content standards encompass the most recognized and accepted guidance for effective staff development available to school and district leaders (see Appendix B, page 233).

Maintain Great Expectations for Student Achievement

Effective building principals believe all children will achieve to high levels. They reflect, support, and encourage the district vision and support district leadership in this mission. The Louisiana School Effectiveness Study long ago concluded the primary role of the principal in effective high-poverty schools was to hold high expectations for student learning, which in turn helped to motivate teachers to motivate their students (Teddlie & Stringfield, 1993). This role provides the motivation and high expectations students need that are often absent in their homes.

Understand Effective Professional Development

Effective leaders provide and support professional development for teams of teachers. In the Illinois Golden Spike study, one of the major policy recommendations was to bring together everyone involved in the teaching of a particular content or skill area to participate as teams in targeted professional development. The principal, teachers, instructional aides, and specialists all came together to learn new skills. In the Louisiana "The Secrets of 'Can-Do' Schools" study, analyzing data was the first step and the driving force that guided their professional learning process. The "Can-Do" leaders and staff looked at test results to identify common needs and individual strengths and weaknesses: "Each school used many types of job embedded staff development—coaching, mentoring, examination, and reflection on student work and instructional practices, visitation to classrooms and other schools, conferences, workshops, serving on curriculum committees" and so on (Richardson, 2003, p. 1).

Develop and Support Teacher Leaders

Research on high-performing, high-poverty schools has highlighted an increasing number of new roles for principals and teachers. They act as tutors, mentors, curriculum developers, and instructional leaders, in addition to many other roles. In many effective high-poverty schools, either the principal or a teacher leader, or both, assumes essential roles in improving instruction: Their primary job responsibility was "to oversee instruction and know what was going on in classrooms" (Richardson, 2003, p. 6). But while principals and teacher leaders guided the learning process of teachers and provided the necessary resources, each of the 12 schools studied was a true learning community. Effective school principals develop the capacity to collaborate and share the challenging work of successfully leading and attaining instructional priorities. No individual can do it all alone.

Leading Through Collaboration and Distributive Leadership

The "go it alone" days of education are over, ushered out by standards, mandated accountability at the federal and state level, and a growing determination among educators that every student counts and will achieve. Improving a classroom's scores requires both a teacher and a grade-level team; improving a whole school's scores requires a school-wide collaborative team approach. Distributing the leadership responsibilities to teacher leaders creates and supports the necessary collaboration needed to effectively teach all students. Mike Schmoker (2004), a noted school improvement author, recommends a:

> simple powerful structure which starts with a group of teachers who meet regularly as a team to identify essential and valued student learning, develop common formative assessments, analyze current levels of achievement, set achievement goals and then share and create lessons to improve upon those levels. (p. 48)

Schmoker goes on to say,

> If there is anything that the research community agrees on, it is this: The right kind of continuous, structured teacher collaboration improves the quality of teaching and pays big, often immediate, dividends in student learning and professional morale in virtually any setting. (2004, p. 48)

The work of Richard DuFour, Robert Eaker, and Rebecca DuFour provides this kind of continuous, structured collaboration. Viewed by many as the originators of the concept of professional learning communities (PLCs), DuFour and Eaker (1998) carefully present a sequential plan to create, nurture, and "live" a professional learning community. Built on a foundation of shared mission, vision, values, and goals, PLCs exemplify teamwork, collaboration, and commitment to addressing any barrier that stands in the way of all children achieving proficiency.

**Secrets of Success
in High-Performing, High-Poverty Schools**

Building a Cadre of Leaders

When Principal Susan Williamson took over Taft School in Boise, Idaho, in 1998, the school's poverty rate was over 70%, its students' reading and math achievement were among the lowest in the district, and low expectations, underachievement, and misbehavior were the norm. Five years later, the school was performing with the best in the district; by 2006, its improvements had become the established culture.

Williamson attributes the school's transformation to its teachers: "We didn't import a program. . . . We created a process . . . one that has succeeded because our teachers have become leaders and have driven our improvements." After launching a campaign to enhance the school's environment and address discipline issues, Williamson focused grade-level teams on understanding student data, aligning instruction to curriculum, and learning together through study groups. She found extra time to meet through hiring substitute teachers and reorganizing the daily schedule.

Perhaps most importantly, Williamson connected the school's adults with each other to focus on the needs of the students. School secretaries teach parents, paraprofessionals fully participate in professional development, university interns are expected to contribute as they learn, and parents are heartily welcomed to visit and collaborate as co-leaders to build and sustain their school community.

Elements of the PLC model are present in every school where high-poverty students are achieving at or above state-mandated standards. A PLC focuses its collaborative teams of educators on collective inquiry followed by action, experimentation, and the ongoing study of interventions. Critical to the process is changing the model of conducting day-to-day business into one of mutually focused continuous improvement. Leaders support and drive effective PLCs by enhancing teachers' ease of access to data through technology and by actively participating in the collaborative teams' action research.

Successful implementation of a PLC requires commitment to the concept of continuous improvement. Eaker, DuFour, and DuFour (2002) have designed a rubric to guide a district or school's implementation of the process. This continuum provides guidance on attaining benchmarks and implementing the core elements of a PLC in a four-stage process that begins with a pre-initiation and culminates with sustaining the PLC. (See Appendix A, page 227, for a copy of the rubric.)

Improving the System

The success of the PLC approach lies in its central influence on the system. Our public school systems were not designed to focus on struggling students—they were designed to serve those prepared and supported externally to achieve. Yet as of 2002 at the federal level and by 2004 in every state, the requirement of basic academic proficiency for all students clearly establishes the need for a systemic shift of previous priorities to one that accomplishes success for all students. DuFour and Eaker (1998) challenge educators to move beyond simply asserting, "All kids can learn," to instead answer the question, "How will we monitor learning and respond to students who struggle?" One might now also ask, "How will we ensure that all students reach academic proficiency?" This is the essential challenge for each of America's 14,571 public school districts.

Accomplishing this challenge lies in the domain of what Michael Fullan refers to as the most important strategy of this decade: leadership. He argues that to achieve the goals of the last decade, which focused on accountability, leadership must become far more assertive and adept at sustaining progress. Leaders must seek to make the comprehensive challenge and work of leadership understandable and coherent to all. Leading schools and districts in the 21st century requires collaboration and the subsequent creation of what Fullan calls deep learning communities focused on the work at hand and the complexities of maintaining progress and sustaining a culture of continuous improvement.

Sustaining Gains

Fullan's book, *Leadership and Sustainability: System Thinkers in Action* (2005), identifies the development of systemic capacity as the cornerstone to an organization's ability to get and stay better. This is particularly true of schools and districts with high enrollments of high-poverty youth. Building and sustaining systemic capacity is the critical challenge confronting our public schools. In fact, Fullan suggests that for a leader to be judged effective in the present and future, that leader must also create sustainability. He has identified eight elements that must be accomplished:

Public service with a moral purpose
A commitment to changing context at all levels
Lateral capacity-building through networks
Intelligent accountability and vertical relationships (encompassing both
    capacity-building and accountability)
Deep learning
A dual commitment to short-term and long-term results
Cyclical energizing
The long lever of leadership (Fullan, 2003, p. 14)

Factors one through six are generally agreed-upon elements in the work of leaders that result in positive gains; however, "cyclical energizing" and "long levers of leadership" set Fullan's work apart. He has concluded that in any improvement effort, plateaus of progress will be followed by implementation dips (when scores drop) or flat lines of improvement. Through these times, effective leaders re-energize and continue their progress, acknowledging that efforts to improve schools will always be accompanied by periods of static growth. The "long lever" element comes from a quote from Archimedes: "Give me a lever long enough, and I can change the world." As Fullan recognizes, the lever for sustainability is leadership. To build lasting improvements in high-poverty schools, leadership is *the* critical element.

Against the Odds: Leadership and School Improvement— A Case Study*

All of the essential elements of leadership can be found in the small microcosm of a high-poverty Native American school in Northern Idaho. Lapwai Elementary School, located on the Nez Perce Reservation, serves a K–6 population of 302 students, 84% of whom are enrolled Nez Perce or other tribal members. Seventy-nine percent of the students live at or below the poverty level. The remarkable success of this school in teaching poor children was acknowledged by the Education Trust when they selected Lapwai Elementary in 2004 as one of five schools nationally to receive the annual Dispelling the Myth Award. Lapwai Elementary represents just one of hundreds of schools nationwide that have reversed a history of under-achievement and low performance among poor students.

In 1999, only 16% of Lapwai's children were achieving at or above the state's reading averages, and only 17% were achieving above the averages in math. Dissatisfied with a tradition of low performance, a group of teachers and administrators sought to permanently improve the achievement of their students. They began from a position of shared core values characterized by collaboration, determination, openness to consider dramatic change, and relentless energy to help children achieve. They studied school data and crafted a 3-year course of action that included measurable goals focused on achievement, attendance, and community engagement and satisfaction. The group sought and was successful in obtaining external funds from the state and federal government and a private foundation. The additional funds increased Lapwai's annual budget of $5 million by approximately 10% and dramatically accelerated their work as they embarked on a complex agenda of improvement.

---

*Reprinted with permission from the January 2005 issue of *The School Administrator* magazine.

First, they tackled creating a curriculum aligned to state standards and assessments. They created time for this work through revising the daily schedule to gain 2.5 hours of common planning and professional development time each Friday afternoon. They researched and implemented results-based reading and math interventions. They initiated full-day kindergarten, modestly reduced class sizes, initiated looping, extended after-school tutoring, and increased daily instructional time in reading for all students. Teachers and administrators participated in assessment-literacy learning teams focused on assessment *of* learning and, more importantly, assessment *for* learning. Frequent assessments, content benchmarks, and clear learning targets became the norm.

District and school leaders consistently focused their attention on building a comprehensive capacity to improve their use of data. Through grade-level and school-wide professional development activities, Lapwai educators became both proficient and comfortable in allowing data to guide decisions. As the state implemented a new testing program, the school district was well-positioned to make immediate use of the additional student performance data.

To build community collaboration, engagement, and satisfaction, a monthly Lapwai Educational Summit was launched. Held in the Nez Perce executive tribal chambers, this group of community leaders, parents, educators, and students gather one morning each month to consider progress data, offer input, and focus their concerns and support toward improving achievement and school success for the students of Lapwai. A multicultural coordinator was hired to work closely with the students' homes and families. Enhancing cultural understanding and appreciation through teaching the Nez Perce language, history, and culture also bolstered their work. Lapwai Elementary succeeded in engaging more parents and community members in the school and more educators in the community.

Most importantly, the administrators stayed the course and maintained a relentless commitment. The results were overwhelming. In 2004, 91% of third-grade students (up from 16% in 1999) and 89% of fourth-grade students (up from 32% in 1999) performed above state averages in math. Seventy-three percent of third-grade students (up from 17% in 1999) and 77% of fourth-grade students (up from 27% in 1999) performed above state averages in reading. Eighty-two percent of Lapwai kindergartners were now reading at or above grade level.

Student attendance rose from 89% to 94%. Parental satisfaction increased from 62% to 92%. Parental dissatisfaction steadily declined from 29% to 5%. Each of these gains and accomplishments resulted from 5 years of focused leadership and relentless work by the Lapwai superintendent and staff. Between 1999 and 2004, the superintendency did not turn over, and the building principals have remained in place, as has most of the teaching staff. Access to additional funds permitted the district to hire its first curriculum director. The school board membership changed frequently during these years, yet the board maintained a constant focus on student achievement. When school board members depart through natural attrition, they are consistently replaced with new members committed to the improvement of learning for Lapwai students.

Lapwai Elementary's success exemplifies what a high-poverty, high-minority school with a history of low student academic performance can accomplish when effective leadership is in place. While many schools rely primarily on the leadership of a single principal, the Lapwai story is one of *comprehensive* leadership engagement and support. The school's teachers and principal receive daily support from the district curriculum coordinator, superintendent, and other central office staff. Members of the school board regularly interact with the school, as do parents and community members. In short, the adult community surrounds the school with support. Evidence of this support is the recent passage (a 79% "yes" vote) of the district's first construction bond in over 20 years to build a new school for grades 7–12. All of the leadership skills so essential to developing high-performing, high-poverty schools are evident in the Lapwai story, and the Lapwai experience illustrates each of the aspects of the pattern of improvement described in this book.

Improvement Through Leadership

High-poverty schools can achieve high academic performance, but this work cannot be accomplished without effective system-wide leadership. Without this leadership, achievement gains among poor and minority students are not likely to be realized and sustained. Yet with this leadership, improvement is all but inevitable. As the Lapwai story demonstrates, even the greatest odds can be overcome.

Research has clearly identified the relationship between effective leadership and improving achievement in high-poverty schools, and we know that new leadership skills and traits are essential for student success. It is important to note that effective leadership is the anchor for each of the other essential elements in the pattern of improvement described in this book, as shown in figure 4.2 (page 76).

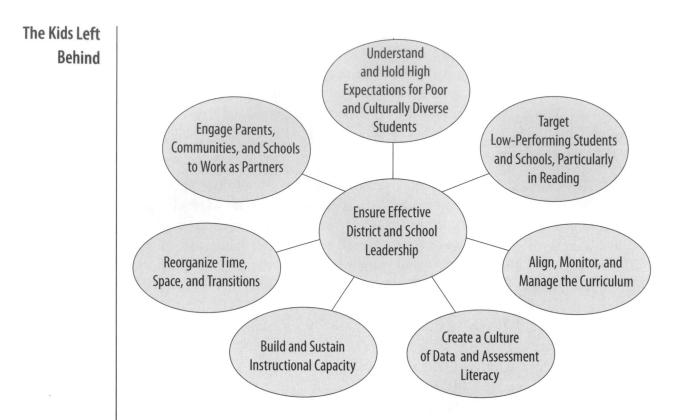

Figure 4.2: Characteristics of High-Performing, High-Poverty Schools

Leading a high-poverty school or district is a challenging task in public education today. Reversing the decades-old trend of low performance and underachievement is a daunting undertaking, one that simply cannot be accomplished without changing the structure and delivery of public education. As the 18 studies in chapter 3 show, we possess the knowledge and capacity to do this work. What remains in question is our willingness to choose to do it. Leadership is the pivotal element that will tip a school or district toward effectively educating all students. Do we really have a choice?

Next Steps

Complete and Discuss the Self-Evaluation

District and school leadership teams should begin or continue their work by completing the following Self-Evaluation Rubric (pages 78–79) and then, in groups, compare their perceptions and discuss the appropriate next steps.

Apply the 11 Leadership Priorities

Two decades of research and practice have identified eight district-level and three school-level characteristics that drive effective schools and programs for low-socioeconomic-status students: Develop long- and short-term plans to implement these components.

Don't Reinvent the Wheel

Scores of recent studies identify the critical leadership strategies of high-performing, high-poverty schools. Access this work, and apply it to your settings.

Don't Attempt to "Go It Alone"

Successfully intervening to increase the achievement of low-socioeconomic-status students requires collaboration from the boardroom to the classroom, but most importantly, among teachers and administrators.

Develop Professional Learning Communities

Effectively leading communities of support and collaboration will dramatically enhance the achievement and school success of low-socioeconomic-status students.

Keep the System in Mind: Build a Culture of Success

Leading improvements in high-poverty schools requires a clear focus on elements of sustainability. Improvements must be embedded in the system to ensure the ongoing successes of all students.

Ensure Effective District and School Leadership
Self-Evaluation Rubric

What is my school's or district's progress?	BEGINNING			EMBEDDING			SUSTAINING		
	No Action Has Been Taken	Efforts Are Limited	Results Are Being Gained	Efforts and Results Are Being Enhanced			Practices Are Widespread, Policies Are in Place, and Results Are Increasing		
Does my school or district . . .	1	2	3	4	5	6	7	8	9
Employ a superintendent and school board that communicate the will and relentless determination needed to ensure success?									
Demonstrate relentless determination through a clear vision of excellence in policies, newsletters, press releases, news stories, and other forms of communication?									
Publicize student performance of all required subgroups, even if the information reflects low school or subgroup performance?									
Have a timeline of measurable achievement goals that reflect the vision of all students achieving proficiency?									
Regularly monitor progress toward the established goals and publicly report results?									
Establish accountability measures to ensure that every principal and classroom teacher is evaluated on the basis of student achievement progress toward goal attainment?									
Possess accountability measures that include sanctions for poor performance?									
Emphasize the importance of using data in all school decision-making?									

(continued)

The Kids Left Behind © 2007 Solution Tree Press • www.solution-tree.com

Ensure Effective District and School Leadership
Self-Evaluation Rubric (continued)

What is my school's or district's progress?	BEGINNING			EMBEDDING			SUSTAINING		
	No Action Has Been Taken	Efforts Are Limited	Results Are Being Gained	Efforts and Results Are Being Enhanced			Practices Are Widespread, Policies Are in Place, and Results Are Increasing		
Does my school or district . . .	1	2	3	4	5	6	7	8	9
Have established policies that prioritize and direct additional funding to the lowest performing students and schools?									
Use student achievement data to identify ineffective, struggling, or outstanding teachers?									
Ensure that schools with high percentages of impoverished students have experienced, well-trained, and certified teachers?									
Seek to staff schools attended by a high percentage of impoverished students with a stable, high-quality faculty?									
Support and provide targeted and embedded professional development for staff members?									
Possess building principals who reflect the school district's vision that all students achieve proficiency and success?									
Provide time for teacher collaboration and support for the development and maintenance of professional learning communities?									
Have systemic efforts in place to monitor, evaluate, and sustain progress?									

Chapter 5

Engage Parents, Communities, and Schools to Work as Partners

"I had never worked much with parents. I didn't really think that it was my job. Even the parents seem to feel that their role was mostly for the elementary years. But wow . . . the more I have engaged parents in my teaching, the more my students have improved."

—Algebra Teacher, Oklahoma

Developing and sustaining effective partnerships between the home, the community, and the school is critical to improving the education of children and youth. More advantaged parents tend to be more involved with teachers and schools, often choosing their families' place of residence to ensure high-quality education and athletic programs. Or, if they are unhappy with the quality of their neighborhood school or the teacher assigned to their children, they have the financial ability to choose private or parochial schools. They are often the backbone of parent/school organizations, volunteer mentoring and tutoring programs, school fundraising projects, and campaigns for bond elections.

The situation is often quite different for the parents, extended family members, and guardians of the children of poverty. Low-socioeconomic-status families, especially new immigrants, minorities, and non-English-language speakers, tend to be unsure and sometimes suspicious and antagonistic toward schools controlled by the dominant middle-class culture (Epstein et al., 2002). Many impoverished family members had negative experiences when they were in school, which may have heightened their uneasiness and suspicion.

Yet there are a growing number of impressive success stories in all areas of the country—urban, rural, and suburban—where families with low socioeconomic status have not only become involved in the education of their children, but have also entered into meaningful, beneficial partnerships with their children's schools. In these schools, family members have become intimately invested in the total school effort—instruction, curriculum, and management—even helping to make budget, staffing, and professional development decisions. When such partnerships are developed and sustained, the children of poverty learn far more effectively, achieve higher levels of academic proficiency, and attend school in safer, more orderly classrooms and schools. All of the major research studies used to identify a pattern of school improvement in this book have recommended or recognized parental involvement and school/parent partnerships as important factors for the success of high-performing, high-poverty schools.

Schools also benefit from community partnerships. There is a growing research base documenting the power of extending teaching and learning outside of the school, involving a variety of business, professional, and technical experts in career themes in the school, and using schools to coordinate the many resources and services of the national, state, and local government. Since poor children and youth are almost universally without adequate nutrition, health services, and health insurance, "full-service" schools are increasingly providing low-socioeconomic-status students with essential health information, referrals, a wide variety of family services, and even food and clothing (Dryfoos, 1994). There is ample evidence to support the African proverb, "It takes a whole village to raise a child."

The challenge is for schools to find ways to make contact with the families of poverty in a positive, nurturing, meaningful manner and to develop mutual trust and understanding, maintain continuous two-way communication, and ultimately join in comprehensive partnerships. Those schools where poor and minority students are learning effectively and closing the achievement gap with their more advantaged peers have shown how essential and effective family, school, and community partnerships can be.

The Old World of Public Education

> *"Our role is to provide good quality schools. There's really not a role for parents beyond the usual volunteer stuff. Too much parent involvement can get in the way of what we're here to do."*
>
> —*Principal, Idaho Elementary School*

The old world of public education was characterized by a significant disconnect between the homes of poor families and the school. Families learned early on in most communities that they were not particularly welcomed or needed in the education of their children. Often families were publicly blamed for the failures of their children in school. Poor families were viewed as the enemy of high-quality education. If schools were successful in the education of poor children and youth, this was accomplished in spite of the students, their parents, and their home lives.

While there have always been isolated examples of schools in poor neighborhoods partnering with low-income families in the education of their children, too often public education has been characterized by just the opposite. A rich historical literature chronicles the negative attitudes, class and racial prejudice, and elitist decision-making of schools in poor communities. *Death at an Early Age* (Kozol,

1967), *Crisis in the Classroom* (Silberman, 1970), and *Savage Inequalities* (Kozol, 1991) are just a few examples of books that explore the class and race wars schools have waged with poor children and their parents and families. It is no wonder so many poor families do not trust, respect, or have confidence in the school's interest in their children's academic success.

Even in good situations, most parents were involved in schools in traditional ways—such as in volunteer roles as office aides, teacher aides, or playground staff. Even in more autonomous schools employing site-based management, parents and guardians were usually excluded from decisions regarding staffing, the budget, and the curriculum. Too often poor parents were not invited to serve on school committees or advisory boards. In the old world of education, schools were usually controlled, operated, and managed by middle-class teachers and administrators; few poor and minority students saw adults in their schools who were from their own backgrounds or cultures.

The New World of Public Education

> *"I feel welcomed and wanted by my son's elementary school. This means so much to our family because we all want to do all we can to support his learning and the staff who work so hard with him."*
>
> —*Parent, Florida*

Beginning in the late 1960s, parent and community involvement in the old world of public education began to change. Significant parent and community involvement in poor communities emerged in community-based "free schools," alternative public schools, and later in charter schools where poor parents joined with local educators to create a common vision for their schools, conduct cross-cultural education programs for students and adults, and actively participate in managing schools. In the late 1980s, a number of school-wide improvement programs such as Success for All, Accelerated Schools PLUS, Expeditionary Learning Schools Outward Bound, and the Comer School Development Program emerged. These programs included family, community, and school partnerships as essential aspects of developing and sustaining effective schools. With the adoption of the No Child Left Behind legislation, educators everywhere finally began to realize that they could no longer absolve themselves of responsibility for students who were failing to learn by blaming parents. They started to recognize how essential cooperation and partnering with parents really are. Almost every school that demonstrates academic success with student populations composed primarily of low-socioeconomic-status families has succeeded through the support, involvement, and partnerships between schools, families, and the community (Chadwick, 2004).

Effective Partnerships

"I don't understand why a principal wouldn't do everything possible to build a relationship with the community. We need all the help we can get!"
—*Middle School Teacher, Tennessee*

In its fourth assessment of evidence related to the value of home/school connections, the Southwest Educational Development Laboratory concluded that there is "compelling, research-based evidence that when schools and families work together, student achievement spikes, particularly in low-performing schools" (Henderson & Mapp, 2002, p. 12). While the exact nature of partnerships varies from community to community, a number of strategies characterize most of the schools where the children of poverty achieve proficiency and beyond. Research at Mid-continent Research for Education and Learning has documented a strong link between parents' emphasis on education and student achievement, but for poor and minority students, schools must be very creative to get parents involved (Goodwin, 2000). To involve parents who speak little English, work multiple jobs, or who are uneasy about or intimidated by going to their children's schools, successful schools use a wide variety of creative approaches, such as offering health care, counseling, and other social services (Goodwin, 2000). A variety of research has documented the strategies that tend to be most effective and significant (Slavin & Madden, 1989; Haberman, 1991).

Joyce Epstein of the Center on School, Family, and Community Partnerships has devoted 25 years to helping schools, families, and communities develop effective partnerships. The Center supports states and districts through coordinating the National Network of Partnership Schools, an organization of 130 school districts and state departments of education committed to building and improving school, family, and community partnerships. Epstein and others have identified six crucial practices schools can use to enrich parent/community partnerships:

1. Assist families with parenting skills.
2. Improve communication with families.
3. Increase school volunteer opportunities for families.
4. Increase family involvement in student learning at home.
5. Involve families in school decision-making.
6. Increase collaboration with the community. (Epstein et al., 2002)

Organizations such as the National PTA, the International Reading Association, and others have also developed detailed recommendations for establishing and sustaining effective family, community, and school partnerships. Overall, parent/

community strategies that seem to be present where poor children and youth are learning effectively include:

- Parent education
- Parent-provided education
- Improved communication between the school and home
- Outreach to parents and families of English learners

Parent Education

"I was never successful in school and I dropped out in the eighth grade. I never liked school and still feel really uneasy every time I walk into a school—any school. I always feel like they think I am intruding. They look at me like 'Well, what do you want?'"

—Hispanic Parent, California

High-performing, high-poverty schools "make every parent welcome. Schools must be a safe, supportive place for parents as well as for students" (McGee, 2004, p. 116). Parent education must be a priority if poverty-level students are to succeed. This includes providing opportunities for parents to improve their literacy skills and learn about parenting (McGee, 2004).

Since children from poor families tend to arrive at school with significant learning differences, such as limited vocabularies and serious health and nutrition problems, many schools have experienced great success in helping to educate parents of elementary, preschool, and infant children about these issues. These schools have also developed prenatal education programs, parenting classes, and a variety of other programs focused on how to help young children get ready to read and learn. Parents of middle and high school students can benefit from education regarding drugs, alcohol, safe sex, gang activity, the media, bullying, and the early warning signs of violence, as well as from education on parenting skills for the teenage years.

A number of organizations provide detailed educational programs for parents, such as *Ten Ways Your Children Become Better Readers* (Center for the Study of Reading, 1989), and *101 Ways Parents Can Help Students Achieve* (Amundson, 1991). Other parent education programs are available through ERIC and the U.S. Department of Education, state departments of education, and an array of other providers. These programs provide educational plans for schools to use in working with parents to significantly help prepare their children for school success. These programs detail how parents can:

- Help their children learn to read.
- Talk to their children, ask questions, and encourage children to make decisions.
- Provide a stimulating environment for children.
- Encourage responsible television viewing.
- Be involved in their children's schools.
- Provide a safe, loving environment for young children.

**Secrets of Success
in High-Performing, High-Poverty Schools**
Family Education

While significant family involvement typically leads to a spike in student achievement, one form of family involvement has proven, primary importance. High-performing, high-poverty schools have documented that the single most effective approach to family involvement is teaching parents and guardians how to help their children learn at home. Improved student achievement can be expected when schools educate families in specific approaches to prepare their children for school and to support teaching and learning during evenings, weekends, and the summer months.

Parent-Provided Education

The more parents and community members help middle-class teachers learn about the culture of poverty and the culture of minority ethnic groups, the more sensitive and effective teachers and administrators will become. Parents and community leaders should be invited to help plan and present professional development that teaches faculty, staff, and administrators about cultural mores and folkways, appropriate behavior and language in the home and neighborhood, effective approaches to developing mutual respect with students, and effective discipline policies and practices. Such cooperative sharing and development can help eliminate prejudice from schools, improve student behavior, establish safe and orderly classrooms and schools, and ease the "clash of culture" that too often typifies public education in poor communities.

The Just for the Kids organization advocates for active parent engagement with their children's schools as a means of supporting improvement and student achievement. Their web site provides parents with tips, recommendations for communication, and even specific questions and advice on how to ask families for help. (Visit www.just4kids.org for more information.) Engaging families of underachieving students will often make a huge difference in the child's success in school.

Improved Communication Between School and Home

Staff members of high-performing, high-poverty schools make "expectations for parents clear and communicate with them frequently" (McGee, 2004, p. 116). To be effective in the education of poor minority students, teachers and administrators must demonstrate continuous two-way communication with parents, extended family, and guardians. Often this two-way communication includes home visits.

Ongoing communication with parents must not simply focus on student problems at school. The communication should share student successes and help families see their children as effective students. The communication should help teachers and parents understand student problems and potential difficulties and upheavals in the home, school, and community. For students and families with a home language other than English, all efforts should be made to translate written and verbal communications into their native language.

To foster effective two-way communication with low socioeconomic-status families, it is essential that schools first establish a trusting, respectful relationship. Research on effective communication has identified a number of communication actions that foster an atmosphere of trust. These actions include:

- Being open, helpful, friendly, and respectful to student families
- Communicating clearly and frequently about policies, programs, and student progress
- Encouraging family feedback
- Encouraging teamwork among the school, student, and family
- Seeking out and facilitating the involvement of all families in a two-way dialogue about student achievement and well-being
- Engaging parents and the larger community in volunteer activities and partnerships with the school (National Parent Teacher Association, 1998, pp. 2–3)

Effective, honest communication with parents and families of poor children makes all the difference in the success or failure of a school to reach and teach underachieving poor students. The National Parent Teacher Association has developed comprehensive recommendations for successful communication (1998). These recommendations are described in the feature box on page 88.

Characteristics of Successful Communication

- Use a variety of communication tools on a regular basis, seeking to facilitate two-way interaction through each medium.

- Establish opportunities for parents and educators to share partnering information such as student strengths and learning preferences.

- Provide clear information regarding course expectations and offerings, student placement, school activities, student services, and optional programs.

- Mail report cards and regular progress reports to parents. Provide support services and follow-up conferences as needed.

- Disseminate information on school reforms, policies, discipline procedures, assessment tools, and school goals, and include parents in any related decision-making process.

- Conduct conferences with parents at least twice a year, with follow-up as needed. These should accommodate the varied schedules of parents, language barriers, and the need for childcare.

- Encourage immediate contact between parents and teachers when concerns arise.

- Distribute student work for parental comment and review on a regular basis.

- Translate communications to assist non-English-speaking parents.

- Communicate with parents regarding positive student behavior and achievement, not just regarding misbehavior or failure.

- Provide opportunities for parents to communicate with principals and other administrative staff.

- Promote informal activities at which parents, staff, and community members can interact.

- Provide staff development regarding effective communication techniques and the importance of regular two-way communication between the school and the family.

(National Parent Teacher Association, 1998, p. 1)

Outreach to Parents and Families of English Learners

All of the concepts and practices discussed so far are essential when connecting with the homes, families, and parents of English learners. Yet effective schools and districts must go further. The needs of an English language learner in a family where limited English is spoken are substantial. Districts and schools that have made remarkable progress have incorporated the following elements into their daily schedules:

- Dual-language classes
- English as a Second Language GED and parenting classes
- Home/school liaisons (with staff fluent in the home language)
- Preschool early literacy programs
- Early assessment
- Community and school activities and events (Sadowski, 2004)

These components characterize a proactive approach and are found in some form in thousands of other programs and communities throughout the nation. Given that the number of English language students has more than doubled in the past decade, interventions such as these must become central to the mission of any district that serves these students.

Comprehensive School and Family Partnerships

"The evidence is convincing: families have a major influence on children's achievement in school and through life. . . . When schools, families, and community groups work together to support learning, children tend to do better in school, stay in school longer, and like school more."

—*Henderson and Mapp (2002, p. 16)*

Effective communication is essential in the successful education of poor and minority students, and it increases exponentially when a comprehensive partnership between the school and home is maintained. Schools where the children of poverty are achieving tend to develop strong, complex partnerships with families. In such partnerships, parents and guardians become intimate partners in the management, curriculum, and instruction of the school. Effective schools often work together with families to develop a common vision for the school, institute advisory committees that establish rules and regulations for the school and classroom, develop behavior standards, and review data about student progress. Partnerships work to review curriculum and instruction and relate the instructional progress to student achievement data. Parents may even be engaged in budget allocation and in teacher and principal hiring decisions. When poor and minority parents become partners in their children's complete school life, students are the ultimate beneficiaries.

In this day of No Child Left Behind, schools must seek to become better partners with parents to foster improved achievement. Schools that receive sanctions for low performance will increasingly experience parents who abandon the failing school to find a more effective school that will welcome their children and their involvement. Even without sanctions, an increasing number of parents are "voting with their feet" and leaving inadequate schools in search of effective educational programs for their children.

Successful Programs

Research on the Comer School Development Program, Accelerated Schools, Success for All, Expeditionary Learning, and alternative and charter schools has documented the power of school and family partnerships at enhancing student achievement (Barr & Parrett, 2001). While each program has built a track record of success, the Comer School Development Program stands apart.

For the past 35 years, Yale child psychiatrist James Comer has devoted himself to creating what many call the Comer Process. Working in predominately inner-city impoverished neighborhoods, Comer and his associates developed a model that engages parents in authentic governance and operations of a school. Throughout his years of work, more than 500 low-performing schools enrolling poor students have become "centers of productive learning and development" (Comer, 2004). A meta-analysis of 29 comprehensive school reform models identified the Comer School Development Program, along with Success for All and Direct Instruction, as the most effective designs for improving school-wide student achievement as well as relationships with parents and community (Borman et al., 2002).

In the Lapwai Elementary School on the Nez Perce Reservation in northern Idaho, parents work closely with the school to implement a more effective approach to reading instruction. Their carefully selected intervention, Success for All, requires enhanced partnership with parents and families to support their children learning to read. The results have been remarkable (see chapter 4 for a detailed discussion). In much the same way, Brazosport Independent School District in Texas developed a comprehensive partnership with parents to reorganize the school day and improve teaching and learning. Working closely with parents, the schools were able to extend the instructional day to "capture" more time to help struggling students.

The Essential Partnership Between Schools and Communities

> *"Our kids don't just go to school here; this is our school. We all share a vision . . . and we share in all the responsibilities of managing and operating the school. It is all of our responsibilities if the school fails or succeeds, and we are determined not to fail."*
>
> —*Parent, Wyoming*

In the new world of public education, it is essential that schools assume the responsibility of working with their local communities. While public schools must continue to seek support from their communities in the traditional ways, such as with school board elections and superintendent contracts, the challenge of No

Child Left Behind to successfully teach all students demands that schools and communities work together in dramatic new ways.

Provide Community Information

Helping teachers, administrators, and school board members understand the new world of education has proven a difficult task. School districts must work to help the entire community understand the new goals for public education and the impact of local school failure. Many parents and community members seem to perceive that "closing the achievement gap" may mean dumbing down the education program for advantaged children in the community. Others worry that targeting low-performing student subgroups will reallocate resources, both human and financial, away from gifted and talented programs and advanced placement classes. At one Iowa school board meeting, for example, affluent parents and students pleaded with the board not to create an alternative program for high-risk students. They opposed a shift in district emphasis from supporting students who were working hard to educate themselves and prepare for college in favor of supporting programs for the "unconcerned and unmotivated." Unfortunately, such examples of prejudice and ignorance still exist. To ultimately be successful in the new world of public education, school leaders must do everything possible to assure community members that low-performing students can be successfully educated without detracting from the education of the best and brightest students.

Use Community Resources and Support

Studies have documented the importance of community resources and support to student academic achievement. The Search Institute of Minneapolis, Minnesota, surveyed thousands of teenagers in hundreds of cities and used this data to identify developmental assets that are essential for student learning (1999). Their findings are presented in figure 5.1 (page 91). This research shows a clear relationship between student achievement and the number of specific assets found in the students' community: The more assets teenagers have in their communities, the more successful they are in school.

Supportive Assets	Boundaries and Expectations Assets
• Family support	• Family boundaries
• Positive family communication	• School boundaries
• Other adult relationships	• Neighborhood boundaries
• A caring neighborhood	• Adult role models
• A caring school climate	• Positive peer influences
• Parental involvement in schooling	• High expectations
Empowerment Assets	**Assets for Constructive Use of Time**
• A community that values youth	• Creative activities
• Youth as resources	• Youth programs
• Service to others	• Religious community
• Safety	• Time at home

Figure 5.1: Developmental Assets Essential for Student Learning
(Search Institute, 1999)

Assets have tremendous power to protect youth from many different harmful or unhealthy choices. The charts in figure 5.2 (page 93) show that youth with the most assets are the least likely to engage in four different patterns of high-risk behavior. The same kind of impact is evident with many other problems, including tobacco use, depression and attempted suicide, antisocial behavior, academic struggles, drinking and driving, and gambling. In addition to protecting youth from negative behavior, having more assets increases the chances that young people will have positive attitudes and behaviors, as figure 5.3 (page 93) shows.

In another study, the Iowa Association of School Boards (IASB) conducted a statewide investigation of school districts in Georgia (Iowa Association of School Boards, 2000). Georgia was selected because the state had a track record of several years of student assessments and statewide standards. The Lighthouse Inquiry examined school districts that on the basis of assessment data were succeeding in teaching high-poverty students effectively in comparison to those that were failing to educate low-income, minority, and special education students. The study discovered powerful new insights into the current school improvement revolution.

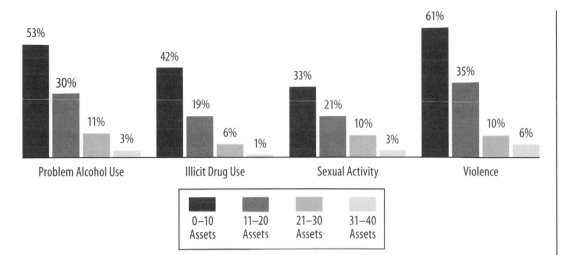

Figure 5.2: High-Risk Behaviors: Protection With Community Assets

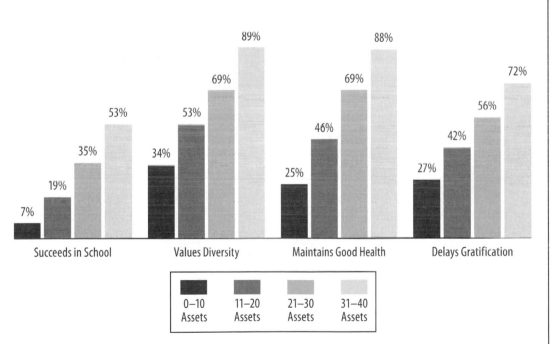

Figure 5.3: Positive Attitudes and Behaviors Promoted With Community Assets

The researchers concluded that when there was a positive perception of schools and support of schools in a community, the schools tended to be successful. When communities did not support their local school district, the district tended to have failing schools for poor and minority students. While no effort was made to explain this causal relationship between schools and communities, the researchers simply concluded that school success seems intimately related to broad community support (Iowa Association of School Boards, 2000). As a result of the Lighthouse Inquiry, the IASB strongly encouraged school boards and superintendents to explore ways to generate widespread community involvement and support.

One of the Lighthouse districts in Sioux Center, Iowa, has worked hard to develop community partnerships. The Sioux Center School District is one of the most effective in Iowa at helping poor and minority students obtain significant levels of academic achievement (Morley, 2004). In Sioux Center, the school board and superintendent have attempted to discover new ways to:

- Sustain community involvement in decision-making.
- Recognize the complete community as true partners.
- Ensure that all school personnel feel connected to the larger community.

The school board went even further, setting a goal to "establish a powerful community connection that will engage parents and community members in school improvement and inspire public will to ensure that all students learn well" (Morley, 2004).

Among the many community-focused strategies the school district attempted was the creation of a broad-based advisory board for the local school board. The advisory board was made up of local leaders representing various community groups: the faith community, private schools, home-schoolers, the county, nonprofits, the media, and so on. Over time, this local board participated in staff development, curriculum, and instruction and encouraged the use of data-driven decision-making in advising the school board. The advisory board quickly began to define the overall plan of action, not simply provide advice. The school district then conducted town meetings and encouraged each school to work directly with their local community.

One of the initial efforts of the Sioux Center School District was to build a "literacy community" in their town. Ray Morley of the Iowa Department of Education described the school district's goal of getting all teachers, students, parents, businesses, and political and community leaders to support literacy and become involved readers: "Their goal was to ensure that every evening at dinner, parents and their children would ask, 'What are you reading now?' and 'What do you think about it?' They wanted everyone to be reading—they wanted their entire community to be model readers" (Morley, 2004).

Develop Full-Service Schools

Schools that successfully teach poor and minority students have made a concerted effort to address the needs of their most challenging students. Since children and youth cannot learn when they are sick, hungry, cold, or afraid, effective schools must try to alleviate these problems as an essential precondition for learning. As a result, effective schools have mobilized services and resources from throughout their communities. These schools help needy students and their families connect with community agencies and offer services such as family health centers and high-quality childcare programs. A major study found that children in high-quality childcare programs demonstrated greater mathematical ability, greater thinking and attention skills, and fewer behavioral problems than children in lower-quality care (Barnett, 1996). Effective schools in poor communities often collect and disperse used clothing, coats, shoes, and even eyeglasses. Some effective schools at the elementary level have installed washers and dryers to provide laundry services for students who have no access to clean clothes. Successful schools have even established health clinics, legal aid centers, and job search services and have made provisions for food stamps and temporary housing for families in need.

Schools that provide a wide variety of services have been referred to as "full-service" schools. For better or worse, public schools are the single social institution that can coordinate the many needs of poor children and their families. According to Dryfoos (1994), to best help poor children learn, full-service schools must:

- Feed children.
- Provide psychological support services.
- Offer health services.
- Offer health screening.
- Establish referral networks related to substance abuse, child welfare, and sexual abuse.
- Cooperate with local police and probation offices.
- Add curriculum for prevention of substance abuse, teen pregnancy, suicide, and violence.
- Actively promote social skills, good nutrition, safety, and general health.

The Community as a Classroom

Schools that have raised the achievement level of poor and minority students have formed partnerships with businesses, organizations, and agencies and blended classroom experiences with learning throughout the community. Nothing seems to help focus student learning, provide relevance to classroom courses, and motivate students quite like reality-based experiences outside the school. Effective schools are increasingly using the entire community as a classroom. In particular, schools that are effective with the children of poverty use service learning and career exploration and development.

**Secrets of Success
in High-Performing, High-Poverty Schools**

Service Learning

For the children of poverty, few educational programs have proven as effective as service learning in the school and community. Students who have low self-concepts and feelings of inefficacy often thrive in service learning opportunities, which build resilience and responsibility and strengthen self-concept. Whether it is tutoring elementary students, working in a day care or senior center, or doing volunteer work at hospitals, service learning has a powerful, positive effect on all students, especially those of low socioeconomic status.

Service Learning

"They [students] learn to give back to their community. They learn not to be takers. . . . What you put into life is what you get out of it."

—*Parent, Maryland*

Service learning has long been recognized as a powerful learning experience and one of the most effective strategies for reducing school dropout (Schargel & Smink, 2001). For the children of poverty, few educational programs have proven as effective. There is a direct relationship between service learning and positive academic achievement. The value of service learning can be seen in the following evaluations:

- Florida gathered data on service learning for 3 academic years, each year consistently reporting strong improvement in attendance, grades, and conduct. Attendance improved in 83% of reporting sites, 80% had fewer discipline referrals, and 76% of students improved their grade point average. At-risk students showed 89% improved attendance and 89% fewer discipline referrals (Learning In Deed, 2006) .

- Service-learning participants scored significantly higher than comparison group members on 4 measures of educational impact: school engagement, school grades (math and science), core grade point average (English, math, social studies, and science grades combined), and educational aspirations (desire to graduate from college) (Center for Human Resources, 1999).

- Among students participating in service learning, 87% reported having learned a new skill that they believed would be valuable in the future (Center for Human Resources, 1999).

- Service-learning participants showed enhanced civic attitudes in terms of social responsibility (Center for Human Resources, 1999).

While service learning may provide practical experience and enhanced motivation, most importantly, it appears to be directly related to academic performance. As one recent report concluded, connecting service-learning activities to core curriculum and requiring children to engage in academic analysis (or reflection) tends to enhance academic performance (Lewis, 1995). In an effective service-learning program:

- Service learning should be voluntary.
- Teachers should be involved in planning and implementation.
- Activities should link with the core curriculum.
- Community partners should be involved.
- Research should demonstrate accountability for meeting standards.
- The service learning activities should connect to more difficult subjects.
- Management should be school-based.
- Resources should be easily identifiable and accessible.
- Time for related student reports and academic work should be built into the schedule.
- Administrative responsibilities should be minimal (Lewis, 1995).

The Simon Youth Foundation in Indianapolis, Indiana, has developed partnerships between regional shopping malls and local school districts in more than a dozen states. The Foundation provides facility space for housing at-risk alternative schools in area shopping malls, professional development for teachers and administrators, and a variety of support services, including an emphasis on service learning. Simon Youth Foundation schools support service learning as an important aspect of their curriculum. "Service-learning is not a distraction from academic study; it enhances academic achievement by showing relevance, increasing student motivation and interrelating studies with real life," reports the directors of one of the schools (Simon Youth Foundation, 2001, p. 4). Two of the most effective Simon Youth Foundation schools—in Seattle, Washington, and San Antonio, Texas—believe service learning is essential to their academic success with poor and minority students.

Career Exploration

For middle and high school students, few learning experiences provide such powerful motivations as career exploration, job shadowing, and career internships. Effective schools give students opportunities to incorporate academic learning with real-world experiences. Students gain firsthand experiences in potential careers, learn specific skills and educational requirements of various occupations, and interact with professionals in their particular field of interest.

Powerful Partnerships

Student cannot learn in isolation. To ensure that teaching and learning are maximized, effective schools have developed powerful partnerships with parents and families as well as a wide variety of community agencies, organizations, and businesses. Effective schools partner with the family for the good of the student through parent education, comprehensive partnerships, and two-way communication. For the children of poverty, few learning experiences have proven as powerful as real-life experiences in the community outside of the school. Effective schools throughout the United States have found service learning and a wide variety of career exploration experiences to be particularly valuable in preventing dropout and enhancing academic achievement of poor and minority children and youth.

Next Steps

Complete and Discuss the Self-Evaluation

District and school teams should begin or continue their work by completing the following Self-Evaluation Rubric (page 101) and then form groups to compare their perceptions and discuss the appropriate next steps.

Help Parents Learn to Support School Learning

Schools should develop and frequently provide educational opportunities for parents of students of all ages. Focus on helping family members understand ways to help their children learn effectively at home.

Facilitate Two-Way Communication

Effective communication includes an invitation for the adults in the home to respond and provide feedback through a variety of options. Two-way communication with teachers is essential for families of poverty to help underperforming students.

Encourage Parents to Communicate

The busy parents of today need as much assistance as possible to communicate with teachers. Teachers can use phone calls, voice mail, e-mail, classroom web sites, and self-addressed postcards.

Be Creative—Employ a Variety of Communication Strategies

Learning packets should regularly be sent home with clearly explained specific roles for parents to assist in their children's learning. Friendly two-way communication regarding classroom and school activities, assessments, special events, and social gatherings will encourage parents and families to become regularly and actively engaged in the classroom and school. If the home language is a language other than English, appropriate translation of all communications is essential.

Require Home Visits

Perhaps the most effective strategy, especially for young children, is to develop trust and close working relationships with poor families through home visits.

Next Steps

Address the Needs of English Language Learners and Their Families

Educators must acknowledge the needs of English language learners and their families and seek to accommodate all issues of translation and understanding between the home and school. Effective school districts develop bilingual, multicultural newcomer and welcome centers and transition programs to provide family orientations, information, and support for new students and their families.

Encourage Families and Community Members to Enrich the School and Classroom

Parents, families, and other community members should be used as tutors and classroom volunteers and should assist with out-of-school activities. Parents can also assist with classroom instruction and provide direct instruction on cultural issues.

Establish Service Learning and Career Exploration Opportunities

Teachers in grades K–12 should work together to provide service-learning opportunities for every student. Students at the middle and high school level should be given opportunities to participate in short-term career explorations and job shadowing. Many students also benefit from extended internships.

Target Professional Development and Create Action Plans

Educators and schools should access the invaluable resources available today on creating effective family/school/community partnerships and make time to develop a school action plan.

Engage Parents, Communities, and Schools
Self-Evaluation Rubric

What is my school's or district's progress?	BEGINNING			EMBEDDING			SUSTAINING		
	No Action Has Been Taken	Efforts Are Limited	Results Are Being Gained	Efforts and Results Are Being Enhanced			Practices Are Widespread, Policies Are in Place, and Results Are Increasing		
Does my school or district . . .	1	2	3	4	5	6	7	8	9
Help parents learn?									
Support and encourage parents to improve communication skills?									
Employ a variety of communication strategies?									
Facilitate two-way home/school communication?									
Create partnerships with parents and families?									
Provide assistance for effective learning at home?									
Require home visits?									
Engage parents and families as resources?									
Have a plan for engaging volunteers?									
Engage parents and families in decision-making?									
Offer or require service learning as part of the curriculum?									
Offer career exploration as part of the curriculum?									
Support targeted professional development and action plans?									

Chapter 6

Understand and Hold High Expectations for Poor and Culturally Diverse Students

"Man, this teacher is so tough! She will not let me say 'can't' in this classroom. She really believes we can learn all of this stuff and she won't even let us say we can't do it."

—*Fifth-Grade Student, Hurst, Texas*

In so many ways, today's teachers are more prepared than ever before. Every year they enter their classrooms with up-to-date training in pedagogy and human development. But too often they have little or no understanding of the different cultural groups that make up their student population. They lack an understanding of the backgrounds, languages, religions, cultures, social structures, community norms, and social classes of the students they work with every day (Epstein, 2001). And most significantly, they fail to recognize the strength and resilience of their underachieving students of poverty, and as a result, many fail to teach these children successfully. The children of poverty cannot learn effectively unless educators have a thorough understanding of the nature, extent, and impact of their poverty—not to excuse their absence of learning, but to ensure that student needs are addressed so they can achieve success in school.

Poverty can affect everything from vocabulary and language use to behavior toward teaching and learning. This does not mean poor children cannot succeed. These students often possess resiliency and a strong set of values from their family and community culture. These strengths often stand in stark contrast to those of the prevalent culture of the white middle class. Unfortunately, for so many of these students, life at school and life at home and in the community require completely opposite coping and survival skills. This dichotomy often leads to a "collision of cultures," which frequently creates personal and family conflict with schools and results in behaviors and actions that undermine student academic success.

This collision of cultures has led poorly informed or prejudiced educators to identify the cultural traits of different ethnic groups as the reason why some groups of students do not meet performance standards: "In the past, low-academic achievement in the African-American, Hispanic and Native American population was interpreted as resulting from a 'deprived home environment'" (Padrón, Waxman,

& Rivera, 2002, p. 56). The negative stereotyping of students in public education has had devastating effects. It has led to assignment to remedial and low-track classes, retention, placement in special education, suspension, and even expulsion. African-American, Hispanic, and Native American students are much less likely to be placed in gifted and talented, advanced placement, college preparatory, or other accelerated educational programs. Such stereotyping often places these students into a situation where they have to choose between adapting to "street culture" values that glamorize academic underachievement or feeling as though they must "act white" to succeed (Kuykendall, 1992; Ogbu, 1992). Herb Kohl (1994) believes it often becomes a point of personal honor for students to simply respond with "I will not learn from you"—in effect living up to the low standards set for them.

The Old World of Public Education

> *"I understand why so many of our poor kids are failing our state's tests. When you look at the examples of test items, you see all of these questions about golfing, yachting, taxi cabs, and credit cards. And then our test experts argue that the tests are 'bias-free.' Yeah, right!"*
>
> —*Legislator, Pennsylvania*

The old world of public education is wrought with tragic examples of institutional racism and class prejudice that have formed the basis for low academic expectations of poor minority students. The "culture of poverty"—the conditions associated with poverty—does create a complex set of problems that make teaching and learning an enormous challenge for poor students. Because of this and a lack of understanding of the challenges of poverty, schools adopted numerous policies, practices, and programs that compounded these problems and created long-term negative effects (see chapter 2). Rather than helping low-socioeconomic-status students remediate, catch up, and accelerate, these approaches stigmatized, isolated, and abandoned the very students they were designed to help. These school traditions that characterize the old world of public education in effect waged war on poor children and youth. In addition to the programs, policies, and practices explained previously, these traditions included:

- The melting pot concept
- The philosophy of equal opportunity
- The practice of blaming poor families and their children

The Melting Pot Concept

"When the tribal leaders decided to try and teach the Arapaho language to our elementary reservation school students, we were surprised that not only did the children not know their native language, but neither did their

parents. We worked with elders to find grandparents who were willing to help teach their forgotten language and culture to the younger generation."

—*Principal, Reservation School, Wyoming*

In the past, the goal of American public education was to embrace the vast numbers of immigrants and assimilate them into mainstream culture. Public education was viewed as a huge cultural melting pot. Native American reservation schools and public schools with large Hispanic populations traditionally prohibited children from speaking their native languages, even on the playground. Many schools even punished students for this. Some schools, districts, and states went as far as to adopt "English only" policies. Others eliminated bilingual education. In addition to prohibiting native languages, schools often punished students for cultural behavior, such as using street slang and wearing clothing associated with a particular ethnic group.

The curriculum inspired by the melting pot concept tended to ignore the historical contributions of ethnic groups. Until relatively recently, school texts included few examples of African-American, Hispanic, and Native American writers, poets, artists, and musicians. Textbooks and curriculum focused primarily on American and European history, art, literature, and social studies. The goal of the melting pot was to welcome immigrants into the classrooms and then work systematically to eliminate cultural differences, replacing the ethnic mosaic of the classroom with a composite middle class—an "Americanized" student who was prepared to fit in.

Poor and minority students who were unable or unwilling to conform to this approach were often tracked into slow-learning ability groups, which were assigned to inexperienced teachers who often lacked the skills to teach effectively. Far too many of these kids ultimately dropped out of school. Even today, dropout rates for poor and minority students in the nation's urban school districts and on the reservations of rural America are more than 50% and in some urban areas as high as 90% (Balfanz & Legters, 2004).

The Philosophy of Equal Opportunity

"We just don't have a level playing field. As long as our neighboring district can fund better facilities and pay their teachers a lot more than we can, we'll never catch up."

—*Elementary Principal, Idaho*

During the past 50 years, public education has gone from the "separate but equal" policy of racial and socioeconomic segregation to "equal educational opportunity for all." Unfortunately, the philosophy of equal educational opportunity has proven almost as destructive as the earlier concept of separate but equal. Poor families and their children have rarely had equal educational opportunity. The practice of using geographic boundaries to assign students to public schools has led to schools being segregated on the basis of socioeconomic status. In most communities, poor families and their children suffer a "savage inequality" (Kozol, 1991) by being assigned to inferior schools along with other poor children. Research continues to document that many schools serving poor children and youth have inferior resources compared to schools in advantaged neighborhoods, as well as more inexperienced teachers who are less likely to be certified, and higher levels of underachievement (Kozol, 1991).

Few issues in public education have proven as tragic and destructive as the philosophy of equal educational opportunity. Schools simply "offered" a high-quality education, and if students failed, it was attributed to the students' supposed lack of initiative and motivation.

The Practice of Blaming Poor Families and Their Children

"It's not our schools that are failing; it is the parents who are failing."
—*School Board Member, Vermont*

Too often, teachers, administrators, and school boards explain the failures of public education by blaming the students and their families. Schools and districts throughout the country serving poor neighborhoods have argued and pleaded with educational policymakers to exempt them from newly legislated academic standards because their schools serve large percentages of poor and minority students. To blame poor children for their deficits is no more productive than blaming poorly developed children for lacking proper nutrition. This attitude is not limited to community members and local educators. A number of scholars continue to maintain that schools cannot overcome the debilitating effects of poverty (Greene & Forster, 2004). But today we have a better understanding of the problems associated with poverty, and we have two decades of research documenting that schools can effectively overcome these challenges.

The New World of Public Education

The new world of public education is replacing blame with understanding, racism and prejudice with a more enlightened view of reality, and destructive policies and practices with effective educational programs. Many of the schools where students attain proficiency have built their educational interventions on the basis of a careful understanding of the needs of poor children and the nature and culture of poverty, which includes holding high expectations for all students.

Understanding poor and culturally diverse students is an essential prerequisite for high-performing schools, according to most of the studies that form the foundation of this book—most often in sections of the reports associated with professional development. In his McREL study, Goodwin (2000) emphasizes how important it is for schools to understand why achievement gaps occur in public schools and encourages educators to understand the implications of poor student self-concept, unsuccessful adjustment to school culture, and class prejudice and racism. Kati Haycock of the Education Trust has also emphasized the importance of understanding why achievement gaps occur if we are to address the obstacles to poor children's performance (Sparks, 2000).

**Secrets of Success
in High-Performing, High-Poverty Schools**
Structured Classes and Proactive Teachers

ABT Associates (Schiller et al., 2006) conducted a study that focused on teachers in high-performing classrooms in 71 Title I schools in 18 school districts and 7 states. Following inquiries and observations of teachers whose students' test scores in reading and math were above the national average, they discovered a number of variables they felt were significant to high-performance in these high-poverty schools:

- Low-income students with little structure in their families seem to benefit from highly structured learning environments that focus on basic skills.

- Teachers in high-performing, high-poverty environments had a strong commitment to their work, spent extra time helping students, and demonstrated respect for their students.

- Teachers had high expectations for all of their students.

- Teachers were knowledgeable about state and school district academic standards, curriculum frameworks, and assessment.

- Teachers assessed their students constantly and used assessment as an instructional tool.

The Illinois Golden Spike Study stressed the need for professional development for teachers and administrators working in high-poverty schools. According to the study, teaching and leadership in high-poverty schools require "different knowledge, skills and attitudes than teaching in affluent schools" (McGee, 2004, p. 121). The study found that teachers in high-performing, high-poverty schools had:

- High expectations
- An "esprit de corps" (a common spirit that inspires enthusiasm, devotion, and a strong regard for the honor of the group)

- A collective work ethic
- Human relations skills
- A missionary zeal
- A variety of characteristics associated with effective teaching (McGee, 2004)

High expectations of student learning among teachers is crucial. Educators must believe all of their students will achieve. Leaders in high-performing schools repeatedly identify this as the top priority for themselves and their teachers. Teachers are not the only ones who exhibit poor attitudes toward students of low socioeconomic status. Research has shown that without proper training, school counselors tend to underestimate poor and minority students' abilities and place them in non-college-bound programs (Goodwin, 2000). Since students live up to (or down to) teacher expectations, it is absolutely essential that teachers are held to a rigorous accountability in their expectations of student learning.

The Louisiana School Effectiveness Study (Teddlie & Stringfield, 1993) conducted multiple studies of schools where poor and minority students were achieving during a 10-year period in the 1980s and concluded that the most important factor is not just well-qualified and experienced teachers, but also caring and demanding teachers. In addition, the studies documented the power of administrators who held high expectations for all students and provided supportive leadership for their teachers. More recently, the Illinois Golden Spike Study found that 90% of the most effective schools included "talented, hardworking teachers who believed that all students can learn" (McGee, 2004, p. 116).

Clearly, one of the ways effective schools address teacher expectations and attitudes is through targeted professional development. Effective schools and districts focus heavily on professional development that increases understanding and expectations of the culture of poverty and minority students (Goodwin, 2000; Massell, 2000).

Educating English Language Learners

"I sat next to a student and read the questions on the math portion of a standardized test he was taking for the third time. He had arrived in the United States only 2 years earlier as a refugee from a war-torn country. His English was actually quite remarkable, but he was still learning. It was obvious that he was struggling with various terminologies in the test. Questions would use terms like 'multiply' and 'times' interchangeably in multiplication problems, and the switching of wording was confusing to him.

I am convinced to this day that he knew how to do the majority of the problems, but he was not really being tested on his math skills; he was being

Understand
and Hold High
Expectations
for Poor and
Culturally
Diverse
Students

tested on his ability to read and interpret English. Now and again he would get so frustrated, he would just start clicking answers on the computer screen without even reading the question. I think this was his way of trying to speed up the process of pain. Then he would stop, take a deep breath, and begin to try again.

The end of the test finally came. We were both exhausted, he was sweaty, and I felt sick to my stomach and helpless in a situation where I was supposed to be the helper. His score flashed on the monitor, and his shoulders sank. He was one point below the cut score, and he knew that this automatically placed him in a mandatory remediation class next semester. He now would be unable to fit auto-shop class, the only subject he really enjoyed in school, into his schedule. I had watched him rollercoaster through numerous emotions throughout the testing process—anxiety, hopelessness, frustration, and finally failure. He dropped out of school the next week."

—*High School English Language Learner (ELL) Teacher, Boise, Idaho*

With the populations of linguistically diverse students increasing at unprecedented rates, leaders must act decisively to intervene when necessary with students to ensure their academic achievement, growth, and proficiency. Principals may begin this work by considering the following eight self-assessment questions (Santos, 2004, p. 91):

1. How much do I know about the English-language learners in my school? How many ELL students are there? What are their countries of origin?
2. Do I know where I can find out more about the cultural backgrounds of these students? What resources exist in my community?
3. What steps am I taking to promote my own professional development in the education of ELL students?
4. What steps have I taken to support the language and literacy development of my ELL students?
5. How do I serve as an advocate for high-quality instruction in all subject areas for the ELL students in my school?
6. What supports exist in my school to help ensure that it is a comfortable and welcoming place for ELL students?
7. What is my definition of "multiculturalism"? What do I think of when I imagine a "multicultural school"?
8. In what specific ways do I model the fair treatment of students and staff from a variety of backgrounds?

The information gained from the answers to these questions will provide direction and guidance to leaders to plan and implement appropriate next steps.

Understanding the Culture of Poverty

An impressive research and literature base on poverty and culture is now available to educators in the publications of the Children's Defense Fund, in Kids Count annual reports, and in the classic work of Ruby Payne, *A Framework for Understanding Poverty* (2001). Learning about situational and generational poverty and ways to effectively intervene with underachieving students gives educators the confidence to work more actively with students and their families. Understanding the characteristics of the culture of poverty also helps to focus educators' attention on what policies and programs are needed in their schools to address the needs of their most challenging students.

Secrets of Success
in High-Performing, High-Poverty Schools
Target Deficiencies of
Low-Socioeconomic-Status Students

Schools and school districts should seek out research on the culture of poverty, language use among low socioeconomic classes, and instructional strategies proven effective with poor and minority students. In the past, culture and language were used to blame poor families or to explain why certain students were not successful in school. Today, these same characteristics of poverty-level families become the target for instructional goals, curriculum, and remediation programs. The more educators understand low-socioeconomic-status and minority students, the better they can target curriculum and instruction to teach these students.

A Feeling of Helplessness

Most teachers and school administrators experienced a successful K–12 education and went on to graduate from college. Many educators have also completed graduate degrees or at least some graduate work. These educators model the success of hard work, dedication, and delayed gratification. Teachers often exemplify self-determination and have an ingrained belief in cause and effect: They believe that hard work leads to success. When confronted with failure or lack of success, they have learned to take charge, try harder, invest more time, and increase their work and their output. All successful people have learned that what they themselves do can largely ensure their personal success. As a result, they can set long-term goals, identify what they need to do to accomplish their goals, and develop a personal plan to ensure success. Successful adults *internalize* an understanding of self-reliance and self-determination.

Many children and adults living in poverty, however, have learned that there are often few rewards, regardless of how hard they work. Many have developed feelings of utter helplessness that at best lead them to passively accept their plight and at worst, to engage in harmful addictions, substance abuse, or other debilitating behaviors. Rather than work harder to improve their condition, they surrender to what they perceive as the inevitable. Too often, they simply give up.

The culture of poverty tends to make people *externally centered*. They come to learn that events and forces outside their own lives and control often overwhelm their best efforts and hard work. Jerry Conrath (1988, 2001) has attempted to explain the externally centered student. Conrath believes that too many children of poverty see hardworking parents laboring in low-paying jobs that do not provide medical care or opportunities for advancement. Thus, they develop an attitude that effort makes very little difference. Because children of poverty see little possibility of hope for a better economic life, they frequently question the value of working hard in school. Many live in homes where none of the adults have a job and perhaps have never had one. Others live in homes where adults work in the lowest paying jobs: serving as field workers, house cleaners, fast-food employees, security guards, hourly workers in factories, and so on. Other children see their parents working two or three part-time jobs and failing to make ends meet. Unfortunately, even with minimum wage, many working parents do not earn enough to afford even a place to live.

As a result, children of poverty grow up being externally centered and believing that external events control their lives. They see no relationship among hard work, sacrifice, self-reliance, and success. These students often arrive at school with little or no concept of educational success or an understanding that this success often depends on their efforts to conform to classroom procedures. Schools must teach externally centered students to take control of their lives and to see that personal effort can bring big rewards.

The Homes of Poverty

Children of poverty typically live in homes with a parent or parents with little education and few marketable skills. The homes rarely have computers and reference materials and may even lack pencils and paper. Poor children rarely have access to a quiet atmosphere conducive to study and homework. As a result, many poverty-level children maintain a poor record of completing homework assignments and arrive at school less prepared than their more advantaged peers. Many schools now provide time during the school day for students to complete their homework. This gives children a quiet, safe work environment and a chance to accelerate their learning, often with the help of adult tutors.

Teachers, especially in the early grades, should schedule home visits to all of their poor students' homes so they can get to know parents, grandparents, or guardians. This is key to developing strong, positive relationships with families and the community. In addition, teachers need to see firsthand the living conditions of their students. This contact also demands frequent and two-way communication. For families living in poverty, this type of communication is essential; it helps the teacher learn more about the problems and needs of his or her students and their families. It also enables teachers to help parents and guardians understand how they can help their children and provides them with informal support and education.

Schools should invite parents to join with teachers and administrators as full partners in the curriculum, instruction, and management of the school (see chapter 5). If the school does not intervene and develop an effective partnership with parents, the gap between poor and advantaged children grows over time.

Lack of Educational Stimulation

Children of poverty often suffer significantly during time spent away from school, especially during the summer months. A study analyzed by Bracey (2002b) found that advantaged students spend their summers going to city and state parks; taking swimming, music, and dance lessons; visiting museums, science centers, and zoos; participating in organized sports programs; and going to the public library. Few of these activities are available for poor students. For them, the summer months are spent without books, educational stimulation, or even nutritious meals. As a result, "students from poor families suffer a significant drop in academic learning when compared to their more advantaged classmates who not only maintain their level of achievement over the summer months, but actually increase their achievement through their non-school activities" (Bracey, 2002b, p. 497). Many effective schools implement summer programs for low-achieving students that include nutrition, recreation, academic acceleration, and remediation.

Lack of Health and Nutrition

The Children's Defense Fund and the Kids Count Program have documented for decades the tragic impacts of poverty on children in each of the 50 states in the nation. The single largest group in the United States without health insurance continues to be families living in poverty. According to a report by the U.S. Census Bureau (Sadowski, 2004), the number of Americans living in poverty and without health insurance rose by more than 1.4 million people in 2003 to a total of 5 million Americans. The report also explained that child poverty was increasing at the fastest pace in a decade. Too many poor children arrive at school with uncorrected vision, decaying teeth, untreated illnesses, and malnutrition.

To teach poverty-level children effectively, schools and communities need to help their students find medical, dental, hearing, and vision care. The Illinois Golden Spike Study suggests major policy changes that focus on the needs of poor children and their families. The report recommended that the state expand food services, community health access, and parent education at school and concluded that all of these recommendations will have little effect if children come to school undernourished and in poor health. Learning occurs best when children are well-nourished and safe (McGee, 2004).

Many communities are creating "full-service schools" to better address the needs of poor children by coordinating health, welfare, and family services through the state and local governments and private nonprofit groups. Schools must also ensure some type of nutrition program throughout the summer months.

Lack of Vocabulary and Reading Readiness

In addition to health problems, poverty-level children often grow up with significant deficiencies in communication skills that impair their ability to read, write, and spell. A study of class differences in verbalization for children aged 1 to 3 years old found that "parents employed in professional occupations talked to their children using almost 2,200 words per hour. Blue-collar parents spoke about 1,300 words per hour to their children. Welfare parents spoke only 600 words per hour to their children" (Bracey, 2000a, p. 432). The impact of this lack of communication with adults severely affects the children of poverty because they arrive at school with significantly fewer communication skills than their more advantaged peers.

More than half of the research reports that form the basis of this book emphasize the importance of early literacy for poor children. The Illinois Golden Spike Study captures the tone of many of the other studies: "When building budgets, schools, school districts, and states will maximize the effectiveness of scarce resources by drawing more funds to programs and services that will prevent reading problems than those that remediate them" (McGee, 2004, p. 120). Since poor and minority students often arrive at school with significantly less vocabulary development, language skills, and pre-reading skills than their more advantaged peers, high-performing, high-poverty school districts recognize the importance and effectiveness of an early start.

Language, Culture, and Diversity

The landscape of America's classrooms is rapidly changing. Michael Sadowski, in his introduction to *Teaching Immigrant and Second-Language Students* (2004), cites recent U.S. census data and the work of Donald Hernandez to illustrate the new trends (figure 6.1). Sadowski further states:

> Given the linguistic and cultural diversity of today's school-age population—which will become even more diverse in the coming decades—it is becoming clearer every day that 'education as usual' will not suffice. Simply put, good intentions—even when combined with vast subject-matter knowledge and a host of pedagogical strategies—are not enough. (2004, p. 2)

- One in five children in the United States comes from an immigrant family (one or both of their parents were born outside the country).

- Children from immigrant families are the fastest-growing segment of the U.S. child population. Since 1990, their number has grown seven times faster than that of their counterparts from U.S.-born families.

- Immigration, once largely confined to a handful of states and urban centers, has been rising in virtually every U.S. state. Yet many states that have had low immigration rates historically have little institutional infrastructure to accommodate recent influxes of newcomer families.

- Whereas the vast majority of immigrants to the United States came from Europe and Canada at the beginning of the 20th century, today more than 80% of immigrant families come from Latin America and Asia.

- Children from immigrant families are more likely than their peers to live in poverty, to be behind in grade level, and to live in overcrowded housing.

- More than 70% of children from immigrant families speak a language other than English at home.

Figure 6.1: Teaching the New Generation of U.S. Students (Sadowski, 2004, pp. 1–2)

Educators need to recognize that different cultural groups (as defined by their socioeconomic status) find very different meaning in common cultural concepts, such as money, possessions, time, education, language, family structure, and world view. In *A Framework for Understanding Poverty,* Payne (2001) explains these differences in cultural concepts. Culture impacts everything about a student's life and plays a major role in a child's expected progress toward proficiency. The complex differences between middle-class language and the street slang of poor and minority students are particularly important for teachers to understand if effective learning is to occur. Classrooms and schools must accommodate the learning needs of students through the implementation of proven and effective interventions and instructional programs that take these differences into consideration. The better teachers understand these often conflicting concepts, the better they will be able to prevent cultural collisions between poor families and middle-class schools.

Mobility

One of the most difficult factors regarding education and poverty is how often low-socioeconomic-status families move. Poor families may be evicted, may move because they cannot pay their bills, or may move to seek work or follow seasonal employment. Poor families may move in with other family members when they are unemployed. Regardless of the reason, this poverty-related mobility means that the students most in need of educational stability, consistent instruction, and strong relationships with adults are often in a school for a very short time. Teachers with large numbers of low-socioeconomic-status students may experience from 20 to 30 transitions a year in their classrooms. Some teachers report 100% turnover, ending the school year with a completely different group of students. The constant, disruptive mobility of families living in poverty often overwhelms schools and significantly affects the interventions they can offer.

To address the challenges of mobility, effective schools successfully use the following approaches:

- **Work with parents.** First, in ongoing work with parents, teachers and administrators need to be sure to help families understand how important stability is in the education of children. Some schools sign contracts with parents in which they commit to doing everything possible to keep their children in the same school for at least 3 years.

- **Align the curriculum.** Because of the high rate of student mobility, curriculum alignment with state assessments helps poor students maintain instructional consistency from school to school. Some school districts have had to modify their site-based school management in order to maintain consistency in textbooks, instructional approaches, and curriculum (see chapter 8).

- **Create successful transitions.** Effective schools also work hard to be significantly involved in student transitions to other schools, even schools in other communities or in other states. Some school districts now employ transition counselors who meet with the families of each student who is leaving school, for whatever reason—even if the student is dropping out. The goal is to help parents and students find the next appropriate educational opportunity and assist them in making the transition. Effective schools keep track of students who leave their community to ensure that all instructional and curriculum records follow the students to their next schools. Some schools even use new technologies to enable learning to continue during family transitions to new communities and new states.

- **Provide transportation.** Start with the objective of keeping students in the same school, rather than allowing a transportation schedule to dictate where students can attend school within a district. When a family moves within the same district, provide bus transfers for students so they have the option of staying in the same school.

Each of these approaches has worked to reduce mobility and its negative effects on students of poverty.

Student Behavior

Children of poverty can pose an extremely complex set of challenges for public schools. Perhaps the most difficult challenge is their behavior and its effects on discipline or behavior modification. Misbehavior of low-socioeconomic-status students often reflects values, attitudes, and survival mechanisms that clash with the middle-class behavior norms of public education. Poor children and youth learn early behaviors that are essential to their survival and well-being in their homes and communities. As a result, when disciplined or corrected, poor students may react to teachers and administrators with laughter, loud and angry arguing, and even inappropriate, vulgar, and disrespectful comments (Payne, 2001). Poor students may react to problems or frustration with physical aggression, lying, cheating, or stealing. They may be extremely disorganized, have difficulty completing even simple tasks, and talk incessantly. So many of the behaviors of poor students that cause disruptions in schools and classrooms are survival tactics they have learned in their homes and communities. The children of poverty have great difficulty in achieving success in public schools because the culture of the family is often so different from that of the classroom. To be successful in schools, students must learn to practice self-control and self-governance—something with which poor, externally controlled students may have had little or no previous experience.

To help bridge the gap between the culture of public education and the culture of poverty, scholars have identified three essential approaches: structure, choice, and participation (Comer et al., 1996; Gathercoal, 1999; Glasser, 1998; Payne, 2001; Rogers, 1994). To be effective with poor children and youth, school and classroom management must "clearly delineate the expected student behavior in a structured environment" (Payne, 2001, p. 101). As William Glasser has discussed, teachers and administrators must use what he calls "reality therapy" or "choice therapy" to ensure that students are helped to understand the consequences of their actions, and also encouraged to make personal decisions that are best for them. Low-socioeconomic-status students will not only fail to respond to the approach of "I will tell you what to do and when to do it and punish you if you do not respond appropriately," but they will often resist in the most negative, vocal, and demonstrative ways.

To be effective in developing safe, bully-free schools and classrooms that are sufficiently orderly for an effective learning environment, schools need to involve parents, guardians, and students in the establishment of rules, regulations, and consequences (Comer et al., 1996; Gathercoal, 1999). Such cooperative development of the behavioral expectations and school or classroom management strategies is essential to educate the children of poverty. Some schools have found developing a detailed contract agreed to and signed by the teacher, parents, and student to be particularly effective. Other schools teach a variety of conflict-resolution strategies and interventions to students, parents, and teachers to help students work out and resolve many of their own conflicts. Payne (2001) recommends teaching students the language and process of negotiation; others recommend peer mediation and teaching students anger management and conflict resolution strategies (Rogers, 1994).

Resilience

Research during the past 15 years has focused on students who have all of the characteristics of being at high risk of school failure but nonetheless perform academically at high levels of proficiency. Identified by researchers as "resilient" children and youth, these students seem to thrive in spite of personal challenges. Over time, research from Johns Hopkins University and the North Central Regional Educational Laboratory (among others) has helped to identify these characteristics of resilient children and youth (Benard, 1991; Krovetz, 1999).

- **Social competence.** Resilient students tend to have the qualities of responsiveness, flexibility, empathy, and caring, communication skills, a sense of humor, and other pro-social behavioral attitudes.
- **Problem-solving skills.** Resilient students tend to have the ability to think abstractly, to be reflective, and to attempt creative, alternative solutions to both cognitive and life problems.
- **Autonomy.** Resilient students tend to have a strong self-esteem and a sense of personal power and independence.

- **Sense of purpose and future.** Resilient students tend to be optimistic about their future and to have healthy, realistic goals. (Barr & Parrett, 2003, p. 52)

There is a growing realization among effective schools that these personality traits are teachable (Barr & Parrett, 2003; Brown, D'Emidio-Caston, & Benard, 2001; Krovetz, 1999). Since personal perceptions and self-concepts are defined in large part by the people around us, teacher perception is highly influential. If teachers care for students, support them, and hold them in high regard, students tend to internalize positive feelings about themselves. Positive self-concepts and feelings of resiliency can also be developed through adult mentoring programs, community-service learning, cross-age tutoring, challenge programs such as Expeditionary Learning Schools Outward Bound, and placement of students in positions of personal responsibility. For children of poverty, few areas (if any) are more important for academic achievement than a strong self-concept, a belief that they can succeed in school, and a growing sense of independence and power over the direction of their lives.

High Hopes for the Underachieving Children of Poverty

"When we respond to the individual differences among students by lowering our expectations and providing inferior educational opportunities, we underestimate the capacity for all children to grow intellectually and we fail to provide adequate tools for learning. In these ways, we confirm our own predictions. To prevent such educational tragedies—a particularly urgent goal given the growing diversity of children attending our schools—we need to both embrace and support pedagogically a vision of possibility regarding the educational achievement of all our children."

—Rhonda Weinstein (2002, p. 2)

Underachieving children of poverty will not learn effectively unless educators understand the nature, extent, impact, and culture of these students and address their needs. Because the culture of poverty affects everything from vocabulary to language use to behavior to teaching and learning, the first essential step of schools that have taught low-socioeconomic-status students effectively is participation in a comprehensive professional development program focused on understanding the culture of poverty. Such a program helps teachers and administrators recognize class prejudice, racist attitudes, and institutional bias. Professional development helps educators understand offensive and destructive school practices and develop new approaches, programs, and procedures, such as early childhood programs, parent education and partnership programs, and instructional approaches to school and classroom management. It is through education and understanding that educators learn the needs and challenges of poor students and then develop school responses and interventions designed to teach all students effectively.

Next Steps

Complete and Discuss the Self-Evaluation

District and school leadership teams should begin or continue their work by completing the following Self-Evaluation Rubric (page 121) and then, working in groups, compare their perceptions and discuss appropriate next steps.

Educate English Language Learners

Educators must understand the needs of ELL students and ensure that they receive high-quality instruction in all areas. Evaluate and support language and literacy development as well as a culturally sensitive and supportive environment.

Understand the Characteristics of Poverty and Different Cultural Groups

Educators must learn the characteristics of poverty and different cultural groups. Without this understanding, teachers and administrators may react to student achievement or behavior with misunderstanding, bias, or prejudice rather than with insight.

Understand the Externally Centered Student

Educators must teach externally centered students to take control of their lives and to understand that hard work and effort can bring big rewards.

Anticipate the "Collision of Cultures"

Middle-class schools need to plan carefully to anticipate and address the "collision of cultures" between the middle-class values of the school and the culture of poverty and minority groups. This might include providing parent education, requiring professional staff development for teachers and administrators, and helping students transition from home to school.

Conduct Home Visits and Form Partnerships With Parents

Teachers should conduct home visits to the families of poverty-level students. These can be invaluable to student success when teachers seek to develop a constructive partnership with parents or guardians based on the mutual desire for all students to learn.

Engage Parents in Meaningful Work

Build relationships with parents and students, and work to cooperatively develop rules, regulations, and consequences for schools and classrooms.

Next Steps

Address Student Mobility

Mobility can be detrimental to student learning; educators need to learn more about its causes and work to develop successful interventions, such as keeping kids in their home school, scheduling alternate transportation, or working closely with the new school.

Foster Resiliency to Improve Student Behavior

Despite what appear to be overwhelming challenges, many students become resilient in ways that allow them to persevere and even thrive. Build resiliency in students by developing school and community programs to enrich their social and emotional growth, such as mentoring programs, service-learning programs, outdoor challenge programs, cross-age tutoring, and conflict resolution training.

Provide Professional Development

Teachers need intensive professional development about the culture of poverty, resiliency, and effective approaches for working with poor children and their families. Teachers need to learn about the growing number of programs that have positive effects on poor children.

Understand and Hold High Expectations for Poor and Culturally Diverse Students Self-Evaluation Rubric

What is my school's or district's progress?	BEGINNING			EMBEDDING			SUSTAINING		
	No Action Has Been Taken	Efforts Are Limited	Results Are Being Gained	Efforts and Results Are Being Enhanced			Practices Are Widespread, Policies Are in Place, and Results Are Increasing		
Does my school or district . . .	1	2	3	4	5	6	7	8	9
Evaluate and support the language and literacy development of ELL students?									
Hold high expectations of all students—especially the underachieving children of poverty?									
Understand the culture of poverty and how it differs from middle-class culture?									
Publicize student performance of all required subgroups, even if the information reflects low school or subgroup performance?									
Understand externally centered students?									
Conduct home visits and improve partnerships with families?									
Engage parents in meaningful work?									
Plan for student mobility?									
Foster and support resilient students?									
Connect the successes of resilient students to the improvement needs of others?									
Build student capacity in anger management, conflict resolution, and peer mediation?									
Provide targeted professional development?									

Chapter 7

Target Low-Performing Students and Schools, Starting With Reading

"Well, it was pretty straightforward. . . . We decided to really focus on the needs of our low-performing students and do whatever was necessary to get them up to proficiency. We've made huge strides in the first year."

—Superintendent, Michigan

Educators have long understood that students live up to or down to the expectations set for them. If educators expect students of low socioeconomic status to achieve high levels of academic proficiency, they must provide them with a comprehensive umbrella of support. A growing body of research documents that students will achieve high academic proficiency if this support is available. Research has also documented the reverse: Students will underperform if schools and school districts are not clearly focused on ensuring that poor children and youth learn effectively. To ensure that specific student subgroups achieve high levels of academic proficiency, the entire school district must be mobilized and focused on increasing achievement. If the school board, superintendent, school administrators, and teachers remain focused primarily on the gifted and talented students, advanced placement classes, and the percentage of students going to college, then only those students will flourish. If similar attention is focused on poor and minority students, they too will achieve, graduate from high school, and go on to college.

The Old World of Public Education

In the old world of public education, poor students were not expected to learn. In fact, public education actually offered these students programs that isolated, stereotyped, and impeded their progress. In the past, poor children were assigned to schools with teachers who were less well-trained and less experienced than those of affluent students. Schools typically failed to teach these students the necessary basic skills, so they were then retained, tracked into slow-learning courses, often assigned to special education, given prescription drugs, sent to detention centers, or assigned to ineffective programs. As a result of these ineffective policies, programs, and procedures, poor children were demoralized, and the cycle of poverty continued as generation after generation of poor children and youth were not educated effectively. Unfortunately, many of these practices continue to thrive in schools and districts despite the No Child Left Behind legislation.

In the old world of public education, low-socioeconomic-status and minority students were often targeted for failure. In the new world of education, effective schools and school districts have demonstrated how targeting the most needy and demanding students in a positive way not only transforms poor children and youth into effective, high-performing students, but can also break the cycle of poverty.

The New World of Public Education

In the new world of public education, school districts target low-performing students and schools with a wide variety of positive, highly effective interventions. Research on schools and school districts where poor and minority students are achieving proficiency has helped to identify the most promising strategies that contribute to high academic achievement. Some of the most significant research efforts predated No Child Left Behind. This research identified a number of interventions that were later mandated in the federal legislation. Central to improving achievement and school success for underachieving students is the acceleration of learning—catching children up with their peers as quickly as possible—as opposed to traditional programs that stress ongoing remediation (Goldenberg, 2004).

Guarantee That All Students Learn to Read

It has always been important for every child and young adult to learn to read. It is absolutely essential in today's world of technology. If children do not learn to read early in the elementary school years, their self-concept suffers. They cannot do their school work or their homework. Inevitably, they fall behind academically and often begin to fail their courses. Many students without adequate reading skills ultimately drop out of school and live out their lives unemployed or underemployed. Many struggle with drugs and alcohol, get in trouble with police, and end up in jail or prison. Over half of the men and women in prison in the United States are illiterate (Barr & Parrett, 2001).

Unfortunately, almost everyone assumes that most, if not all, children in the United States know how to read. The sad reality is that more than 40% of elementary school students in this nation do not read well, and 25% enter the fourth grade reading at the first- or second-grade level (Fielding, Kerr, & Rosier, 1998). Until recently, even elementary teachers and principals assumed that only a small percentage of students would ever learn to read effectively. One of the primary findings in the research used as the foundation for this book is that teaching effective basic and early literacy skills is essential in all high-performing, high-poverty schools (McGee, 2004; Richardson, 2003; Barth et al., 1999; Jerald, 1991; Education Trust, 2002). Almost all of the schools studied in the various research investigations found that specialized professional development in reading for teachers and extra instructional time in reading and math for students were key components to the success of the under-achieving children of poverty.

The field of education now has reliable research evidence demonstrating that virtually every student can be taught to read well. In fact, schools across the United States have even begun to guarantee students that they will learn to read.

- "In 1998, four California schools began a new 1,000 Days to Success Program that was designed to ensure that all students learned to read by the end of the second grade. Each student in the school district is provided a printed reading warranty card" (Barr & Parrett, 2003, p. 308).

- In the late 1990s in Idaho, state legislators passed the Idaho Reading Initiative that established a goal of 90% of all K–3 students reading at grade level by 2005. The initiative led to the development of a short grade-level assessment tool, the Idaho Reading Indicator, which is used three times per year in grades K–3. Within 3 weeks of the test, teachers receive student results and a diagnosis online for each student. Lower-performing students begin receiving immediate intervention. When the state passed the initiative, only 40% of K–3 students were reading up to grade level. As of 2005, Idaho's K–3 student proficiency averages have climbed to above the 70th percentile. (Idaho Department of Education, 2004)

- In Kennewick, Washington, the school board established a goal of 90% of all students reading up to grade-level proficiency by the end of third grade. In May 1996, the school district had achieved 55% literacy with K–3 students; in 1998, they achieved 71% literacy. Of the 13 elementary schools, 2 achieved the 90% goal in 1998, and 3 others were in the 70–80% range (Fielding, Kerr, & Rosier, 1998).

One program for reducing achievement gaps between underachieving, disadvantaged, or poor students and their peers is the Reading First program, which focuses on early reading in high-poverty schools. The program has posted impressive gains with underachieving poor students in many states. To provide better instruction to low-performing early readers, the Idaho Reading First project provided:

- Increased instructional time
- Instructional leadership
- Embedded professional development
- Classroom coaching
- The implementation of a scientifically-based reading program

---

**Secrets of Success
in High-Performing, High-Poverty Schools**

Start Early

Research clearly documents the power of effective preschool programs. The earlier poor and minority students are engaged in an educational program, the quicker they gain the basics, accelerate their learning, and catch up academically. Few interventions offer such long-term benefits in school and in life than developmentally appropriate early childhood education, preschool, and all-day kindergarten.

The results have been dramatic. The gains achieved in one Idaho Reading First school illustrate this success. New Plymouth Elementary School had a serious problem in reading. Its kindergarten and first-grade students needed help sounding out words. Students in second and third grade were not reading as fast as their peers in other Idaho schools:

> It was time for a change, and the New Plymouth staff members responded. They eliminated pull-out programs, purchased a new reading curriculum, lengthened the school day, and agreed to spend more focused time working and planning together. The change worked. In spring 2003, only 58% of New Plymouth's kindergarten students could read at grade level. By spring 2004, that number had risen to 70%. The difference was even more dramatic in first grade, where scores rose from 47% in 2003 to 86% by spring 2004. (J.A. & Kathryn Albertson Foundation, 2005, p. 8)

The gains of New Plymouth Elementary are representative of others across Idaho and the nation. The architect of the Idaho Reading First model, Marybeth Flachbart, summarizes the progress and future of the program:

> "The Reading First Program has reduced the number of students being referred for special education services. For many of these kids, we can prevent reading disabilities. If they get the right instruction, with the right intensity, at the right time, they'll always read [at] grade level." (J.A. & Kathryn Albertson Foundation, 2005, p. 8)

Educators have learned so much about how to teach reading effectively that the field of education has compiled a growing list of reading materials and programs with reliable evidence documenting their effectiveness in teaching reading to elementary, middle, and high school students. Yet while progress is being made, many hold serious doubts that the No Child Left Behind goal of 100% reading proficiency by the year 2014 is possible. A Carnegie Corporation–sponsored report prepared by the RAND Corporation states it bluntly:

> Achieving state and national literacy goals is a long uphill road. Recent reform efforts in education have yielded positive results in improving reading achievements for the nation's children in the primary grades, but many children are not moving beyond basic and developing skills to fluency and comprehension. Our findings suggest some major concerns about the ability of states to meet the ambitious goal set by [the federal law] of 100% proficiency for all students. (McCombs et al., 2004, p. 24)

Meeting the national goals of reading proficiency will require a large, sustained effort. Will it be easy? No. Can it be achieved? Yes—if schools choose to target the reading interventions that work for underachieving students. And while effective reading remains the single most important instructional goal for poor and minority students, schools and districts must also target underachieving students with other strategies. These include protecting these students from destructive school practices, as well as developing a comprehensive program of school improvement.

Protecting the Children of Poverty From Destructive Policies, Programs, and Practices

The first step in transforming low-performing students into high-performing students is to purge districts, schools, and classrooms of the negative approaches that all but guarantee academic failure.

Eliminate the Manufacturing of Low Performance

Mid-continent Research for Education and Learning (McREL) commissioned more than 300 research papers on the strategies that schools and districts are using to ensure academic achievement for low-socioeconomic-status students. Of the strategies identified through these research efforts, eliminating destructive programs that "manufacture" low performance was one of the most important recommendations to policymakers (Goodwin, 2000). Similar proposals have been offered for over a decade (Barr & Parrett, 1995, 2001, 2003). Such negative programs and practices as retention, tracking, pull-out programs, detention centers, and suspension were identified by McREL and others as not only failing to help poor students learn, but, in effect, actually *creating* low achievement.

Schools that are committed to all students achieving academic success have eliminated these programs and placed underachieving low-socioeconomic-status students in a rigorous curriculum taught by well-trained teachers and supported by a comprehensive array of effective interventions. Unfortunately, the current emphasis on barrier testing has led to a resurgence of the use of retention. Rather than retaining students, effective schools and districts provide intense remediation and acceleration of learning for underperforming students. They attack the causes of low scores on barrier tests so that students who are not successful can often pass a make-up test within a few weeks, several months, or by the end of an intense summer of support.

Protect Students From Unqualified, Inexperienced Teachers

If low-performing students have any hope of ever catching up, the most important factor is to provide them with highly qualified and experienced teachers with high expectations regarding their ability to learn. Unfortunately, research has documented that poor children and youth are five times more likely to have uncertified, misassigned, or inexperienced teachers than affluent students (see chapter 2).

In a McREL policy brief, Goodwin (2000) explains, "All too often low-performing schools serve as training grounds for teachers who are then promoted to high-performing schools" (p. 6). For years, the Brazosport Independent School District in Texas had a policy of assigning every new teacher hired to one of their poor Hispanic schools. The new teachers were required to sign a contract agreeing not to ask for a transfer to a more affluent school for 3 years. This policy guaranteed that poor students in Brazosport always had the most inexperienced teachers in the school district. The results were tragic.

Schools where children of poverty are achieving high levels of proficiency have made teacher assignment a number-one priority. A variety of studies have compared the effects on student achievement of hiring from the top tier of teacher candidate pools as opposed to the bottom tier, and the results were dramatic: "Poverty students with top-tier teachers significantly outperformed affluent students with bottom-tier teachers" (Haycock, 2004, p. 2).

Eliminate Policies and Practices That Encourage Students to Drop Out

The actual dropout rate in American public schools is perhaps as high as 32%. For poor and minority students, the disparity in graduation rates (perhaps 50%

or higher) is unconscionable (Swanson, 2004). The disturbing secret of the No Child Left Behind legislation is that while states are held accountable for both achievement scores and graduation rates, they are allowed to establish their own goals for graduation, which vary from 5% to 100%. Any amount of progress can be considered adequate, even a minuscule improvement (Swanson, 2004). Even more disturbing, schools may feel so pressured to raise the test scores of all student subgroups that "pushing out" low-performing students from school would seem to be the best and quickest way to improve student performance data. Investigations into district practices in Houston, Texas, and New York City have generated considerable suspicion and evidence that some schools are systematically pushing out poor and minority students (Swanson, 2004).

Collecting accurate data on high school dropout rates is challenging. Efforts by school districts vary from apparently deliberate falsification of records to the genuine challenge of accurately tracking student data through multiple years of enrollment. This task is especially difficult with poor and minority students from families that move often; however, it is clear that high (or increasing) dropout rates, especially for poor and minority students, are not the result of increased assessment and accountability. A number of recent studies have documented that increased accountability does not directly increase the number of students leaving school (Greene & Winters, 2004; Education Trust, 2003d; Swanson, 2004).

If poor and minority students are to learn effectively and not be left behind, schools and communities must demonstrate an unwavering determination to gather accurate dropout data, close the achievement gap between various student subgroups, and close the high school graduation gap. A number of school districts have established policies designed to eliminate programs that have led to high dropout rates (Gehring, 2004).

- In Boston, Massachusetts, where a policy of retention led to a growing pool of 400 freshmen who too often dropped out of school, a significant policy change is being considered. Previous school district policy required ninth-grade students to repeat the entire school year if they failed either English or mathematics. The school board is working on a more forgiving policy so that students can move to the tenth grade while doing remedial work in the subject they failed.

- In Baltimore, Maryland, where 40% of ninth-grade students drop out of school, the school board has reduced the number of credits needed for promotion to tenth grade. (Gehring, 2004, p. 1)

- In Rochester, New York, a number of different paths toward graduation have been established, including 3-, 4-, and 5-year programs. Many students take the 5-year program to earn advanced credit and college credit with no tuition fees.

- In Houston, Texas, the school board replaced a policy that required students to pass core courses in each grade before being promoted to the next. Now students have until the end of 12th grade to pass all the core tests.

- In Harlingen, Texas, the school district focused on data to reduce the dropout rate. They evaluated where they were losing students and how they could prevent this loss or recover students after they left. With help from the Harlingen Area Foundation, this commitment led to the creation of many innovative programs: eighth-grade counselor sessions facilitated by a social worker, a new alternative school that enabled students to complete a school year in an accelerated semester, a team of seven new attendance officers, parent centers, and a community-wide tutoring and mentoring program. The dropout rate in Harlingen has gone down from 15.97% in 1990 to a present rate of less than 1% (Shields, 2004, p. 1). Figure 7.1 (page 131) describes some of the programs created to help reduce the dropout rate in Harlingen.

Other school districts have used career-theme academies, smaller schools, block-scheduled classes, and alternative schools to improve the graduation rate of poor and minority students (Gehring, 2004).

Use Data to Plan, Target Policy, Monitor Student Achievement, and Rigorously Hold Teachers Accountable

In effective school districts, the school board and central administration use data throughout the year to identify and monitor low-performing schools and provide extra time, attention, planning, and professional development as needed (Massell, 2000). The former practice of only using an annual review of standardized test results to assess progress has all but disappeared: "Relying on end-of-year assessments is not a check-up, it is an autopsy" (Jerald, 2004).

Eric Smith, former North Carolina Superintendent of the Year, maintains that for poor and minority students to learn effectively, individual teachers must be rigorously held responsible. "Don't let teachers off the hook!" Smith explains (2003, p. 4). In his district, when teachers are failing poor and minority students, they are provided with additional professional development and training, specialist observers to ensure that teachers are covering required topics, and help with using assessment data to diagnose student needs and re-teach (Smith, 2003). In a major

- **New Directions.** This tutoring and mentoring program provides at-risk high school students with a taste of success by giving them the opportunity to work with adult mentors from the community.

- **New Horizons.** In this club for at-risk sixth to eighth graders in four middle schools, a social worker leads and facilitates regular group counseling sessions during the school day. Students learn how to accept responsibility, manage emotions, communicate effectively, make decisions, and solve problems.

- **KEYS Academy.** Aimed at dropouts, this alternative school offers students accelerated classes so they can complete a year's worth of work in one semester.

- **Aggressive dropout recovery efforts.** A team of seven attendance officers make regular home visits to help convince dropouts to come back to school.

- **A nationally recognized parenting program.** This program features parent centers on each campus where parents can volunteer and take parenting classes throughout the year. Administrators also bring parents along to state-level conferences.

- **Rising leaders.** Through a series of seminars, panel discussions, and activities with community leaders, student participants become familiar with community needs, services, and resources while building interpersonal and leadership skills.

- **Texas Scholar Program.** This program for students and parents emphasizes how good, well-paying jobs go to those who have prepared themselves by obtaining a fundamentally sound academic education. It stresses on-level and above-level academic courses, including languages other than English. Course grade requirements are passing or better, with an emphasis on better. Students who complete the requirements are honored at an awards banquet at the end of the year.

- **Technology academies.** These training sessions provide students with computer-assisted instruction, particularly in math, science, social studies, and language arts.

Figure 7.1: Programs for Reducing Dropout Rates in Harlingen, Texas (Shields, 2004, pp. 1–2)

study of successful school districts linking assessment data to instruction, a school administrator identified one of the greatest challenges of using data:

> One of our biggest challenges right now in the district, I think, is to help schools look at student achievement indicators and try and connect them back to what they are doing, what aren't they doing . . . to really help them understand how to look at data, how to look at student

work, how to interpret. We have sent schools multitudes of pages of data over the years, but we have [not] . . . done a very good job . . . in helping them understand what to do with it when they got it. (Massell, 2000, p. 6)

Representatives for the Louisville, Kentucky, public schools, selected as one of five Broad Foundation's outstanding school districts in 2003, emphasized the importance of holding teachers accountable for effective teaching. Before any interventions are considered, school administrators must make sure that each student, especially poverty-level students, are getting adequate instructional time, adequate attention, and effective instruction. It is only after working directly with teachers to ensure that they are doing everything possible, that the school leader should inquire, "How can we help?" Teams visit low-achieving classrooms, observe instruction, revise the taught curriculum, and relate these factors to student achievement. To monitor student achievement, the number one goal is to get teachers to embed assessment in their classroom instruction and use their data for instructional decisions. When a school is failing in Louisville, it is believed that either the teachers are not providing instruction in the required curriculum, or they are not using internal or embedded assessment in their classrooms.

Improve Instructional Support Programs

More and more schools and districts are providing additional staff, services, and resources to target low-performing students. Even with an aligned curriculum, better-trained teachers, and improved classroom instruction, poverty-level students may still lag behind. Consequently, a common strategy found in high-performing, high-poverty schools is the allocation of a wide variety of additional resources and supports.

Implement High-Performance Instructional Programs

Schools, districts, and states effective in educating poor and minority students have identified instructional programs with documented effectiveness in increasing student achievement. When it comes to selecting textbooks, instructional interventions, and content-specific programs, educators in effective schools demand that publishers "show us the evidence" for new programs. In the Northwest, state reading experts from Idaho, Washington, and Oregon jointly reviewed research on effective adolescent reading interventions and identified several programs that focused on specific reading skills and had sufficient research to support their recommendations (see figure 7.2, page 133).

DECODING	
Corrective Reading: Decoding	Written for students who have difficulty reading accurately and fluently, the Corrective Reading: Decoding program provides a unique blend of teacher-directed instruction and high-frequency practice to accelerate decoding. (www.sraonline.com)
Language	Designed for students in grades four and above, the program includes instruction in each of the five components of reading: phonemic awareness, phonics, fluency, vocabulary, and comprehension. (www.sopriswest.com)
Rewards Plus	Beginning with fourth-grade material, multisyllabic words account for 10 to 80% of the words students will encounter in a passage; unfortunately, many older students struggle with decoding longer words. Rewards Plus is designed to teach older students the structure of syllables. (www.sopriswest.com)
FLUENCY	
QuickReads	The QuickReads program consists of three levels: B, C, and D. Each level contains three books, and each book contains 30 texts (90 texts per level). These texts support automaticity with the high-frequency words and phonics/syllabic patterns needed to be a successful reader at a particular grade level. Additionally, with topics in social studies and science, texts in the QuickReads program encourage meaning and comprehension. (www.quickreads.org)
Read Naturally	Read Naturally's products are designed to improve reading fluency and measure student progress. The products include passages, books, tapes, and software. (www.readnaturally.com)
The Six-Minute Solution	Students team with partners in daily 6-minute sessions, practice repeated readings, and get peer feedback. The book also provides a way to track student progress. It contains 160 nonfiction passages— 20 each for grade levels 1–8. (www.sopriswest.com)
COMPREHENSION	
Corrective Reading Comprehension	Designed for students who read without understanding, the Corrective Reading Comprehension program develops vocabulary, information, and comprehension strategies. (www.sraonline.com)

Figure 7.2: Reading Programs That Work for Teenagers (M. Flachbart, personal communication)

Many low-performing or failing schools have adopted the school-wide Success for All reading program and have experienced significant results. Some other reading interventions that have proven effective include Breakthrough to Literacy, Corrective Reading, Direct Instruction, Reading Mastery, and Reading Recovery. Other schools have implemented highly effective school-wide improvement programs like the Comer School Development Program, Accelerated Schools PLUS, Expeditionary Learning Schools Outward Bound, High Schools That Work, the Coalition of Essential Schools, Talent Development, High/Scope, HOSTS Learning, and a variety of other tutoring-based approaches.

Many districts have also dramatically increased their offerings of advanced placement (AP) courses. Districts such as Anne Arundel in Maryland set goals for increasing AP enrollments, particularly of poor and minority students. The College Board's Advanced Placement Program found that Hispanic and low-income students remain grossly underrepresented in AP classes. During the 1990s, AP incentive programs primarily subsidized test fees for low-income students, but this provided "no incentive for low-income and rural schools to expand their AP course offerings and did nothing to strengthen the weak academic preparation of low-income, African-American, and Hispanic students. Recent federal funding changes have provided a step in the right direction by supporting a comprehensive approach to increasing the AP access and participation of traditionally underserved students" (Klopfenstein, 2004, p. 1).

Increase Instructional Time

Virtually every study of high-performing, high-poverty schools identifies increasing instructional time as a critical factor of improvement. If students arrive at school below grade level academically, and quickly fall further behind, they must be provided with extra instructional time. If not, it is unlikely that they will ever catch up (see chapter 11). However, this additional time must not include the failed approaches of the past. The instruction must have an individual and intense emphasis on the specific areas in the required curriculum in which students need help. Schools and districts provide this extra time in a number of ways:

- **Starting school early.** Districts are expanding preschool, Head Start, and all-day kindergarten to give students an early start on the first grade.

- **Reorganizing the school day.** A growing number of schools have re-organized the school day to provide an hour-long period for remediation and enrichment.

- **Extending the school day, week, and year.** Effective schools have found before- and after-school programs and Saturday programs essential to increasing student achievement. In Louisville, poverty-level students have an extended school year that provides 20 extra instructional days each year. Each student is also given an individual success plan that includes extra targeted instruction each week (Education Trust, 2003c).

- **Extending graduation.** More and more effective schools are working closely with parents at the middle-school level to help them understand that some students need additional time to graduate, just as some students need less than the traditional 12 years. All students may delay graduation until the 13th year in order to complete remediation, pass high-stakes tests, or take advanced or college-level classes free of charge and during a more relaxed time frame.

**Secrets of Success
in High-Performing, High-Poverty Schools**

Extra Instructional Time

Research has verified what common sense tells us: Poor students who arrive at school far behind their more affluent classmates will quickly fall further behind unless they receive additional instructional time to remediate and accelerate their learning. Dramatically increased time for reading instruction has shown particularly strong results (Freedman, 2004; Barr, Joyner, Parrett, & Willison, 2004). Extra hours can be added before or after school, on weekends, during summer, and during the regular school day, with some rearrangement.

Provide Targeted Professional Development

The new world of public education requires different skills and knowledge than the old world. The need for targeted professional development has never been greater. The Consortium for Policy Research on Education study identified "building teacher knowledge and skills as one of four essential components of high-proficiency schools and districts that had successfully built capacity to increase achievement" (Massell, 2000, p. 6).

Teachers and administrators in high-poverty schools require a different set of knowledge, skills, and attitudes than educators working in more affluent schools (McGee, 2004). Ongoing support and professional development are needed to provide teachers with a highly specific understanding so that they can be successful with students in the most challenging situations.

Many school districts implemented effective strategies for improving low student performance through professional development long before No Child Left Behind. One school district that was part of a CPRE study describes the extra attention, services, and support they provide as follows:

> A district intervention team spends about a half-day at each school visiting every classroom and focusing on four areas: school organization and management, culture and climate, curriculum and instruction, and parental involvement. They present their observations and recommendations to a school team, which then reports to the faculty to develop an improvement plan. The district follows up with ongoing technical assistance. (Massell, 2000, p. 6)

The Louisville, Kentucky, public schools provide teachers with instructional coaches—even before a school has been identified as failing. Depending on the degree of problem, the coaches are made available for 1 to 4 days each week. The district also provides a variety of other services and supports: scholastic audits, highly skilled instructional coaches, extra financial resources, leadership teams, talent pools, optional programs, and an alternative calendar in which classroom instruction occurs Tuesday through Friday. Monday is reserved for remediation, when master teachers work with the neediest students.

More and more effective school districts are providing teachers with extra days (without students) for the purpose of planning, analyzing assessment data, and getting professional development training. Louisville teachers have 8 to 10 full days during the school year without students. Many other districts, such as Lapwai in Northern Idaho, provide weekly 2-hour blocks of time for targeting professional development in addition to the full-release days (see chapter 5 for further details). A number of school districts are using assessment data to identify teachers who are unusually successful with poverty-level students and arranging for them to lead study groups, lesson study sessions, and other instructional leadership activities for other teachers (see chapter 10). This is called embedded professional development, and some states have experienced dramatic increases in student achievement by using this homegrown approach to professional development.

A Targeted Focus

Research has documented that the children of poverty can learn effectively and achieve high levels of proficiency, but accomplishing this demands a comprehensive effort focused specifically on these needy students. Although much of this type of targeted focus is now mandated or recommended by No Child Left Behind, high-performing, high-poverty schools are going far beyond basic interventions to provide a rich set of enhancement strategies and opportunities that lead to academic success for their students.

These interventions must first target reading instruction as the single most important aspect of effective classrooms, schools, and districts. Each and every student must learn to read well at the earliest possible age. Fortunately, research in the field of reading has led to remarkable developments in understanding what skills students need to learn at each developmental age, which instructional strategies are effective with poor and minority students, and which reading programs are most effective. Schools and districts must target low-achieving students and then address the needs of these students in the most rapid and effective manner possible.

Target Low-Performing Students and Schools, Starting With Reading

Next Steps

Complete and Discuss the Self-Evaluation

District and school leadership teams should begin or continue their work by completing the Self-Evaluation Rubric (page 140) and then, working in groups, compare their perceptions and discuss the appropriate next steps.

Establish District Policies That Focus on High Achievement for Poor and Minority Students

School policies must reflect the vision of all students achieving to proficiency, measurable instructional goals for all students, the careful monitoring of progress toward goals, and policies that direct the necessary resources and instructional support to the students and schools in greatest need of improvement.

Focus on Reading

School and district leaders should use all available performance data to assess the reading proficiency of all students. Use thorough and frequent assessment to guide interventions for students who need help. Ensure that all students are reading up to grade level, especially by the end of the third grade.

Eliminate Destructive Programs, Policies, and Practices

Use data to identify the programs, policies, and practices that are ineffective or, worse, destructive to student achievement. Each of these ineffective or destructive approaches should be quickly eliminated from the school district.

Use Data

Use data to identify ineffective teachers, schools, and school district policies, programs, and practices and to target interventions and improvements.

Employ Well-Prepared, Qualified, and Experienced Teachers

Schools and districts must ensure that well-prepared, qualified, and experienced teachers are working with poor and minority students.

Reallocate Resources

Often, schools and districts must reallocate resources and staff to provide the support necessary to focus on and successfully intervene with the students in greatest need.

Provide Additional Instruction Time

If poverty-level students are performing at an unsatisfactory level, schools and districts must provide additional instructional time, support staff, effective instructional programs, and ongoing professional development for teachers, administrators, and counselors.

Provide Targeted Professional Development

Provide teachers with professional development opportunities to acquire knowledge and skills in teaching underachieving poor students. Build non-teaching time into the schedule for planning and analyzing assessment data, provide instructional coaches, and use embedded professional development to ensure that effective teaching strategies are shared throughout the school or district.

Next Steps

Target Low-Performing Students and Schools
Self-Evaluation Rubric

What is my school's or district's progress?	BEGINNING			EMBEDDING			SUSTAINING		
	No Action Has Been Taken	Efforts Are Limited	Results Are Being Gained	Efforts and Results Are Being Enhanced			Practices Are Widespread, Policies Are in Place, and Results Are Increasing		
Does my school or district . . .	1	2	3	4	5	6	7	8	9
Eliminate destructive policies, practices, and programs that manufacture low achievement?									
Establish policies that focus on high expectations for underachieving poor and minority students?									
Frequently assess reading levels of all students?									
Use data to make decisions and to evaluate and monitor progress?									
Employ well-prepared, qualified, certified, and experienced teachers?									
Ensure early proficiency in literacy and math for all students?									
Ensure proficiency in reading and math for adolescent students?									
Reallocate resources for targeted goals?									
Provide additional instructional time for students who have fallen behind?									
Target professional development toward the needs of low-performing students and schools?									

The Kids Left Behind © 2007 Solution Tree Press • www.solution-tree.com

Chapter 8

Align, Monitor, and Manage the Curriculum

"Five years ago, we started contacting every publisher of algebra textbooks we could find. We asked one question: 'If we adopt your text, can we expect student achievement in algebra to improve?' We were often met with either a stammered reply of some confusion or silence. The most common response was, 'Well, our text has been adopted in 14 states.' Only two replied that their text was linked to our state standards. Not a single textbook publisher at the time had any statistical evidence, let alone independent reviews, regarding the effects of their instructional material on student achievement. Thankfully, that is now changing, and more and more publishers are recognizing that to survive, they must demonstrate the positive effects of their textbooks on student achievement."

—*Curriculum Director, Kentucky Department of Education*

Curriculum is the support structure—the steel girders—in the high-rise of K–12 education. Curriculum is made up of what is taught, when it is taught, to whom it is taught, and how it is tested. It is what is written, taught, and tested in our schools. Curriculum is a complex mixture of aspects that are formal, informal, and even "hidden" (English, 2000). The written curriculum includes guidelines and textbooks (formal aspects), tracking or flexible grouping plans (informal aspects), and the unwritten rules that are used to manage the curriculum (hidden aspects). For the taught curriculum, there is content that is taught (formal), the personality variables of the teacher (informal), and the authority role of the teacher (hidden). In the tested curriculum, there are standardized and teacher-made tests (formal), the test behavior of students (informal), and the cultural norms relating to socioeconomic status (hidden). All of these aspects affect how the school curriculum is developed, written, taught, and tested. These complexities of the school curriculum greatly affect student achievement—especially the achievement of low-performing students of poverty.

The Old World of Public Education

In the past, no one was ever certain about what was being taught and tested behind the closed doors of individual classrooms. The curriculum decisions of the past were thought to have been based on educational philosophy, theories, research on human development, the structures of knowledge in academic disciplines, and the emerging science of teaching and learning. Yet the realities of curriculum decisions were far different. Too often, curriculum decisions were based primarily on commercial textbooks, and to a lesser degree were influenced by college admission and teacher certification requirements. They were often motivated by tradition, institutional racism, classism, prejudice, patriotism, politics, and the demands of pressure groups. The public school curriculum has almost always been organized into various learning tracks that purported to reflect student ability. In reality, curriculum tracking tended to be based on race and socioeconomic class.

Curriculum: The Way It Used to Be

The curriculum of most public schools was largely a loose but complex structure that differed from teacher to teacher, school to school, district to district, and state to state. Some districts, until recently, had no written curriculum document. Other than the dominating impact of textbooks and the pressures and recommendations of various national organizations, there has been no national curriculum. While substantial energy and resources have been invested in textbooks, curriculum planning, and development, most of public education has been characterized by a patchwork of differing written and taught curricula.

The old world of curriculum was characterized by six distinct features:

Unused curriculum guidelines
The dominance of textbooks
Teachers as free agents
Minimal use of planning and coordination
Tracking and ability grouping
Pressure from special-interest groups

Unused Curriculum Guidelines

Over the years, most schools and districts assembled teams of teachers, administrators, curriculum specialists, and university scholars who spent their summers preparing curriculum guidelines for every grade level and every subject. Unfortunately, there is little evidence that teachers used or even consulted these documents. Curriculum guidelines can be found in almost every classroom and school office, too often unopened, unused, or gathering dust on a shelf.

The Dominance of Textbooks

There is considerable research documenting that the primary curriculum guidelines that most teachers used were the adopted textbooks for their courses. This tradition of using textbooks as the standard curriculum for K–12 courses has given textbook publishers an enormous influence on what has been taught in schools. Unfortunately, until very recently, there has been little or no independent research on the effects of particular texts on student achievement. In the absence of data on effectiveness, state and district textbook adoption committees have often made selection decisions based on commercial marketing ("This text has been adopted in California and Texas!" "It has sold over two million copies!"), the attractiveness of graphic designs, accompanying teacher instructional aides, tests, and cost.

Teachers as Free Agents

In the past, teachers have operated as educational "free agents." Like freelance journalists, teachers have enjoyed almost unlimited freedom to decide what to teach and how much emphasis to give each topic. Teachers have always used textbooks and their own personal interests, skills, expertise, and prerogatives to plan their courses. As a result, courses with the same titles often varied widely in their content. As Fenwick English (2000) has explained:

> School structure isolates teachers in self-contained classrooms with children and alone they make independent decisions about what they teach. The decisions of a teacher can void the best developed curriculum plans by ignoring them. (p. 1)

In addition, far too often schools have allowed teachers to teach outside of their areas of certification. This phenomenon continues in rural schools and in schools with high poverty and high populations of minority students.

Minimal Use of Planning and Coordination

The history of public education is filled with teachers at all levels blaming the preceding teachers for their students' inadequacies. University professors blame high school teachers who blame middle school teachers. The middle school teachers blame the elementary teachers who blame the parents. The reality is that there has been a disheartening absence of curriculum planning and coordination across subjects and between grade levels. Traditionally, teachers rarely met with other teachers in the same subject area or grade level. As a result, teachers had no way of anticipating what students could be expected to know upon arrival in their classrooms and what students were expected to know when they left.

Tracking and Ability Grouping

Perhaps the most tragic reality of the K–12 curriculum of the past has been the widespread use of ability tracking. Ability tracking has led to a highly structured set of very different instructional curricula. "Able" students studied in college preparatory or advanced placement courses, while the poor and disadvantaged minority students tended to be assigned to general education courses, vocational courses, or watered-down academic courses like "opportunity math" (supposedly designed for students who could not learn algebra). The slow-learning tracks too often were assigned to the most inexperienced teachers. The most needy and challenging students pursued low-level content through mundane learning experiences (worksheets, questions at the end of the chapter, and drill) that were significantly lacking in academic rigor. The disastrous effects of this multitrack curriculum on poor and minority students have been documented for decades (Barr & Parrett, 2003).

In the old world curriculum, the "victim" was blamed. Low test scores were the result of "dumb students." But poor students were tracked into a less challenging curriculum where they had almost no opportunity to succeed academically. The result has been a vicious cycle of low expectations, which results in underachievement (English & Steffy, 2001).

In spite of the possible loss of some instructional creativity and freedom for classroom teachers, everyone should welcome the end of the inconsistent, chaotic, and destructive old world of curriculum. The old world did little more than widen the achievement gap between the various socioeconomic classes and intellectually and socially devastated generations of poor children and youth. The old curricular approach tended to stigmatize, isolate, and abandon the very students most in need of a high-quality education. Research has documented that the predictability of socioeconomic determinism ends when poor and disadvantaged students are assigned to a rigorous curriculum with well-trained teachers. Poor and minority students can achieve if they are taught a legitimate curriculum and taught effectively (English, 2000).

Pressure From Special-Interest Groups

Many organized commercial, professional, social, and religious organizations in this country have lobbied at one time or another to exclude or include some particular information in the curriculum of the public school system. For years elementary schools have been the battle ground of proponents of phonics versus those of whole language. School boards and state legislatures have on occasion banned the teaching of evolution and replaced it with "scientific creationism" or, more recently, "intelligent design." Recent federal policy has temporarily ended the debates over sex education by limiting the public school curriculum regarding human sexuality and reproduction exclusively to the concept of abstinence. Similar issues have impacted the field of history and the social sciences. It is widely known that until recently, social studies textbooks and curriculum reflected racial and sexist attitudes, a narrow focus on Western civilization, and more patriotic themes than accurate, research-based historical and social science knowledge. Over the years, pressure groups in many states have succeeded in using "watered-down" versions of the curriculum through their state textbook approval processes. Most teachers complain that there is simply no way to teach everything that is important to everyone.

The New World of Public Education

Beginning in the early 1990s, a new and powerful development began to emerge that would further complicate the K–12 school curriculum and lead to one of the most dramatic changes ever to occur in public education. As state after state began adopting new content standards, high-stakes assessments, and policies to hold teachers, schools, and school districts publicly accountable, it quickly became evident that teachers would lose considerable freedom in their classroom instruction. Teachers would now be required to follow a prescribed, written curriculum aligned with state standards and assessments. The sudden introduction of the new world of curriculum development, deployment, coordination, and monitoring significantly altered the age-old traditions of local control and classroom autonomy. As a result of the No Child Left Behind legislation, teachers, schools, and districts are leaving an old world of scattered, confused, and often idiosyncratic curriculum and entering a new world of standards-based, aligned, prescribed, and monitored curriculum.

Curriculum: The Way It Is Today

The new world of curriculum is often referred to as one of "deep curriculum alignment" (English & Steffy, 2001). Without careful and complete alignment between the written, taught, and tested curriculum, students will be unable to perform successfully on mandated assessments. Teachers must follow the written curriculum explicitly, and the written curriculum must relate directly to the standardized tests. Any misalignment penalizes the students. Administrators, teachers, and parents must understand deep alignment, which begins with the written curriculum that guides what educators teach and what standardized tests assess.

The curriculum must also be connected between the classroom, the school, and the school district. This grade-by-grade articulation, from kindergarten through grade 12, ensures that everything students must learn is taught effectively at the specified time. Schools and districts must also coordinate the curriculum between all teachers of the same grade level and subject in order to ensure continuity between classrooms. Any breakdown in these complex interconnections will negatively affect student (and school) achievement. For effective instruction to occur, each specific curricular factor must be in place, aligned, articulated, and coordinated.

Schools and school districts that have successfully turned around failing and low-performing schools have often done so by first focusing on dramatic changes in the school curriculum. A focus on the school curriculum and policies that relate to low-socioeconomic-status students appears as a major finding in almost every study of high-performing, high-poverty schools (Jerald, 2001; Goodwin, 2000; Massell, 2000; McGee, 2004; Togneri & Anderson, 2003). The Education Trust identifies high-performing, low-income/minority schools—"high flying schools"—on their web site (www.edtrust.org). Inevitably, these districts and schools focused on curriculum alignment as one of their first steps in turning around their previously low-performing students. Nationally recognized school districts in Aldine (Texas), Jefferson County (Kentucky), and Long Beach (California) each started their efforts towards teaching poor children by focusing on significant changes in the school curriculum.

Research has found a number of successful curriculum strategies used in schools where poor and minority students are achieving at high levels.

Establish a Rigorous Prescribed Curriculum for All Students

The Effective Schools research of the late 1970s (Edmonds, 1979), the Louisiana School Effectiveness Study (Teddlie & Stringfield, 1993), and research on the High Schools That Work project (2000–2004) (Bottoms & Anthony, 2005) have each clearly documented that students enrolled in a rigorous curriculum will achieve more. If a student is placed in an algebra class with an effective teacher, the student will learn algebra. If placed in a low-level math class like Opportunity Math, he or she will not learn algebra. There is no mystery here: If we do not teach students algebra, biology, or literature, they will not learn these subjects.

At the original Kipp Academy, which began in Houston and as of 2005 operates in 38 schools coast to coast, poor minority students are challenged with a demanding academic curriculum and immersed in superb teaching, structure, and high expectations (Thernstrom & Thernstrom, 2003). (See the *No Excuses: Lessons from 21 High-Performing Schools* study in chapter 3 for further details.) In Hobart Elementary School in Central Los Angeles, another successful school with large percentages of poor and disadvantaged minority students, fifth-grade teacher Rafe Esquith has had truly remarkable success with kids left behind. He explains why his students score at the 82nd percentile in reading and the 95th percentile in math: "I have a definite point of view [that] kids need to work much harder than they've been working, much longer than they have been working and with much more discipline than they have been working" (p. 54). His approach is to immerse the students in a rich, rigorous curriculum, including an in-depth study of Shakespeare: "We go over everything word by word, explaining conflict, every bit of symbolism" (Thernstrom & Thernstrom, 2003, p. 58).

Another project documenting the impact of rigorous curriculum for low-socioeconomic-status students is the High Schools That Work project (HSTW). Years of research on this project continually document that students perform well when they are enrolled in college preparatory coursework. HSTW allows no "low-level" classes in its curriculum. Further evidence indicates that students who complete the full college preparatory sequence perform much higher in mathematics on the National Assessment of Educational Progress (NAEP) test than those who complete only one of two courses (Bottoms & Anthony, 2005). The reverse is true of the traditional "watered-down" vocational courses: The more vocational education courses students take, the lower their performance on the NAEP. Although some of these differences are clearly due to the fact that higher-scoring students are often assigned to tougher classes, research shows the positive impact of more rigorous coursework even on formerly low-achieving students (Haycock, 2001).

Since research has shown that low-achieving students benefit more when they are placed in rigorous, heterogeneously grouped courses (Goodwin, 2000), the first step in teaching poor children and youth effectively is to dismantle all student tracking systems (Calderón, 1999; Slavin, 1995; Wheelock, 1992) and assign all students to a rigorous prescribed curriculum.

Implement a Research-Based Curriculum

Research also demonstrates the effectiveness of providing all students with a curriculum that is research-based with evidence of proven success (MacIver & Balfanz, 2000). More and more curriculum materials and school-wide instructional programs have now been carefully tested in school settings. As schools and school districts seek to redesign and implement curriculum, instructional materials, and programs, they must be cognizant of independent studies and other efforts to document the positive effects of their redesigns on student achievement. This seems especially true for literacy curricula. A study of nine high-performing, high-poverty schools found that research-based programs appear to be an essential element in improving student performance (Goodwin, 2000). Robert Slavin and his colleagues at Johns Hopkins University have reported similar findings (Slavin & Madden, 1989).

Coordinate Vertical and Horizontal Curriculum Planning

Schools and districts effective in teaching poor students have invested considerable effort to ensure that the curriculum is articulated across each subject and grade level. The goal is to carefully determine what each teacher must teach at each grade level and in each subject area. Teachers must be clear about what students are expected to know and ensure that students complete their courses with the essential knowledge and skills expected to be learned in the course or grade level. Vertical planning teams start by using state standards to begin planning at the 12th-grade level and work down to the first grade. This type of "backmapping" is used to break down the ultimate instructional goals so that each grade level is responsible for specific content. Vertical planning requires that teachers for each secondary subject area and elementary grade level work closely together to ensure a thorough K–12 content articulation.

The use of horizontal planning, collaboration, and assessment is absolutely essential in ensuring that all teachers of the same grade level or subject meet regularly to plan and coordinate the instruction and also develop and use regular weekly or bimonthly self-developed assessments that are embedded in the instructional program's benchmarks. Many collaborative teacher groups require that students pass each of these benchmarks before moving on to the next. Often after a benchmark assessment, students will be temporarily grouped into "those ready for enrichment," "those who need a little extra support," and "those who need to be re-taught." This temporary grouping often moves students between multiple teachers. The goal is to quickly get all students up to benchmark proficiency, either during class time or in before- or after-school programs. This approach encourages an instructional process that is consistent among teachers as well as with the written curriculum.

**Secrets of Success
in High-Performing, High-Poverty Schools**
Backloading and Benchmarking

Both horizontal and vertical planning are necessary to ensure that each and every student receives the essential content of the K–12 curriculum. K–12 teachers in each subject area must meet, analyze data, and plan, asking, "If our goal is for every student to pass algebra in the eighth grade, what must students learn in seventh-grade math, sixth-grade math, fifth-grade math, and so on, to make this a reality?"

Horizontal planning teams must then meet and plan year-long courses at each grade level to ensure that all of the necessary content is taught. These courses are then organized into a sequential set of small units, or benchmarks, that all students must master as they progress through every course. The team then works to develop benchmark assessments so that teachers can assess who has mastered the benchmark material, who has almost mastered the requisite learning, and who needs re-teaching. Next, schools must be organized to quickly provide "leveled" instruction for enrichment, remediation, or re-teaching. The goal is for every teacher of every subject and grade level to understand exactly what students will know and be able to do when they arrive in their courses and what they are expected to know upon completing their courses.

Use Standards and Assessment to Align the Written Curriculum

Schools where low-socioeconomic-status students are achieving proficiency carefully compare state standards with the written curriculum for each subject and grade level and identify areas of omission in the instructional program. Test results become the diagnoses for advanced planning, professional development, and targeted teaching.

While this work of aligning standards to curriculum has demonstrated promise, it is important to note that the standards being used must be of high quality and in reasonable breadth and depth. Many states are currently reviewing their standards to ensure these aspects as well as improve alignment with state assessments.

Teachers of advanced placement courses have traditionally studied standardized tests to be sure that their curriculum covered all of the essential areas of the assessments. At Bennett-Kew Elementary School near Los Angeles, Principal Nancy Ichinaga set out to improve the teaching of mathematics by directing teachers to study the major standardized tests for mathematics. The teachers then categorized and sequenced the content found in the tests and developed a comprehensive curriculum for their school. "This process took several years," the principal reported, "but the result was a program that elevated student test scores up to and beyond the 50th percentile on standardized tests" (Klein, 2000, p. 4).

**Secrets of Success
in High-Performing, High-Poverty Schools**
Informal Alignment

When the Springfield Public School District in Oregon first began working with teachers to encourage curriculum alignment, they used a quick, informal process that was unusually effective. For example, they assembled all fourth-grade teachers at each school for staff development sessions and asked each of them to bring along their curriculum-planning material for writing. They then created a large matrix on the wall, with each teacher's name down the vertical side, and for the horizontal side, they included the six comments of effective writing that were used to organize state writing assessments. Teachers then worked through their writing lessons and wrote the specific types on a small yellow self-stick note. After they finished, teachers went to the matrix and posted their yellow slips of paper under the appropriate assessment area. In a few minutes, each school had a rather dramatic snapshot of their fourth-grade writing curriculum, including assessment areas that were not covered and topics that seemed to be over-emphasized. All of these findings led to involved discussions and quickly to curriculum planning.

Monitor the Written and Taught Curriculum

Unfortunately, developing a prescribed, rigorous curriculum and aligning the curriculum to state standards and assessments are not enough to ensure instructional success with poor children and youth. It is critical to ensure that the written curriculum is consistent with the *taught* curriculum. Three means of monitoring consistency are "walk-throughs," surveys of enacted curriculum, and curriculum audits.

- **Walk-throughs.** Many instructional leaders use a brief classroom "walk-through" on a weekly basis to monitor the instructional curriculum and determine if what is being taught in classrooms is consistent with the written curriculum. Lasting only a few moments, this approach is quite effective in spot-checking for content teaching, pacing, and alignment. Frequently, walking through a classroom also encourages and supports classroom teachers in their challenging work.

- **Surveys of enacted curriculum.** The Council of Chief State School Officers (CCSSO, www.ccsso.org) has recently made composite tools for aligning instruction, standards, and assessments available to states, districts, and schools. Based on the earlier research of Andy Porter and John Smithson of the Wisconsin Center for Education Research, Rolf Blank and Associates at CCSSO created the Surveys of Enacted Curriculum for K–12 math, science, language arts, and reading. Data from the teacher survey instruments and reporting tools allow states, districts, and schools to objectively analyze instruction as it relates to required content standards. The Surveys of Enacted Curriculum system provides data and reports to educators and policymakers for the purpose of providing assistance in:

- Alignment among instruction, standards, and assessment
- Improvement of instruction
- Needs assessment and program evaluation
- An indicators system for monitoring progress
- Interpreting assessment results with instructional data (Council of Chief State School Officers, 2006)

The use of Surveys of Enacted Curriculum provides educators with usable tools to rapidly assess their efforts to successfully deliver standards-based instruction.

- **Curriculum audits.** During the past 15 years, a growing number of school districts have initiated, contracted, and conducted a formal audit of their curriculum. These audits are performed by an external team of certified auditors who compare the state standards and assessments to the written curriculum of a school district and then observe actual classroom practice to assess consistency between documents and actions. The team moves throughout a district visiting classrooms to observe the focus or topic of the day's lesson, examine teachers' instructional plans, and determine the degree of agreement or disagreement between the classroom and the written curriculum. Following the audit visit, a formal, highly detailed written report is completed and presented to a district school board meeting. Curriculum audits provide an invaluable look at a district's effectiveness in delivering curriculum. Every audit provides a springboard for improvement (English, 2000).

Ensure a Diverse Curriculum

One of the greatest concerns of students, parents, and educators is the danger of "narrowing" the curriculum and teaching exclusively to the test. The fear is that teachers will abandon all instructional content except what is covered on high-stakes standardized tests. To ensure that public education continues to have a diverse, comprehensive curriculum that capitalizes on the unique expertise and experiences of each teacher, many schools and districts are developing a rigorous prescribed curriculum that consists of approximately 70% of the standards-based instructional curriculum. The other 30% is targeted for enrichment, student interest, unique teacher experiences and expertise, and "teachable moments" arising from world, state, and local events or student questions and experiences (Education Trust, 2003c).

Use Curriculum Mapping

The curriculum mapping approach is particularly helpful in establishing a rigorous and prescribed curriculum. Curriculum mapping advocate Heidi Hayes Jacobs (2004) suggests that this approach will clearly establish:

- Who is doing what
- How work aligns with goals
- Which operations are effective and efficient

Curricular maps guide teachers through the arduous process of teaching an aligned, standards-based curriculum. They also have proven particularly valuable to new teachers as they begin to build, implement, and assess their classroom instructional design and process.

Use Pacing Guides and Assessment Calendars

To meet the challenges of state and district content standards, many classrooms have successfully implemented pacing guides and assessment calendars to direct their daily or weekly instructional progress. These tools provide teachers with expected checkpoints of learning and detailed instructions that emphasize specific lessons and assessments to be used for each content benchmark. Most importantly, these tools give teachers a needed timeline for ensuring that all required content is taught and learned. Pacing guides and assessment calendars also frame the agenda for weekly grade-level meetings and are most helpful in improving parent and home communications.

Use Flexible Skill Grouping

The research is clear: Segregating students for extended periods of time by ability has negative effects. Temporary flexible grouping has proven to be highly effective as an intervention to accelerate the gains of underachieving students. This approach ties weekly assessment of skill gains to targeted instruction with a goal of rapid acceleration of skill development. Students are separated from the class for brief intervals during which focused "skill shots" provide intensive learning opportunities. Once a student has caught up, the intervention is reduced or discontinued. This approach may also be used to promote deeper learning and understanding of both required and advanced content.

Identify Model Lessons

Perhaps the most promising approach to connecting the written, taught, and tested curriculum so that poor students learn effectively is through the use of model lessons. The concept is quite simple. While many school districts in the past have used curriculum specialists and university professors to develop instructional model lessons, today, more districts review student assessment data and identify the teachers who are most effective in raising the achievement of the most needy and challenging students. School districts then invite these teachers to work together in a lesson study format to share and study their lessons; identify the single best lesson for each topic, theme, or benchmark; and then organize these lessons into a coherent course of study. The models provide assignments, optional instructional strategies, optional student activities and assignments, handouts, background reading, and research summaries. Each lesson provides teachers with everything they need to teach an active, effective lesson (see chapter 10 for more information on model lessons).

A growing number of school districts use these effective teachers to provide professional development for other teachers. Houston Public Schools used the model lessons approach (www.houston-texas-online.com/htoeducation.html) when they decided to focus on fifth-grade mathematics and raise student achievement scores for poor and minority students. Student performance rose by more than 8% when the district's fifth-grade instructional staff began using the model lessons. The Jefferson County Public Schools in Louisville (www.jefferson.k12.ky.us) has also placed their approved model lessons on their web site. The Illinois State Board of Education (www.isbe.state.il.us) is preparing and posting model lessons on their web site as well. Many independent web sites such as LessonLab (www.lessonlab.com), headed by Jim Stigler (*The Teaching Gap*), also provide teachers with high-quality model lessons.

The Challenges of Implementing a New Curriculum

The work of developing, aligning, and monitoring curriculum may well be one of the most demanding tasks in schools today, particularly in schools with large numbers of students of poverty. Several issues further complicate the process and demand thoughtful attention:

- Building an effective, aligned curriculum
- Developing diverse instructional materials

- Narrowing the curriculum
- Implementing site-based management

Building an Effective, Aligned Curriculum

When a district chooses to construct an aligned curriculum, the task often presents an overwhelming challenge. Who analyzes the existing curriculum? How are the state standards addressed? Who monitors horizontal and vertical alignment? Who checks textbooks and other resources for content alignment? Who analyzes the state tests for congruence with district curricular and instructional application? Addressing these other issues can be very costly, time-consuming, and frustrating to board members, superintendents, and the educators who must do the work. Many state departments of education provide model-aligned curricula and instructional lessons for districts to use as starting points. Several districts, including Houston (Texas), Anderson #5 (South Carolina), Montgomery (Maryland), and Chicago (Illinois), market their curriculums nationally (Archer, 2006). Districts with sufficient resources may find it more cost effective to purchase an existing curriculum and revise it to meet local and state standards and assessments.

Developing Diverse Instructional Materials

Most states provide local school districts great freedom to independently select their textbooks and other instructional material. One school district in Kentucky with a highly mobile student population found that the lack of consistency between the textbooks used in various individual schools created a significant problem in learning and school performance. The school district negotiated a new policy that permitted the district to identify a common set of textbooks so that a more coherent curriculum was provided to all students (Massell, 2000). But there can be significant issues in choosing common textbooks.

While most agree that textbooks have improved over the years, the politics of textbook approval continues to be problematic because it is dominated by one state: Texas. As an editor of a major publishing house recently commented, "If you're creating a new textbook, you start by scrutinizing the Texas Essential Knowledge and Skills (TEKS) test." The Texas test "describes what Texas wants and what the entire nation therefore will get" (Ansary, 2004, p. 32). Texas spends 42 billion annually on its education system (as much as California), so every major publisher knows it has to meet the Texas standard. The highly political adoption process for textbooks results in what most concede is a dull product that will offend no one. This is what most teachers are given to teach.

Narrowing the Curriculum

Perhaps the greatest danger in the new standards/assessment approach to education is the tendency to narrow the curriculum and limit the instructional program to the state standards and assessments. Since even the best assessments commonly question a small sample of the written and instructional curriculum, educators must be careful not to limit instruction to the tests. Curriculum narrowing is not only a fear of parents and teachers; it is too often a reality. Without careful planning, courses will focus exclusively on assessment items and lose the rich side issues that broaden student interest and motivate students and teachers alike. Many of these experiences also connect the content to a student's life and experience in the real world. Planning must provide for opportunities for teachers to use their unique interests, experiences, and skills to provide for content enrichment. If not, courses may be bland and boring, focusing too narrowly on test items. The 70/30 curriculum planning concept is designed to prevent curriculum narrowing.

Secrets of Success
in High-Performing, High-Poverty Schools
70/30 Curriculum Planning

Many districts have adopted a 70/30 approach to address the need to align the taught curriculum with the approved written curriculum and the states' standardized tests while still providing teachers with the opportunity to use their own special skills, experiences, and training. Approximately 70% of the instructional time in any course is carefully prescribed, while the remaining 30% is open to enriched classroom teaching. This helps teachers to avoid feeling overwhelmed by pressure to "teach to the test" and provides them with the freedom to be creative.

Yet in an environment of mandated standards-based assessment, teaching to the test is a necessary reality and must be a part of a well-balanced curriculum. Failing to teach the prescribed content jeopardizes the student's achievement in the course. When taught well, students will achieve proficiency on required assessments.

Implementing Site-Based Management

In the new world of state standards and assessments, local control and site-based management can lead to serious conflict. The national trend in the 1990s to decentralize decision-making in school districts moved responsibility for curriculum, instruction, and resources from the superintendent's office to individual schools. While this process may lead to autonomy, it can also lead to challenges in a district's responsibility to ensure progress toward required proficiency levels in all schools.

If any school varies significantly from the school district's prescribed, written curriculum, students in that school are in jeopardy of taking a high-stakes test on material they have not been taught.

Achieving Deep Curriculum Alignment

Dramatic curriculum transformation may well be the most demanding, complicated, and time-intensive aspect of the new American educational revolution. The task of developing, aligning, managing, and monitoring a curriculum that is consistent with standards, assessments, and instruction (the taught curriculum) is a highly challenging, long-term process that never ends. Yet without it, efforts to provide improved professional development, high-quality instructors, research-based classroom instruction, and extra instructional time may be ineffective. Students of poverty must have the opportunity to attend schools that have or are currently undertaking this work.

Next Steps

Complete and Discuss the Self-Evaluation

District and school leadership teams should begin or continue their work by completing the Self-Evaluation Rubric (page 159), and then in groups, compare their perceptions and discuss appropriate next steps.

Eliminate Tracking

School boards and school administrators must immediately eliminate all forms of traditional tracking of K–12 students into low-level classes.

Develop a Rigorous Prescribed Curriculum

School boards and administrators should provide leadership in developing a rigorous prescribed curriculum for all K–12 students and aligning the curriculum with state standards, assessments, and the approved local curriculum.

Ensure Ongoing Vertical and Horizontal Planning and Coordination

School boards and administrators should provide leadership to ensure ongoing vertical and horizontal planning and coordination of the approved curriculum.

Use Curriculum Mapping

Work teams should map strategies to ensure effectiveness and efficiency in aligning content and required student work with district goals.

Implement Pacing Guides and Assessment Calendars and Flexible Skill Grouping

District and classroom leaders should work together to support the use of pacing guides, assessment calendars, and appropriate interventions like flexible skill grouping ("skill shots") to ensure that all students meet achievement goals.

Next Steps

Implement Walk-Throughs and Surveys of the Enacted Curriculum

School and district leaders should use strategies such as walk-throughs and surveys of the enacted curriculum to ensure alignment and consistency of the taught curriculum and to encourage and support teachers in their work.

Audit the Curriculum

District leaders should have their curriculum audited to establish a baseline for improvement. A successful audit will review the taught curriculum to ensure that it is consistent with the written curriculum.

Enrich the K–12 Curriculum

School administrators should provide planning, coordination, professional development, and classroom monitoring to prevent a narrowing of the curriculum. They must support teacher efforts to enrich the written curriculum with their own unique interests and expertise. Teachers must be encouraged to capitalize on "teachable moments," even if they do not relate directly to the prescribed written curriculum.

Keep Students of Poverty in Mind

District and school efforts to create and institute an aligned curriculum must always accommodate the needs of underachieving students of poverty.

Align, Monitor, and Manage the Curriculum
Self-Evaluation Rubric

What is my school's or district's progress?	BEGINNING			EMBEDDING			SUSTAINING		
	No Action Has Been Taken	Efforts Are Limited	Results Are Being Gained	Efforts and Results Are Being Enhanced			Practices Are Widespread, Policies Are in Place, and Results Are Increasing		
Has my school or district . . .	1	2	3	4	5	6	7	8	9
Eliminated tracking?									
Developed a rigorous prescribed curriculum for all students?									
Ensured ongoing vertical planning, articulation, and alignment?									
Ensured ongoing horizontal planning, coordination, and alignment?									
Implemented curriculum mapping?									
Developed a 70/30 curriculum plan for each subject and each grade?									
Implemented pacing guides and assessment calendars?									
Implemented flexible skill grouping?									
Implemented classroom walk-throughs?									
Implemented surveys of enacted curriculum?									
Conducted a formal curriculum audit?									
Enriched the K–12 curriculum to increase relevance?									
Kept the underachieving students of poverty in mind while creating and instituting an aligned curriculum?									

Chapter 9

Create a Culture of Data and Assessment Literacy

"On the surface, it would appear that the most important assessments in schools are the annual standardized tests. After all, they command the attention of the President of the United States, who demands more of them to be sure 'no child is left behind.' They receive major attention in news reports. . . . They command an investment of tens of millions of dollars annually as communities across the nation hold schools accountable for student learning. But the fact is that these politically important tests pale in their contribution to school success when compared to the assessments teachers develop, administer, and use day to day in the classroom. Given the decisions influenced by classroom assessments, it is not an overstatement to contend that a child's academic well-being hinges on the quality of these assessments and on the manner in which they are used."

—*Rick Stiggins (Chappuis & Chappuis, 2002, p. i)*

Improving achievement and school success for the underachieving children of poverty begins with the student's experience in the classroom. If a teacher is confident and positive and provides a welcoming environment that includes clearly defined learning targets, goals, and support, then there is a high likelihood that the child's learning will flourish. The teacher's clear understanding of grade-level learning goals, assessments, and appropriate student data will translate into an instructional plan for accomplishing success. If an underachieving poor child is not provided with this environment, his or her continued low performance and failure is likely.

No Child Left Behind requires that all students steadily progress toward state-determined proficiency standards. Faced with this unprecedented challenge, districts, schools, and classrooms are hastily responding to what Ted Hershberg of the University of Pennsylvania describes as "the greatest social policy ever enacted for low-performing students" (Hershberg, 2005). The legislation and accompanying state policies mandate student participation in assessments; the disaggregating of student assessment data by socioeconomic status (SES), ethnicity, special needs, and language proficiency; and the monitoring of adequate yearly progress toward proficiency goals—all with consequences and sanctions for underperformance.

Never before have classroom teachers and building principals been confronted with performance expectations quite like these. Yet thousands of classrooms and schools are demonstrating that the requirements of our federal and state governments can be met, that proficiency, achievement, and school success for underperforming, low-socioeconomic-status students are attainable. To best meet this challenge, we must start by creating a culture of assessment and data literacy.

The Old World of Public Education

> *"Turning data into information has long been a staple in fields such as business and medicine, but the use of student data for educational improvement has not been widespread. Until only recently, examining student data was a difficult chore for most educators: Data was difficult to access and manipulate, and most educators were unprepared to generate information from data. Further, there were no sanctioned incentives for participating in data use. Consequently, data use was relegated to a few educators with unusual motivation and skills."*
>
> —Wayman (2005, p. 235)

In the not-so-distant past, the federal government and most states required a nationally normed assessment of student academic growth at the elementary, middle, and high school levels. Many states also required specific testing in reading, writing, and mathematics. Rarely, if ever, were these assessments tied to state standards (which, for the most part, did not exist), or to a district-approved curriculum. It did not matter if students missed school the day tests were administered. Scores were reported by whole-group cumulative averages. A bell-curve mentality deemed it acceptable for the lower quartile (or more) of students to underperform. Everyone knew that the majority of students in that lower group were either poor or minority (or both).

Teacher's classroom assessment environments mirrored those of their districts. Occasional state and national tests were administered. The results, which arrived months later, had little (if any) impact on classroom instruction, were minimally understood at best, and were rarely used by teachers. The test results were almost always inadequately presented to the parents who chose to come to the one or two parent/teacher conferences held each year.

Within the classroom, most teachers used a combination of text-provided assessments and some of their own creations. They assigned grades ranging from

A to F based on attendance, homework, and test performance. Assessment strategies varied considerably from teacher to teacher and often had little alignment to the national- or state-required exams. Many districts had no approved curriculum on which to base instructional assessment. If there was an approved curriculum, it was usually ignored. Students, having virtually no input in assessment decisions, usually passed these teacher-determined tests, but those who did not were retained for another year at the same grade—and then often lost hope and fell permanently behind.

This lack of a systematic approach to assessment characterized far too many of our nation's districts and schools—particularly those that enrolled significant numbers of poor and minority students.

The New World of Public Education

> *"The other second grade teachers and I began meeting in August to set our targets. We started with the state testing schedule, state standards, and our district curriculum for second graders. We conferenced with the first-grade teachers and reviewed all previous scores and available data on each of our incoming students. From there, we planned our semester, but mainly our first several weeks of instruction, both individually, but most importantly, as a team. I don't know how we ever managed this before. The easy answer is, I guess, that we didn't —and the kids suffered."*
>
> —*Second Grade Teacher, California Elementary School*

For so many of today's classroom teachers, this vignette represents the reality of the significant change in the way they work. Central to this shift are the new policies about what we expect of all children and how we assess their progress and success. Advances in digital technology have enabled districts to create sophisticated student-information systems, data warehouses, and instructional-management programs. These changes have dramatically enhanced a classroom teacher's ability to accurately assess student achievement on a daily basis. This new world of assessment and data literacy is characterized by:

- Federal- and state-required tests and student assessments
- Ambitious federal and state benchmarks for achievement goals
- Mandated reporting of student achievement data disaggregated by socioeconomic status, ethnicity, special needs, and limited English proficiency (LEP)
- Data-driven district, school, and classroom accountability
- Incentives, rewards, consequences, and sanctions
- Assessments aligned with state standards and district curriculum

- Tracking of individual student, classroom, and school progress
- Teacher- and district-developed benchmark assessments
- Clear learning targets
- Assessment literacy learning teams
- Student involvement in assessment decision-making
- Student-led conferences
- Improved communication with parents and homes

This new world of data and assessment literacy is here to stay and exists to some degree in every public school in the United States. The further developed and more sophisticated the implementation, the better the results for students. This can be seen in the case studies of high-achieving schools with predominately high-poverty student enrollment.

The Education Trust examined schools that have managed to outperform far more affluent schools in their states (Jerald, 2001). The study found common characteristics in those schools that clearly identify the significance of attention to data and assessment. They found that high-achieving, high-poverty schools promote:

- Extensive use of state and local standards to design curriculum and instruction, assess student work, and evaluate teachers.
- Substantial investment in professional development for teachers focused on instructional practices to help students meet academic standards.
- Comprehensive systems to monitor individual student performance and to provide help to struggling students before they fall behind.
- Parental involvement in efforts to get students to meet standards.
- State or district accountability systems with real consequences for adults in the school.
- Use of assessments to guide instruction and resources and as a healthy part of everyday teaching and learning. (Jerald, 2001, p. 3)

Numerous other national and regional studies and case studies of individual schools have identified the same characteristics (see the studies outlined in chapter 3). In its landmark 2000 study of high-performing districts, the Consortium for Policy Research in Education (CPRE) found interpreting and using data necessary to achieving success and building capacity.

A study of California schools that are narrowing the racial and ethnic gaps in achievement among their students found that it is not whether schools test students, but what they do with the results that impacts student achievement (Viadero, 2004). The Bay Area School Reform Collaborative compared "schools that are shrinking the achievement gaps separating white and Asian-American students from their lower-scoring black or Latino peers with schools that are not. The study sought to pinpoint what the successful schools were doing differently" (Viadero, 2004, p. 9).

Based on data collected from 32 schools, the study found that gap-closing schools "tested their students often and used the results to change their instructional programs. They changed schedules or made other arrangements to give teachers time to discuss assessment results, and they used experts and coaches to help teachers alter their instruction accordingly" (Viadero, 2004, p. 9).

A careful approach to collecting, monitoring, analyzing, and prescribing interventions from well-maintained data on low-performing children is essential to their success in school. When interventions are based on accurate data, the intended results can be far better understood and continuously improved. This work starts with classroom teachers constructing individual profiles of their students and using this data to reform their teaching.

Data Literacy: Start With a Focus on Data

"What gets measured gets done."

—*Tom Peters (1987, p. 486)*

Virtually every study of high-performing, high-poverty schools identifies as their foundational building block an organized, comprehensive capacity to collect, analyze, and monitor data. Every student has a mosaic of data that portrays his or her progress, performance, and a variety of individual assets and needs (figure 9.1, page 166). Successful teachers know the needs of each individual student and build the necessary trust to intervene effectively. The student and the family must also understand the data and the purpose for its collection.

Creating this mosaic of data for students of poverty can be daunting. The mobility of many of these students complicates the task of keeping records. Often their files are incomplete, poorly maintained, or missing and may contain gaps, misinterpreted analyses, and ignored recommendations. Despite these challenges, federal and state mandates require leaders to accelerate their efforts to implement systems of collecting student data that will provide classroom teachers with the composite information they need to guide instruction, particularly for underachieving students. The cooperation and participation of teachers is critical to constructing usable and understandable records of student data so that timely interventions can be initiated.

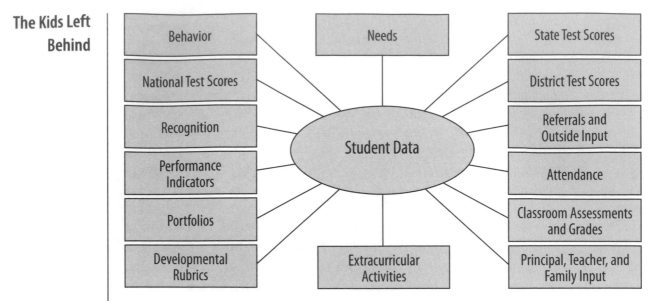

Figure 9.1: Student Mosaic of Information

Go Beyond Mandated Tests

Of course mandated state tests should be a part of each school's assessment plan, but schools must also include multiple measures of learning that go far beyond those tests. A study of comprehensive accountability approaches provides direction for districts and schools in their efforts to create balanced approaches to student assessment. Nathan and Johnson (2000) present the approaches and successes of 21 schools (many with significant enrollments of low-socioeconomic-status students) from 12 states. These approaches create a landscape of methods and tools for better understanding and documenting the learning of students.

- **Set clear goals.** The schools in the study set clear, explicit, and measurable learning goals, outcomes, or standards for their students. They designed curriculum to assist students in reaching the goals, and their assessment systems measured the students' progress toward these goals.

- **Understand outcomes.** The schools made certain that teachers, parents, students, and community members understood and supported the outcomes and standards set by the school. Students and parents were given examples of the standards and opportunities to engage with teachers to improve their performance.

- **Use multiple measures.** The schools varied methods of assessment, beyond standardized or criterion/norm-referenced testing.

- **Link assessment to school improvement.** Assessment results were used to modify instruction and guide professional development.

- **Consider language proficiency.** Assessment accounted for language proficiency and accurately measured what students knew, despite disabilities or linguistic differences.

- **Assess all students.** The schools measured the academic progress of every student. (Nathan & Johnson, 2000, pp. 11–12)

The schools in the study also engaged several other valuable approaches beyond mandated tests. Assessment involved an outside person or persons to help judge student work and also measured the attitudes of people who graduated from the school. The schools had committees of parents, educators, community members and, in secondary schools, students, to help plan, carry out, and monitor the student assessment system.

The schools in the study were driven by a commitment to create fair, balanced, and appropriate systems of accountability for students. Multiple measures of student learning characterize the schools' approach, which both acknowledges the required state measures and augments them with a variety of authentic, performance-driven assessments. This far better reflects a student's mastery of school goals and also better connects the students, parents, and community members in these schools, making a critical connection for students and families of poverty.

Build Student, School, and District Profiles

A helpful approach for going beyond mandated assessments is to build student, school, and district profiles. Who are your low-socioeconomic-status students? How are they achieving? What are their needs? How are they impacting classrooms other than their own? The answers to these and other questions are critical. They combine to form a "snapshot" of student needs, and many educators report that building these profiles is the best place to start when creating your school's assessment plan.

Student Profiles

Student profiles help a classroom teacher to better understand the individual needs of each student. Individual profiles also assist teachers in clustering students for group work, pacing their content, assessing progress toward benchmarks, reteaching, and providing them with necessary remediation and enrichment. Figure 9.2 (page 168) provides an array of available data sources from which to assemble student profiles. The data necessary to create these snapshots is almost always readily available in schools.

- Disaggregated achievement data
- Extracurricular activities
- Retention data
- Suspension and detention data
- Number of Ds or Fs
- Behavior reports or problems
- Academic or behavioral referrals
- Free- or reduced-lunch status
- Student IEP or 504 plan information (prescribed medications and inclusive supports)
- Recognitions and awards
- Employment
- Attendance, absences, and tardies

Figure 9.2: Student Profile Data Sources

School and District Profiles

While classroom teachers create individual student profiles and use the information to guide instruction and improve achievement, school and district leaders should work to assemble more comprehensive profiles of district data. Information and trend data will often prove quite revealing and can guide both short- and long-term goal-setting to increase the achievement of all students, particularly of underachieving poor children. Sources of pertinent information regarding the district's existing support and structures, and the performance and needs of low-performing students, can be found in the sources shown in figure 9.3 (page 169).

Each of the components in figure 9.3 represents a direct or indirect influence on the progress and success of underachieving students of poverty. District leaders should assess these components as well as educators' beliefs, dispositions, and perspectives regarding the school's demographics, needed services, and current program effectiveness to serve low-socioeconomic-status children.

District, school, and student profiles can yield invaluable data for the effective development of immediate and long-term plans to support classroom teachers in their work to improve the achievement of these students.

- Federal and state program budgets
- Per-pupil expenditures
- Ethnic diversity of staff and students
- Achievement data disaggregated by grade level
- Data for:
  - Free- and reduced-lunch service
  - Student mobility
  - Counseling and other support groups
  - Dropout and teen pregnancy rates
  - Special education enrollment
  - Rates of student pullout or interruption
  - Participation in extracurricular activities
- Number of limited English proficiency (LEP), English language learners (ELL), and English as a second language students (ESL)
- Kindergarten and early-childhood screening results
- Course offerings, staff assignments, and teaching load
- Teacher turnover, attrition, and sick days
- Out of area and uncertified teaching assignments
- Advanced degrees of certified staff
- Professional development topics and participation rates
- School communication to parents
- Family attendance at school events and activities
- Costs of school participation (sports, activities, field trips, yearbooks, and so on)

Figure 9.3: School and District Profile Data Sources

The goal of building data literacy should be to develop baseline portraits of the targeted student group. Holcomb suggests using the KISS approach: "Keep it simple and succinct" (1999, p. 73). This is particularly true for classroom-level snapshots. Clarity and accuracy of both the classroom snapshots and the larger school and district profiles are critical because the results will highlight current needs and lead to further study.

Many districts and schools now assemble and provide these snapshots in the form of report cards that are posted on web sites and distributed through newsletters to staff, parents, and the community. Classroom teachers also may receive electronic individual classroom and student reports and profiles. While this district-provided data may vary in design, it should include student achievement, behavior, and attendance data. A classroom teacher may then augment these data with his or her own snapshot data to construct a composite student profile. Profiles and snapshots should also include recommended actions and timelines.

Assessment *for* Learning

> *"Now the kids [and I] are clear about the specific learning target we are going for, and their engagement has soared. The students, all of them, really want to succeed and their assessments are showing that they are! You know, most of my students are Title I kids. Tests used to scare them and me! Participating in our assessment literacy learning team has changed all of that."*
>
> —*Elementary Teacher, Wyoming*

Who likes to be tested? Even high-achieving students usually voice disdain at the amount and frequency of classroom and district assessments. What if a student is a poor test-taker? What if his or her entire testing experience has been characterized by under-performance and failure? It is not surprising that testing can provide the motivation for many students to leave school.

Many teachers also display apathy, confusion, and anger toward mandated assessments. These feelings can create a negative environment for students and have a serious impact on the results of assessments. The expectations of the current federal legislation and state and district requirements for proficiency demand that we as educators do all we can to help our students reach learning targets and goals. Becoming assessment literate is no longer an option—it is a requirement of classroom teaching.

Assessment scholar Rick Stiggins (2001) considers this requirement in a message for every teacher:

> Take your students to a place where they no longer need you to tell them whether they have done well—to a place where they know in their minds and hearts how they have performed because they know the meaning of success. We seek classrooms where there are no surprises and no excuses. (p. 17)

Stiggins and Chappuis (2006) encourage educators to embrace the concept of assessment *for* learning while also acknowledging the value of assessment *of* learning to serve as an early warning system to determine which students have met state standards. The authors suggest that assessment *of* learning only identifies problems. Assessment *for* learning occurs within the classroom, building student confidence by engaging kids in all components of their personal assessment process: "It [assessment] rests on the understanding that students, not just adults, are data-driven instructional decision-makers" (Stiggins & Chappuis, 2006, p. 11).

Building Student Confidence

Ultimately, effectively teaching underachieving poor and minority students is all about building student confidence. Rick Stiggins, one of the nation's leading experts in assessment, has helped to focus the attention of educators on a rarely recognized issue: In order for students to achieve the new high standards of academic proficiency, they must believe that they can.

Too often, poor and minority students arrive at school unprepared to learn, and rather than assisting these students, schools assign them to inexperienced and poorly prepared teachers in the most dilapidated building in the community. Rather than remediate and accelerate our neediest students, schools tend to provide far less enrichment and encouragement than they do for more able, affluent students. In fact, many teachers do not believe that poor and minority students *can* learn, and they project their low expectations onto the students. In this destructive environment, poor and minority students come to believe that they are "not very smart," cannot learn, and so cannot succeed in school. This creates a sense of personal hopelessness, manifests itself in a lack of confidence and a lack of effort—a lack of willingness to continue trying to learn—and leaves these students with little opportunity to catch up and achieve the high standards of excellence so essential today.

Assessment has always been the source of evidence students use to determine their chance of success, and the new emphasis on standards and assessment may only exacerbate this situation. In the old world of education, Rick Stiggins has argued, educators believed that to get better student achievement, they had to demand it more vigorously, warn of the negative consequences of failure, and use adult authority to hold students accountable for more learning. If a little intimidation did not work, then teachers would use even greater threats. Testing and assessment have always been a key part of this emotional intimidation. We know the results of this approach: More able, motivated students responded productively to the challenge, while large numbers of other students simply gave up, failed, and dropped out of school. That result is no longer acceptable.

For all students to meet standards in the new world of educational assessment, it is imperative for teachers and students to become partners in the assessment process and work together to identify deficiencies, plan for growth, and focus instruction. Clear assessment targets help students understand where they are now, where we want them to be, and how to get there. Learning must be organized into meaningful, reasonable blocks, and assessment must be used to help each student achieve these sequential benchmarks. Assessment must help every student to reach the conclusion, "I *can* learn this. I *can* succeed."

To be effective with underachieving poor and minority students, schools must not only make all of the structural, organizational developments that lead to higher achievement, they must also plant a seed of hope in our neediest students and nurture a strong and growing sense of personal efficacy and determination. Teachers must believe students can learn, hold high expectations for them, and help students believe in the possibility of success. Schools must use assessment to help students learn that they can indeed learn.

Sound Classroom Assessment

In *Classroom Assessment* for *Student Learning: Doing It Right—Using It Well* (2004), Rick Stiggins, Judy Arter, Jan Chappuis, and Steve Chappuis identify five essential principles of sound classroom assessment practice:

Clear purposes
Clear targets
Sound design
Effective communication
Student involvement

Stiggins and his colleagues further explain how teachers apply each of these five essential principles in their classrooms (see figure 9.4, pages 174–175).

Successfully implementing these components transforms a classroom environment from a focus on assessment *of* learning to assessment *for* learning.

> In short [when students] . . . understand the definition of success from the outset and we generate an ongoing flow of descriptive feedback that permits students to watch themselves grow . . . [they] . . . become partners [with their teachers] . . . in the classroom assessment process." (Stiggins & Chappuis, 2006, p. 10)

Applying the five principles of assessment for learning in a thoughtful and consistent manner has demonstrated "remarkable if not unprecedented gains in student achievement, especially for low achievers" (Stiggins & Chappuis, 2006, p. 11; Black & William, 1998). Assessment-literate classrooms embody the five principles of assessment for learning. Teachers in these environments are both confident in their practices and collaborate with each other. Teachers rarely gain this expertise in teacher preparation programs. Instead, becoming assessment literate requires a commitment to improve; an ability to question established theory and practice; a desire to work with parents and families; high expectations for every student, particularly underachieving, poor children; and a willingness to collaborate in professional development with colleagues.

Underachieving children of poverty will experience an increase in their achievement scores when given the opportunity to learn in an environment focused on assessment for learning.

Secrets of Success
in High-Performing, High-Poverty Schools
Assessment Literacy Learning Teams

Creating an assessment-literate classroom takes time and work. Rick Stiggins has designed a process for teachers and school leaders to acquire the capacity to develop assessment literacy through self-directed learning. Following initial training, focus groups of teachers and administrators work through the materials to integrate their learning with the work of building an assessment-literate classroom.

As these teams progress in their work and implement the learned concepts in their classrooms, the expected benefits of their team's work are transferred to classrooms. One particular strategy, student-led conferencing (see chapter 10), often emerges as teachers and students become more comfortable with classroom assessment and the need to involve parents and families.

As of 2006, thousands of teachers and principals have become assessment-literate. This accomplishment has directly contributed to the increases in student achievement that are being reported throughout the nation. (www.ets.org/ati)

---

1. Why Assess? **Assessment Processes and Results Serve Clear and Appropriate Purposes**	a. Teachers understand who the users and uses of classroom assessment information are and know their information needs. b. Teachers understand the relationship between assessment and student motivation and craft assessment experiences to maximize motivation. c. Teachers use classroom assessment processes and results formatively (assessment *for* learning). d. Teachers use classroom assessment results summatively (assessment *of* learning) to inform someone beyond the classroom about students' achievement as of a particular point in time. e. Teachers have a comprehensive plan over time for integrating assessment *for* and *of* learning in the classroom.
2. Assess What? **Assessments Reflect Clear and Valued Student Learning Targets**	a. Teachers have clear learning targets for students; they know how to turn broad statements of content standards into classroom-level targets. b. Teachers understand the various type of learning targets they hold for students. c. Teachers select learning targets focused on the most important things students need to know and be able to do. d. Teachers have a comprehensive plan over time for assessing learning targets.
3. Assess How? **Learning Targets Are Translated Into Assessments That Yield Accurate Results**	a. Teachers understand what the various assessment methods are. b. Teachers choose assessment methods that match intended learning targets. c. Teachers design assessments that serve intended purposes. d. Teachers sample learning appropriately in their assessments. e. Teachers write assessment questions of all types well. f. Teachers avoid sources of bias that distort results.

(continued)

174

4. Communicate How? **Assessment Results Are Managed Well and Communicated Effectively**	a. Teachers record assessment information accurately, keep it confidential, and appropriately combine and summarize it for reporting (including grades). Such summary accurately reflects current level of student learning. b. Teachers select the best reporting option (grades, narratives, portfolios, conferences) for each context (learning targets and users). c. Teachers interpret and use standardized test results correctly. d. Teachers effectively communicate assessment results to students. e. Teachers effectively communicate assessment results to a variety of audiences outside the classroom, including parents, colleagues, and other stakeholders.
5. Involve Students How? **Students Are Involved in Their Own Assessment**	a. Teachers make learning targets clear to students. b. Teachers involve students in assessing, tracking, and setting goals for their own learning. c. Teachers involve students in communicating about their own learning.

Sound classroom assessment practice = Skill in gathering accurate information + effective use of information and procedures.

Figure 9.4: Indicators of Sound Classroom Assessment Practice (Stiggins, Arter, Chappuis, & Chappuis, 2004, p. 27. Used with permission.)

We're All in This Together: Use Data to Embed Assessment in All Aspects of Teaching and Learning

As schools and districts labor to enhance data literacy, they must heed the caution of scholar Jeffrey Wayman: "Data have been like a Roach Motel. . . . Data check in, they just don't check out" (2005, p. 14). Wayman noted that because many districts are now data rich, educators must make sure that the data are used to address everything from student needs to resource allocation: "Too often, data languish in central repositories, used for little but accountability reporting" (2005, p. 17). We now have sufficient data, so the challenge is to build data literacy in all of our schools and districts.

> ## When We Are Responsible for Every Child . . .
>
> - We set growth targets for each student.
>
> - We assign teachers based on student needs.
>
> - We assign resources based on student needs.
>
> - We assign adequate instructional time.
>
> - We select and develop staff based on student needs.
>
> - We hold all in the district responsible.
>
> —Allan Olson, Executive Director, Northwest Evaluation Association (2002)

Creating an environment of assessment for learning and building the capacity of classroom teachers to lead this challenge are critical first steps to helping children of poverty succeed in school. Of equal importance is fostering a far better understanding in educators, policymakers, parents, and our communities of the critical relationship that exists between student motivation and assessment soundly embedded in all aspects of teaching and learning. Many high-performing, high-poverty schools will testify that when their focus shifted from testing to teaching and motivating students, the test scores "took care of themselves," and they experienced improvement. Jan and Steve Chappuis' book *Understanding School Assessment* (2002) is an excellent resource for schools to use in their work to improve the comprehensive understanding of assessment literacy for parents, families, and community members.

For students of poverty, success in school is imperative to their future. By creating assessment-literate classrooms, educators will teach these students the skills necessary to be confident in the assessment of their learning. Assessment-literate classrooms will also improve instruction and the relationships between teachers, parents, and students.

The new world of mandated accountability creates a long overdue opportunity for the children of poverty—and for every child enrolled in our public schools. From this point forward, the playing field begins to level. Unfortunately, these dramatic changes will take time as districts, schools, classrooms, and the educators who inhabit them build the capacity to successfully teach low-performing poor students. Creating a culture of data and assessment literacy is a critical step in this process.

Secrets of Success
in High-Performing, High-Poverty Schools
Obtaining Immediate, Dramatic Increases in Student Achievement

In his research on high-performing, high-poverty schools, Mike Schmoker (1999) has identified a remarkable process for quickly increasing student achievement: Students will often experience an immediate, dramatic increase in achievement if teachers in a common course or grade level target low-performing students; establish two to four specific, measurable goals; develop a plan to achieve the goals; and meet frequently as a collaborative team to review assessment plans, share experiences, and develop additional plans.

Create a Culture of Data and Assessment Literacy

Next Steps

Complete and Discuss the Self-Evaluation

District and school leadership teams should begin or continue their work by completing the Self-Evaluation Rubric (page 180) and then, in groups, compare their perceptions and discuss the appropriate next steps.

Focus Improvement Efforts on Data Literacy and Assessment for Learning

All students, particularly those who are underachieving, need clear targets. Educators must be data proficient and assess learning effectively.

Go Beyond Mandated Tests

Use a variety of assessments, not just standardized multiple-choice norm- or criterion-referenced tests. Set clear goals, and communicate them to students and their families.

Create School and District Profiles and Classroom Snapshots

Examine sources of readily available data at the district and school level, and compile snapshots of data for individual students. Teacher-developed student profiles will provide critical data to design appropriate interventions. Recommendations should be widely shared and should include an action plan. Data should be prioritized by level of student need.

Use Assessment *for* Learning

Use the results of assessments to modify instruction to improve learning, and involve students in setting goals and tracking their own progress.

Engage All Stakeholders in Assessment

Assessment impacts everyone. Build capacity among all stakeholders (administrators, teachers, parents, and the community) to understand and participate in the process. Support teachers in their work.

Create Assessment-Literacy Learning Teams

Every school should establish small, focused teams to accomplish the goal of building capacity in assessment literacy.

The Kids Left Behind © 2007 Solution Tree Press • www.solution-tree.com

Embed Assessment in All Aspects of Teaching and Learning

Make assessment a part of the learning process for students. Using clear targets for students and teachers to drive instruction will yield immediate achievement gains, particularly for the underachieving children of poverty.

Next Steps

Create a Culture of Assessment and Data Literacy
Self-Evaluation Rubric

What is my school's or district's progress?	BEGINNING			EMBEDDING			SUSTAINING		
	No Action Has Been Taken	Efforts Are Limited	Results Are Being Gained	Efforts and Results Are Being Enhanced			Practices Are Widespread, Policies Are in Place, and Results Are Increasing		
Does my school or district . . .	1	2	3	4	5	6	7	8	9
Focus improvement efforts on assessment for learning and data literacy?									
Build student, school, and district profiles?									
Create classroom snapshots?									
Use multiple assessments to evaluate student learning?									
Use the results of assessments to modify instruction?									
Engage students, parents, and stakeholders in all assessment issues?									
Establish classroom and school goals of assessment literacy?									
Support assessment literacy learning teams?									
Embed assessment in all aspects of teaching and learning?									

Chapter 10

Build and Sustain Instructional Capacity

"High-performing districts and schools know that good teaching matters more than anything else."

—Kati Haycock (2005)

"As many of my colleagues retire, change jobs, or contemplate doing something different, I find myself reinspired. The changes we are making, the support from our principal, and most importantly, watching the faces of kids who were used to stumbling in school now succeeding has caused me to enjoy teaching more than ever. So much is different, but for the first time ever, I know I'm reaching all of my students. They will go on to the fourth grade equipped to succeed."

—Third-Grade Teacher, Iowa Elementary School

Building and sustaining the instructional capacity to teach students of poverty requires changing long-held mindsets and institutional structures. It requires an understanding of the culture of poverty and a belief that all children can achieve proficiency. Schools that have demonstrated sustained success with high-poverty students have reversed past trends of low performance by improving the way their days are structured and equipping each classroom with a competent, caring teacher—a dedicated professional who holds high expectations for all students and is relentless in fostering an environment in which every student achieves the state-required grade-level proficiency. Accomplishing this work requires leadership, time, and support.

The studies of high-performing, high-poverty schools that form the basis of this book show that leaders in these successful schools collaborated closely with teachers to create additional time for catching up, reteaching, acceleration, and professional development. They also maintained a supportive environment for teachers and learners with early and targeted interventions (particularly in reading), increased instructional time, an aligned curriculum, data and assessment literacy, engagement of parents and the community, and most importantly, with improved classroom instruction. Unfortunately, these conditions have not always been the norm in the classrooms of America's public schools.

The Old World of Public Education

"For years, I organized my room, planned my lessons around the textbook that matched our district curriculum, graded a lot of homework and tests, and tried to devote daily time to helping students who were lagging behind. I worked hard and was usually exhausted by the end of the year. Most of my kids were ready for the regular eighth-grade math, but there were always several that had to retake my class."

—*Seventh-Grade Math Teacher, Ohio Middle School*

For decades, classroom teaching in the United States has been an isolated profession. Following a year or so of formal training, new teachers landed their first jobs in lower-paying districts characterized by high teacher turnover and were usually assigned to the most challenging students. Their classroom locations, equipment, materials, and pupils were often viewed as the least desirable. These novice teachers knew that in time they could escape to better-paying districts with higher proportions of economically advantaged students.

After the mandatory meetings and preparation time before the start of the school year, new teachers were pretty much on their own. Equipped with preselected textbooks, some form of district curriculum guide, and a daily bell schedule, beginning teachers embarked on what is generally thought to be the most challenging year of their careers.

The new teachers decided how to meet the expectations of the district curriculum, designed his or her own instruction, created assessments or borrowed text-supplied assessments, established classroom rules, initiated some (if any) communication with parents and families, learned the location of the copy machine and overhead projector, and created his or her own grading structures to evaluate student achievement. Novice teachers also quickly learned that a student discipline plan was necessary for each class.

In the best situations, a veteran teacher or principal would mentor each new teacher throughout the year; however, most entry-level teachers report this to be the exception. Over the course of the year, new teachers learned to adapt to a steady flow of interruptions, such as students being "pulled out" and state- and district-required testing. They became used to the daily instructional inconsistencies between teachers of the same grades or courses, the regular use of ability grouping and tracking, and frequent disparities in homework, grading, and discipline. In addition, they came to expect an evaluation process that usually provided little guidance for their work.

New teachers often found their classrooms, schools, and district to be driven by a bell-curve mentality. An annual standardized test indicated how the district's average performance measured up nationally and provided data that teachers were usually ill-prepared to apply to their own classrooms or explain to parents. Under-performing students, frequently those of color and poverty, were held to low expectations. Instruction for these students was often characterized by a parade of worksheets, drills, and inactive teaching practices—those characterized by Martin Haberman (1991) as the "pedagogy of poverty"—that emphasized lower-order thinking skills. The consequence for failure was assignment to special education, retention at grade level, or repeating the course, often with the same teacher. When students failed to learn, there was little effort in remediation or reteaching. Many poor students arrived behind academically, failed to master basic skills, fell further and further behind, and ended up dropping out or struggling through school because they lacked basic skills.

The school culture significantly impacted underachieving students, but it also impacted the new teacher. Educators came to realize that teachers do not change the school; rather, the school changes the teacher. Far too often, an enthusiastic new teacher was met with resistance, pessimism, and the familiar, "We don't do that in our school." For new teachers, eager to respond and implement practices they have recently learned, reality dampens enthusiasm and often causes them to reconsider their career choice. Fortunately, in the new world of public education, new teachers are less likely to face this challenge.

The New World of Public Education

Federal and state policy shifts, advancing research in teaching and learning, enhanced teacher instructional capacity, and two decades of political attention to improving schools have resulted in a new reality of effective instructional practice. In a relatively short time, classrooms and schools throughout the country have made remarkable gains toward leaving no child behind by reducing achievement gaps and striving for universal proficiency.

Today, the most significant element separating high-achieving, high-poverty schools and their low-performing counterparts is a willingness to change the manner in which instruction is delivered. Those classrooms and schools that are making improvements based on research and in a prescribed manner are realizing steady and often dramatic gains. Those that are stuck "doing the same" are getting the same unacceptable results.

Many educators now understand that every time instruction occurs, some students already know the content, others eagerly learn the new information, still others come close to understanding the information, and some students are confused or lost. In high-performing, high-poverty schools, teachers assess learning continually and follow every lesson with enrichment for those who have mastered the material, remediation for those who almost learned, and individualized reteaching for those who need more time and help.

So if classroom instruction needs to change and improve, how does a district, school, or classroom select the best route to improvement? The educational marketplace is replete with research-based strategies, practices, text materials, and programs that claim to be the answer. Efforts to market and sell these "answers" have never been more intense. To best answer this question, we turn to the studies of high-performing, high-poverty schools that have succeeded in this challenge.

Leading the way in this research is the work of the Education Trust, the Northern Illinois University Center for Governmental Studies, the Consortium for Policy Research in Education (CPRE), the Learning First Alliance, and a number of federally supported regional education laboratories and privately funded research institutes (see chapter 3). While the recommendations of these organizations are unique to the schools they studied, they have much in common in relation to school and instructional improvement.

The Education Trust learned that instructional improvement is driven by a culture of no excuses, clear goals, common assessments frequently administered and acted upon, rigorous and aligned exit standards, and the understanding that good teachers matter more than anything else (Barth et al., 1999; Jerald, 2001; Education Trust, 2002). The Northern Illinois University Center for Governmental Studies (McGee, 2004) found a combination of attributes for improved classroom instruction. Among them were strong, visible leaders who advocated "high learning standards, high expectations, a culture of success for all, and the extensive staff use of data to drive instructional decisions" (McGee, 2004, p. 115). The Consortium for Policy Research in Education (Massell, 2000) identified a successful improvement structure as one that is embraced from the boardroom to the classroom and encompasses effective use of data, enhancement of teacher knowledge and skills, alignment of curriculum and instruction, and targeted intervention for low-performing students.

When teachers use data to guide instruction, work to enhance their knowledge and skills, align their instruction to the required curriculum, and target interventions toward low-performing students, they will see improved results. These strategies are key to building program coherence—the first step in building and sustaining instructional capacity.

Building Instructional Program Coherence

> *"We had to make it fit together. Teachers, principals, parents . . . everybody had to understand the necessity of being on the same page. We had to stop doing things that didn't directly connect with the reason we're here—to help all of our students achieve and succeed in school."*
>
> —*Superintendent, Maryland*

In a study of Chicago schools, many of which enrolled substantial numbers of high-poverty students, the authors found that those settings with enhanced levels of instructional program coherence had heightened student achievement (Newmann et al., 2001). Many of the schools and districts from the research studies in this book credit at least a portion of their success with high-poverty students to their high level of instructional program coherence. Three major conditions appear in a coherent instructional program:

1. A common instructional framework guides curriculum, teaching, assessment, and learning climate. This framework combines specific expectations for student learning with specific strategies and materials to guide teaching and assessment.
2. Staff working conditions support implementation of the framework.
3. The school allocates resources such as materials, time, and staff assignments to advance the school's common instructional framework and to avoid diffused scattered improvement efforts. (Newmann et al., 2001, pp. 13–14)

Building this framework for instructional coherence begins with an analysis of district, school, and grade-level disaggregated data and an examination of the policies and standards set forth by the state and district. Once the district curriculum is aligned to state or local standards, the real work of improving instruction begins. For a classroom teacher, this means first examining the required state assessment data on reading, language, math, and in some states, science. Collaboration and teamwork among grade-level or department staff are critical, as well as a clear focus on instructional benchmarks and ultimately, the creation of a model that fits the classroom, school, and district.

Use Collaboration and Teamwork

Schools that are successful with the underachieving students of poverty commit to collaboration among staff and leadership as the driving force in their work. This collaborative work provides educators with the incentive to focus on continuous improvement. While cases exist of teachers providing the key leadership support of their collaborative teams, an engaged *principal* will dramatically enhance and accelerate the process. A district curriculum coordinator or a cluster of teacher leaders could also assume this role.

Every school's approach to collaboration and teamwork is unique. Lapwai Elementary School (discussed at length in chapter 5) focused their initial efforts to improve instruction on grade-level teacher teams. The teams first agreed to implement a research-based reading program (Success for All) complemented by frequent work sessions in the grade-level teams. The work of the grade-level teams was further supported by weekly 2-hour professional development targeted at building staff capacity in data, curriculum, assessment, and instruction.

As the grade-level teams became more comfortable with their use of data, they focused on increasing their knowledge and use of the assessment *for* learning approach (discussed in detail in chapter 8). They became assessment literacy learning teams and met as a study group to acquire skills. Once teachers became adept at using assessment as a tool for creating clear learning targets and engaging students in the assessment process, their students' scores began to rise. These early successes fueled continued work and capacity building in differentiating instruction; using research-based instructional strategies; using lesson study to critique, analyze, and share effective lessons; and creating school-wide student-led conferencing as a means for students to engage their families in their learning. The teams also carefully monitored the performance of their underachieving students, particularly in reading. They targeted additional intervention through their Success for All reading program by adding other research-based interventions focused on students' specific literacy needs.

As a result of these efforts, Lapwai has experienced dramatic growth in the academic success of their elementary students. Part of what drives the work of teams in successful schools such as Lapwai is the use of instructional benchmarks.

Set Instructional Benchmarks to Focus and Drive Learning

Content benchmarks reflect what is expected to be learned and when. They provide teachers with guideposts for designing instruction, assessments, and interventions. They provide students with a roadmap for demonstrating that they have learned. The Aldine district north of Houston is a high-poverty, high-minority district that has experienced impressive results. Instructional improvements at the district level have cleared the way for all Aldine schools to significantly close the achievement gap between their African American, Latino, and white students, the vast majority of whom are poor. The successful use of benchmarks has driven the remarkable gains in learning for the students of the Aldine district. The district credits adherence to the "Gospel of Benchmarks" for their students' dramatic gains in improvement (Togneri & Anderson, 2003).

Aldine leaders identify two essential questions that drove their instructional improvement:

- What do I need to teach this year?

- What do students need to know to be successful next year? (Togneri & Anderson, 2003, p. 18

These questions guided the collaborative teacher teams in their work to create the instructional benchmarks for every classroom and the necessary framework to achieve them (Togneri & Anderson, 2003). Following the alignment of the district curriculum to state standards, the classroom teachers created short-term learning benchmarks (through extended day and summer work) to coincide with the district and state learning goals for each class and subject area by grade level. These benchmarks were then used to assess the students' content mastery of the taught lessons and to guide a process of reteaching, remediation, or enrichment, depending on the needs of the individual student.

Create a Model That Fits

The Brazosport District, located south of Houston, Texas, was perhaps one of the first districts in the United States to achieve widespread gains and effectively chronicle and disseminate their improvement process. Over the past decade, their high school, two middle schools, and three elementary schools—all with significant populations of poor students (ranging from 65% to 87%)—established a pattern of significant achievement gains that earned each school and the entire district distinguished recognition from the state. Most importantly, their students of poverty were no longer failing to learn (Barksdale & Davenport , 2003).

The approach the district developed to accomplish this work was to create a model for improvement that fit their unique needs. They created the Eight-Step Instructional Process, which combined elements of total quality management, effective schools research, and careful attention to data (see figure 10.1, page 188).

> ## Brazosport Independent School District's
> ## Eight-Step Instructional Process
>
> 1. Disaggregate data.
>
> 2. Develop a timeline of skills and topics to be taught.
>
> 3. Deliver instructional focus.
>
> 4. Administer frequent assessment.
>
> 5. Provide enrichment opportunities.
>
> 6. Provide tutorials.
>
> 7. Provide ongoing maintenance.
>
> 8. Monitor progress.

Figure 10.1: The Eight-Step Instructional Process (Barksdale & Davenport, 2003, p. 13)

Classroom teachers are key to Brazosport's success. They have become adept at focusing their instructional delivery around a timeline aligned to standards and assessment and coordinated with disaggregated student data that illuminates the specific needs of students. Frequent assessments of progress toward learning benchmarks enable teachers to deliver a blend of needs-based differentiated instruction ranging from enrichment activities to targeted interventions. Finally, their model emphasizes a variety of test-taking strategies, which have proven beneficial at reducing student (and teacher) text anxiety, clarifying expectations, and improving scores (Barksdale & Davenport, 2003).

As in Brazosport, districts and schools need to create a model that fits. As standards and assessments vary by state, so do district and school demographics, needs, and capacities. Drawing from the effective practices of successful high-poverty, high-performing districts and schools, a comprehensive plan should be developed to address the most immediate needs while maintaining a clear focus on the goal—all students achieving proficiency and success.

Underachieving students of poverty require extra help and time. Successful schools have reorganized their instruction and school days around the needs of all of their children. This commitment means that every teacher must understand the content to be learned, the use of frequent assessments and benchmarks, and the importance of reteaching and remediating students who do not achieve minimal or expected proficiency on common assessments. Effectively reteaching content through small group instruction, tutoring, and individualized instruction—each of which often requires additional time—is necessary if a district/school desires to successfully educate all students (see chapter 11).

The implementation of research-based instructional practices is another important step in building and sustaining instructional capacity in a school or district.

Research-Based Instructional Practices

High-performing, high-poverty schools focus on improving instruction as the key to making gains in student achievement. The following approaches and practices are found in successful schools:

- Study groups
- Lesson study
- Research-based instructional practices
- Differentiated instruction
- Student-led conferences
- Action research
- Attention to multiple intelligences, relevance, and action learning

When used together, these practices will directly contribute to the quality and sustainability of instructional improvement.

Study Groups

"We knew that just creating teams, just putting people together and creating time, wasn't going to do the job. Whole faculty study groups helped us put everything into reality."
—*Staff Development Director, Springfield, Missouri (Richardson, 2005, p. 6)*

Learning is at the heart of improving instructional capacity. For decades, learning has been shaped by the school calendar, which has been influenced by everything from agricultural needs to school bus schedules to state-required seat time to teacher contract agreements. Professional development—the learning of teachers—was relegated to a few days a year. The mindset was that time is constant and learning is the variable. Study groups reverse this mindset. With renewed attention on student learning, teachers are requesting revised calendars and schedules that allow for weekly 60- to 120-minute blocks of time to collaborate, plan, analyze, and learn. A portion of their collaborative time is devoted to reading, discussing, and applying the strategies and lessons they have learned from a growing literature base on school improvement. This literature base could include study of assessment *for* learning (Stiggins, 2001), understanding the culture of poverty (Payne, 2001), research on how to organize collaboration (Schmoker, 1999), professional learning communities (Eaker, DuFour, & DuFour, 2002), and strategies for teaching at-risk youth (Barr & Parrett, 2003).

For study groups to be effective for whole faculties or grade-level teams, teachers must be provided time, materials, professional development, and other support. Many districts also use this strategy at the principal level. In many districts, even school superintendents and school board members are using this tool to enhance leadership learning and improvement.

Secrets of Success
in High-Performing, High-Poverty Schools

Model Lessons

One of the most promising strategies to emerge from the research on high-performing, high-poverty schools is the use of model lessons. In this strategy, school districts assess their student achievement data to identify the teachers most effective with poverty-level students. These outstanding teachers are then invited to work together to review all of their lessons and, as a group, select what they consider to be the best, most engaging, most effective lessons. They then organize these model lessons into a coherent set of course materials. When the Houston, Texas, public schools used this approach with fifth-grade math, student achievement increased by 8% the following year. (Education Trust, 2003c)

Lesson Study

"I thought I had it all figured out. Fourteen years of successful teaching, nothing but exemplary evaluations from principals, and every year kids that worked hard and learned a lot despite their poverty and other challenges. Then I was asked to participate with a group of colleagues in something called lesson study. I was skeptical at first, but very quickly had my eyes opened—wide. I was amazed at how this rather simple process dramatically improved what I thought was my great teaching. I'm a convert!"

—*Middle School Teacher, Idaho*

As standards-based curriculum and accountability have taken hold in the United States, classroom teachers have been faced with immediate demands to ensure the achievement growth of all students. In the past, "great teaching" did not necessarily mean universal growth toward standards-based proficiency for all students; today, it does. How can a teacher improve his or her quality of instruction to facilitate this growth? Jim Stigler, a noted authority on teaching and learning, believes the solution is clear: lesson study (Stigler & Hiebert, 1999).

Originating in Japan as a common and highly successful practice known as *kenkyuu jugyou* (research lessons), lesson study has steadily gained popularity and respect in the United States. According to Nick Timpone, a New Jersey teacher and pioneer of lesson study:

> Lesson study keeps me on my toes, keeps me from getting complacent, keeps me challenged professionally. . . . [It] allows me to build relationships with my colleagues. Lesson study opens the classroom doors and minimizes isolation. (Lewis, 2002, p. 27)

Simple in concept, lesson study involves small groups of four to six teachers collaborating to observe and critique an agreed-upon lesson, create modifications, and then reteach, assess, and analyze the results. The goal is improved efficiency and quality of lesson delivery and student learning. Catherine Lewis, a leading authority on lesson study, recommends a schedule that outlines participants, pre-work, meeting frequency, tasks, and activities associated with the process (figure 10.2, p. 192).

Secrets of Success in High-Performing, High-Poverty Schools

Lesson Study

Significant increases in student learning occur when small groups of teachers collaborate through lesson study. Teachers first meet to identify a specific classroom lesson and then observe one another teaching the lesson. Next, they meet to critique the lesson and share their observations. This leads them to modify the lesson, reteach the lesson, and then reassess and reanalyze the results. This process demands that teachers are committed to collaborating to improve their teaching and ensures that they are willing to invest the necessary time and energy in this task. Student learning gains can be remarkable when teachers use this approach.

While successful lesson study requires teacher commitment, time, leadership support, and sometimes outside help or consultation, the results in improved student achievement can be remarkable. In addition, lesson study builds improved relationships among teachers and deepens their knowledge base. In a time of high frustration with the challenge of more effectively teaching diverse learners, lesson study opens a much-needed path to improving instruction to teach all learners, particularly underachieving students of low socioeconomic status.

NUMBER OF MEETINGS	TASK	PARTICIPANTS	ACTIVITIES
1–3	Select research theme and subject area.	All groups together	Agree on a research theme based on discussion of long-term goals for students. Select a subject area (such as mathematics).
3–6	Plan research lesson.	Research lesson planning group (4–6 members)	Select a topic for the research lesson. Outline the unit, and plan the research lesson. Write a thorough instructional plan.
1 (a class period)	Conduct research lesson.	Research lesson planning group (other invitees may include other teachers, administrators, paraprofessionals, or parents)	One member teaches research lesson; others observe and collect data agreed upon in advance.
1	Discuss research lesson.	Research lesson planning group, other invitees as desired	Discuss data from the research lesson soon after conducting the research lesson (the same day).
1–2	Reflect and revise.	Research lesson planning group	Consolidate what was learned from the research lesson, and summarize participants' reflections. If desired, revise the lesson for reteaching.
1 (a class period)	Conduct second teaching of research lesson.	Research lesson planning group and other invitees, or whole faculty, as desired	A second group member reteaches the research lesson to his or her own class; others observe and collect data agreed upon in advance.
1	Discuss research lesson.	Research lesson planning group and other invitees, or whole faculty, as desired	Discuss the second teaching of the research lesson soon after it has been retaught (the same day); revise lesson again if desired.
1–2	Reflect and revise.	Research lesson planning group	Reflect on the lesson study and its goals, and continue or modify them.

Note: Shaded box contains optional steps that may be repeated one or more times.

Figure 10.2: Lesson Study Schedule (Lewis, 2002, p. 42. Used with permission.)

Differentiated Instruction

Build and Sustain Instructional Capacity

"The blonde girl in the back desk is smarter than me. The boy by the window is always angry. That child is loved by both parents. This one forgot his medication, while that one 'self-medicates.' The sleepy-looking one watches television all night. The young-looking girl is a perfectionist. The parents of the one looking out the window are getting a divorce. That one's father died last year. The smiling one can't learn enough, and that one can't read. What can I teach these children?"

—Middle-Level Teacher, Idaho (Barr and Parrett, 1997, p. 69)

Standards, accountability, and the requirements of adequate yearly progress have changed the job description of America's public school teachers. How does a teacher meet the needs of diverse learners? They do so in the same way that competent teachers always have: through differentiated instruction. The challenge today is that *all* teachers must possess this capacity.

The concept of differentiating instruction seems straightforward: Educators ascertain individual student needs and design instruction and assessment to meet these needs and to encourage steady, increased achievement. The complexity of this practice lies in the range of student needs, confines of the classroom, available materials, and individual teacher capacity to deliver the instruction. Many teachers have learned to successfully differentiate their instruction through lesson study with focused teams of colleagues. These groups collectively work to identify highly successful approaches to delivering a particular concept or unit of content. Jointly planned, the team observes and critiques each other while teaching. Following the lesson, the group reassembles to assess quality and determine appropriate adjustments. Other teachers learn to differentiate instruction through collaboration, professional development, or self study. Whichever approach is selected, the needs of the individual student must drive the process.

Carol Ann Tomlinson, author of *How to Differentiate Instruction in Mixed-Ability Classrooms* (2001), leads a growing body of research and practice aimed at helping classroom teachers learn to improve their ability to differentiate. While the concept has always accompanied good teaching, far more is known today about how to best implement the practices than ever before. Tomlinson suggests the process illustrated in figure 10.3 (page 194) for differentiation of instruction. Guided by an understanding of individual student attributes and needs, effective teachers establish appropriate content process or product targets for the student and design an instructional sequence from the range of practices and management strategies per figure 10.3.

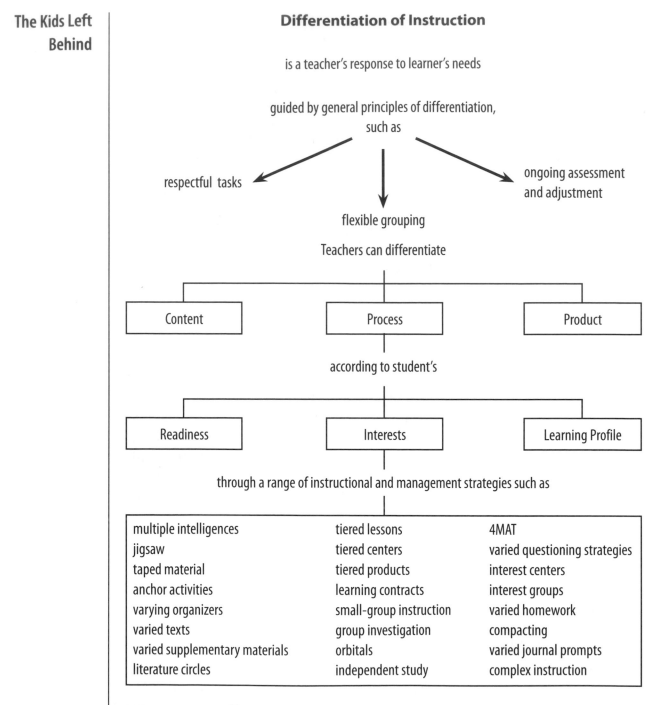

Differentiation of Instruction

is a teacher's response to learner's needs

guided by general principles of differentiation,
such as

respectful tasks

flexible grouping

ongoing assessment
and adjustment

Teachers can differentiate

| Content | Process | Product |

according to student's

| Readiness | Interests | Learning Profile |

through a range of instructional and management strategies such as

multiple intelligences	tiered lessons	4MAT
jigsaw	tiered centers	varied questioning strategies
taped material	tiered products	interest centers
anchor activities	learning contracts	interest groups
varying organizers	small-group instruction	varied homework
varied texts	group investigation	compacting
varied supplementary materials	orbitals	varied journal prompts
literature circles	independent study	complex instruction

Figure 10.3: Differentiation of Instruction. (From *How to Differentiate Instruction in Mixed-Ability Classrooms* [2001, ASCD], by Carol Tomlinson [p. 15]. Reprinted by permission. The Association for Supervision and Curriculum Development is a worldwide community of educators advocating sound policies and sharing best practices to achieve the success of each learner. To learn more, visit ASCD at www.ascd.org.)

Successfully differentiated classroom instruction offers a classroom teacher the means to reach diverse learners and offers an underachieving student of poverty his or her best chance to access the needed support to acquire content and demonstrate learning.

Strategies for English Language Learners

"Two adolescent ELL students were not attending school and not completing work when they did attend. In their principal's words, 'They did not do school. . . . It wasn't something they were interested in at all.' After adopting the SIOP model, and its eight components in sheltered and mainstream core classes, things changed for the two students. They began arriving at school 30 minutes early. They completed their assignments in all classes and were truly excited to be at school. Results from the state achievement test reflected this renewed excitement. After just one full year of SIOP implementation, the two students who didn't 'do school' gained between 3 and 4 years each on the assessments."

—*Teacher, Fairmont Junior High School, Boise, Idaho*

One in five students in the United States has come from an immigrant family and is likely to live in poverty; therefore, public schools must be prepared to meet the challenges that accompany these children. Reino Makkonen (2004) identifies four characteristics of successful instruction for these students:

1. 1. A workplace focused on instructional improvement
2. 2. High expectations for all students
3. 3. Student-centered instruction focused on problem-solving
4. 4. A spiraling curriculum emphasizing constant review (pp. 81–82)

One particular approach, the SIOP model (Sheltered Instruction Observation Protocol), embodies these characteristics and has proven to be particularly effective. The SIOP model provides structure to sheltered instruction, "an approach that can extend the time students have for getting language-support services while giving them a jump-start on the content subjects they will need for graduation" (Echevarria, Vogt, Short, & Short, 2004, p. 10). The SIOP model addresses eight key components of lesson design: lesson preparation, building background, comprehensible input, strategies, interaction, practice/application, lesson delivery, and review/assessment. One of the most unique components of this model is the focus on both content and language objectives; students learn content standards while also focusing on language objectives.

The components of the SIOP model reflect best practices in research on brain-based learning and poverty. This comprehensive approach to instruction produces benefits for all students, not just English learners. Effective SIOP lessons assist all students by helping them reach content standards as they strengthen their skills in reading, writing, speaking, and listening (Farris, 2005).

The SIOP model's eight components drive its instructional effectiveness with English-language learners. School districts should carefully study the original SIOP model to ensure correct and complete implementation of those eight components. In addition, the SIOP framework can accommodate other research-based instructional practices, brain-comparable learning theories, and models for understanding poverty. Districts should analyze which practices and theories show positive correlations with their populations and incorporate them into an individualized SIOP model.

Student-Led Conferences

"I cannot believe the difference student-led conferences have made in the engagement of my students in their learning and their parents in both our classroom and the support of their kids. It's like they now know what the kids are really doing and how to help!"

—*Middle School Teacher, Illinois*

For years, teachers have recognized the powerful relationship of student-led conferences to student learning, achievement, and success. The strategy originated as an attempt to engage students in direct communication with their parents through the use of portfolios illustrating their achievement and learning. Students take the lead in walking their parents through a selection of accomplishments and demonstrations of their work. Teachers interact only as observers, as the student explains their goals and provides examples of progress and learning. Parents are asked to reflect and respond in writing as well as actively engage in a discussion of progress with their child. Student-led conferences bring students to the center of classroom assessment. When implemented appropriately, the conferences unite the student, classroom, school, and home together in a productive critique and celebration of learning. For students and families living in poverty, successful student-led conferencing may be the most effective means of connecting or reconnecting the family with the school. Many high-performing, high-poverty schools identify the practice as intractably connected to their instructional success.

Action Research

"I really wanted to know if my approach to US history was working for my students. They could complete the assignments, journals, and group tasks and do well on the test, but were they really learning to appreciate and enjoy the study of history—particularly my disadvantaged students? But how could I ever find the time to study this question? My principal helped me answer that through getting several of us involved in doing action research. After my first experience, I'm a different teacher, and I know I'm more effective."

—High School History Teacher, Alaska

Teachers, like any professionals, want to know if what they do is effective. Today success is often measured by a single composite score from a single measure (usually an objective test), making this issue of teacher effectiveness even more pertinent than ever before. The question is not, "Do we need to do research on our effectiveness?" but rather, "What is the best way to fit this research into a busy teacher's life?" The answer is action research.

Action research originated for the simple purpose of providing a means for teachers to pose and answer questions about their instruction and to improve their efforts. It has been embraced by teachers and administrators throughout the country as the best means of engaging classroom teachers with research for the improvement of their work. Richard Sagor, a noted authority on school improvement and author of *The Action Research Guidebook* (2005), defines action research as "a disciplined process of inquiry conducted by and for those taking the action" (p. 1). The primary reason a teacher engages in this type of inquiry is to assist the action or to improve or reaffirm his or her actions.

Sagor proposes a four-step process for action research. These four steps describe what teachers, instructional or assessment learning teams, lesson study groups, or grade-level teams attempt to *do* when they meet to discuss data and improve their teaching. Action research provides a simple template for this work.

1. **Clarify vision and targets:** What do I want to accomplish?
2. **Articulate theory:** What do I believe is the approach with the greatest potential for achieving my goals?
3. **Implement action and collect data:** What data do I need to collect to understand the efficiency and workings of my theory of action?
4. **Reflect on the data and plan informed action:** Based on the data, how should I adjust my future actions? (Sagor, 2005, p. 4)

For example, teachers in one rural elementary school used action research to address a pressing concern: the need for more instructional time. First, they set goals of increased learning time for each student. They strongly believed a lack of time was directly impacting achievement. Next, they collected data on what they considered inappropriate uses of in-school time. They collectively reviewed the data and formulated a plan for reducing these daily interruptions. To their surprise, their principal and other administration wholeheartedly embraced their recommendations, which included strict limitations of any type of interruption from anyone during scheduled class time. They also sought to reduce early releases and minimize external noise (such as lawnmowers or vacuum cleaners) during class time. The result? Within days, students began noticing that school was a lot more "serious" this year, and over the course of the year, achievement data revealed increased learning.

Attention to Multiple Intelligences, Relevance, and Active Learning

A main challenge facing the classroom teacher is determining a child's strengths and interests and connecting them with the school's curriculum. This is a key strategy for low-socioeconomic-status students, whose success is largely based on the teacher's ability to assess their individual needs and assets and provide appropriate instruction. Like all children, low-performing poor children often excel in multiple areas of Gardner's eight intelligences (1991): linguistic, logical-mathematical, spatial, musical, bodily-kinesthetic, interpersonal, intrapersonal, and naturalist. A teacher who is committed to best reaching the child will learn which strengths or intelligences best connect him or her with the content and adjust instruction accordingly. All kids possess multiple intelligences. Some may learn math best with manipulatives, given their need to be active and use hands-on materials. Others may prefer individual to group assignments. Many students will respond positively when background music is played, while others might not. Children bring unique aspects of linguistic diversity that will best grow when encouraged and celebrated in classrooms.

Another key to a student's motivation to learn lies in a teacher's ability to see this connection to the content and to find its relevance to a student's everyday life and the world. Teachers can make content relevant only by acquiring a keen understanding of their students' environment and lives. This knowledge often comes from a commitment to take the necessary time to become better acquainted and connected with their students, families, and their communities.

Educators must also seek to make learning active, hands-on, and whenever possible, enjoyable. For decades, classroom teachers have recognized the power of diversifying their lessons to provide learners with regular opportunities to apply what they are learning in activity-based lessons. Whether they are dissecting in a biology lab, hearing an economics lesson in a bank, journaling in the school yard, or learning history through debate, most students, particularly those who are underachieving, will be more excited about their learning and schooling when provided the opportunity to actively learn.

Success for All Students

> *"Improving something as complex and culturally embedded as teaching requires the efforts of all players, including students, parents, and politicians. But the teachers must be the primary driving force behind change. They are the best positioned to understand the problems that students face and to generate possible solutions. In fact, almost all successful attempts to improve teaching have included teachers working together to improve students' learning."*
>
> —*Stigler and Hiebert (1999, p. 135)*

Effective instruction is an underachieving poor child's best hope for success in school. When it is absent, the student's chance to achieve both in the classroom and in life is diminished. When it is present, the baggage of poverty falls aside. All of our children deserve the chance to succeed. Our vast wealth of knowledge about teaching and learning makes it possible to build and sustain the capacity for success in every classroom. Schools and classrooms throughout the United States continue to demonstrate that when appropriate, research- and results-driven instructional practices are deployed, the students often demonstrate remarkable, immediate gains. While there is no single strategy that will "fix" the complex needs of most classrooms, the array of strategies presented in this chapter provides a roadmap for all teachers to improve their capacity to instruct the underachieving children of poverty. All that remains is the will to proceed.

Next Steps

Complete and Discuss the Self-Evaluation

District and school leadership teams should begin or continue their work by completing the Self-Evaluation Rubric (page 202), and then in groups, compare their perceptions and discuss appropriate next steps.

Start With Data

Improving the achievement of the students of poverty begins with building educators' capacity to use data as the driving force in planning and implementing improvements.

Build Instructional Program Coherence

When instruction reflects a common instructional framework, support to implement the framework, and the resources needed to focus on the framework, the under-performing students of poverty will catch up.

Collaborate

Teacher teams at the school, grade, and subject level must drive the work of instructional improvement.

Link Instruction to Learning Benchmarks

Explicit efforts should be made to directly link specific instructional practices to aligned curricular and learning standards. Reteaching and remediation must occur for under-performing students.

Guide Professional Development With Study Groups and Lesson Study

Every school should seek to equip its educators with research-based knowledge of proven instructional interventions, practices, and strategies with the use of study groups and lesson study.

Implement Research-Based Instructional Practices

Teachers of underachieving students should implement research-based instructional interventions, differentiated instruction, and proven strategies for their students.

Initiate Student-Led Conferences

Schools should seek to engage students and families in the proven practice of student-led conferences.

Initiate Action Research

Schools should encourage and support teachers in action research projects focused on improving their classroom effectiveness.

Teach to Multiple Intelligences With a Relevant and Active Learning Environment

Every teacher should address student intelligences and seek to provide a relevant, active environment for learning.

Next Steps

Build and Sustain Instructional Capacity
Self-Evaluation Rubric

What is my school's or district's progress?	BEGINNING			EMBEDDING			SUSTAINING		
	No Action Has Been Taken	Efforts Are Limited	Results Are Being Gained	Efforts and Results Are Being Enhanced			Practices Are Widespread, Policies Are in Place, and Results Are Increasing		
Does my school or district . . .	1	2	3	4	5	6	7	8	9
Use data to design improvements?									
Link instruction to learning benchmarks?									
Create a model for improvement that fits?									
Provide opportunities for enrichment, remediation, and reteaching?									
Seek to improve teaching by implementing research-based practices?									
Initiate and support study groups?									
Initiate and support lesson study?									
Differentiate instruction?									
Address the needs of English language learners?									
Initiate and support student-led conferences?									
Initiate and support action research?									
Encourage teaching to multiple intelligences through relevant, active learning?									

Chapter 11

Reorganize Time, Space, and Transitions

"It took our school awhile to get it, but we finally figured it out. If we really wanted to teach all kids effectively and leave no one behind, then one had to abandon our old, failed programs and practices and really get creative in finding ways to provide remediation and enrichment. This led us immediately to reorganize the school day, the school week, and the school year."

—Superintendent, Arkansas

The organization of time in most public schools is a product of history, tradition, and a variety of internal and external pressures. The school schedule originated during a time when agriculture was the dominant lifestyle and children and youth were needed to work on family farms during the growing season. This situation continues to exist in a few agricultural areas today, but for most of the United States, there is little or no need to organize the school year around a 9-month schedule; it is simply how we have always scheduled public education in the past.

> "We have created a learning system where student proficiency is paramount, but children's acquisition of skills and knowledge still takes place within a school system that too often places priority on the preservation of institutional practices and structures rather than their transformation. . . . There is no institutional structure that has historically resisted (and continues to resist) change more than the school schedule."
>
> *(Davis & Farbman, 2004, p. 52)*

Powerful forces drive school planning. State law has usually prescribed daily, weekly, and yearly school calendars. In most states, the legislature has specified the exact number of minutes each student must be enrolled in school. Thus, school success has been based on "seat time" and teacher-assigned grades. Almost all schools have used the Carnegie unit to measure course completion, rather than measuring academic progress toward proficiency. The Carnegie unit has existed for decades as the standard for evaluating high school graduation and college entrance requirements. Further resistance to changing school schedules comes from the terms of union contracts, athletic agendas, bus schedules, and the perpetual challenge of reaching consensus on needed changes. School planners also are influenced by parent work schedules, childcare needs, and even daylight saving time. These varied forces have all but paralyzed educational planners and created a school schedule that seems to be embedded in stone.

The Old World of Public Education

"I believe that it would be easier to move a cemetery than change our high school schedule."

—*Superintendent, Illinois*

"We have been working on a plan to transform the high school schedule into a block schedule that provides 90-minute instructional periods. We have been working on this for 2 years, and we still are unable to get consensus. I have finally come to the realization that we need to involuntarily transfer about a dozen of my fellow teachers to ever make the block schedule happen. So much for democracy in action."

—*Principal, Washington*

In the old world of public education, all students participated in exactly the same schedule. Students all started school at the same time, ended at the same time, and enjoyed the same summer vacation. Until very recently, secondary students were in classes for approximately 50 minutes per day per course, 5 days per week, for 9 months; elementary schools have been equally regimented. Most states specify the exact number of minutes per course. Students graduated after completing 12 years of school. Remediation was conducted by "pulling out" students from regular courses: Students with the greatest educational needs missed essential course work in order to receive special interventions or were grouped by ability with other students in slow-learning tracks.

Authors Milt Goldberg and Christopher Cross (2005, p. 36) refer to the "uniform six-hour day and 180-day year as the unacknowledged design flaw in American education." They suggest that we have constructed our "learning enterprise on a foundation of sand" based on five false premises:

1. The assumption that students arrive at school ready to learn in the same way, on the same schedule, all in rhythm with each other

2. The notion that academic time can be used for nonacademic purposes with no effect on learning

3. The pretense that because yesterday's calendar was good enough for us, it should be good enough for our children—despite major changes in the larger society

4. The myth that schools can be transformed without giving teachers the time they need to retool themselves and reorganize their work

5. The new fiction that it is reasonable to expect world-class academic performance from our students within the time-bound system that is already failing them (Goldberg & Cross, 2005, p. 36)

Public education has traditionally been organized into elementary, middle-level (or junior high), and high schools, with the middle and high school levels organized into very large schools. The transition from elementary to middle school is dramatic and can be difficult. In elementary school, students are in a more supportive environment where they are with one teacher each year and approximately the same group of students for 5 to 6 years. When they make the transition to middle school, they enter an environment where every 50 minutes, they are assigned to a different teacher with a completely different group of classmates. Students typically have as many as seven different teachers and more than 150 different students in their classes each day.

In this traditional school schedule, many children of poverty arrive at school academically unprepared to learn, quickly fall further behind, and rarely ever catch up. These needy students receive the same amount of instruction as everyone else, so catching up is all but impossible. Too often, the children of poverty feel isolated and ignored in large middle and high schools and in large classes. Likewise, teachers are caught up in a system that isolates them from one another and provides little or no time for cooperative planning and professional development. Teachers tend to be overwhelmed with large classes and large schools. School schedules allow few opportunities for interrupting the relentless march of the school curriculum and the repetition of the daily schedule. Other than assigning students to slow-learning tracks or using temporary pull-out programs, there is little flexible time to address urgent student needs for remedial or accelerated learning. Interrupted classes and early releases rule the day. The overall goal of public education in this traditional format focuses not on performance, but on seat time, specified minutes of instruction per course, the number of weeks of instruction in the school year, and a specific number of years of successful school participation required for graduation. Successful transitions to school and between levels are solely the responsibility of the child and his or her family.

The New World of Public Education

"It didn't take a rocket scientist to figure out that if some students were academically far behind their more affluent classmates, they would need a lot of 'extra' instruction if they ever hoped to catch up."

—*Assistant Superintendent, New Hampshire*

"If something is not worth doing, then don't do it! At our school we invest our time and effort into what is important."

—*Teacher, New Mexico*

With successful interventions, classroom instruction is where the rubber hits the road. In order for schools to gain instructional "traction," they must use a variety of strategies that have proven successful. The pressure driving this creative search for new and more effective approaches to instruction has been the shift in focus from measuring seat time to measuring academic performance. The focus on academic performance has also helped schools to decide what is important during the school day and what is not. As effective schools have been energized by the new focus on student academic performance, the old, static single school schedule for all students has been giving way to a remarkable array of creative schedules and new approaches to school organization.

Effective schools have abandoned trying to do more of the same thing and are attempting to do things smarter and more creatively. Research on high-achieving, high-poverty schools has repeatedly identified the need for extra instructional time, extra support, and new ways of organizing schools as essential characteristics of effective schools (see chapter 3). Examples of recommended actions include:

- Give students extra help (Haycock, 2001).

- Provide students with more academic time (McGee, 2004).

- Give students extra time for instruction in math and reading (Jerald, 2001, p. 3).

- Identify which students need extra help, and then employ creative schedules, such as after-school and summer school sessions, to give students the additional instructional time they need (Goodwin, 2000, pp. 4–5).

- Provide the time and support necessary for system-wide instructional improvement (Togneri & Anderson, 2003, p. 11).

A review of these strategies and recommendations should help educators break out of the box of traditional school schedules, organization, and transitions.

Provide Extra Instructional Time

"Once we decided that all of our students would learn to read, it was easy to figure out. We had to create more instructional time. We did this and our low-level kids are reading like never before."

—*Elementary Principal, South Carolina*

In order to help children of poverty gain academic proficiency, it is critical to provide additional instructional time. Nothing could be more straightforward; students who perform below academic standards are given extra instructional time and attention. Schools need to maximize instructional time during the day, providing for larger blocks of uninterrupted time for reading, language arts, and mathematics, plus ensuring opportunities for before- and after-school, weekend, and summer programs (McGee, 2004). How different schools create this extra time is as diverse as the communities they serve.

For example, in Gainesville Elementary School in Gainesville, Georgia, 125 students were lagging a grade or two behind in reading and math. Almost all were poor and minority; most were the children of immigrants who recently arrived from Mexico to work in local chicken processing plants. The school mandated that the students attend an extra 3 hours of instruction each weekday and 7 hours on Saturday. This additional instruction amounted to the equivalent of an 8-day school week. Under the leadership of Shawn Arevala McCallough, 95% of the Gainesville Elementary School students passed the state English language arts test, and 94% passed the math test. This reflects the classic 90-90-90 pattern: 90% minority, 90% poor, and 90% meeting standards. The school also aligned their curriculum with state tests, implemented 9-week tests to measure achievement, developed specialized lessons to focus on areas of student weakness, and used drills in phonics and mathematics in daily lessons (Freedman, 2004).

Sacajawea Elementary School in Caldwell, Idaho, a school comprised of 60% Hispanic and 78% low-income students, increased the instructional time in reading from the 40 hours required by the state to more than 200 hours. This additional instructional time focused on language development, on beginning reading and writing, and on reading skills (phonemic awareness and phonics). On the state-mandated reading test, 89% of the Sacajawea kindergarten students were reading at grade level in 2003 compared to the state average of 72% and the district average of 77%. What is remarkable about this success story is that in the fall of 2002, only 14% of Sacajawea kindergartners read at grade level. In 1 year, the school raised the percentage of students reading at grade level from 14% to 89% (Barr, Joyner, Parrett, & Willison, 2004).

Start Early

"Being in kindergarten all day has my daughter ready for first grade. It has helped her more than I could have ever imagined."

—Parent, Arizona

Since students from low-socioeconomic-status homes too often arrive at school with language skills deficiencies, a limited vocabulary, and few technology advantages, effective schools have done everything possible to enroll young children in preschool programs, Head Start programs, and all-day kindergarten. Because it is imperative that all students achieve literacy proficiency as early as possible, and retention is not an effective option, the focus of the first three grades should be on developmentally appropriate instruction to achieve grade-level proficiency. Students also benefit from remaining with the same teacher for 2 to 3 years (looping). Since poor and minority students need extra instructional time in reading and math, high-performing, high-poverty schools redesign the curriculum and the daily and weekly class schedule to strategically increase instructional time in reading, language arts, and math. Research has documented the lifelong, positive effects of effective preschool and all-day kindergarten programs on children (Barr & Parrett, 2003; McGee, 2004).

Secrets of Success
in High-Performing, High-Poverty Schools
Redesign the Early Grades

Students who arrive at school from economically disadvantaged homes need to start their educational programs as early as possible. Many successful schools, such as the Sioux Center School District in Iowa, invite parents and their preschool children to come to their local school to have a fun, informative time with their future teachers. Other school districts conduct short, effective "reading readiness" tests to identify student deficiencies at the earliest possible time and provide parents with games, strategies, and ideas for helping prepare their children for school. Almost all effective elementary schools engage students as early as possible in preschool programs (see chapters 7 and 12).

Reorganize the School Day and Week

"People ask us how we were able to provide an extra hour during the school day for remediation and enrichment. It was really quite easy; we reduced the amount of time that we had scheduled for everything that was less important."

—Principal, Texas

"After meeting with all of the parents in our school and agreeing among ourselves that remediation, enrichment, and reteaching was just as important as initial classroom instruction, we reorganized the entire weekly schedule and started teaching four days a week and using Fridays for follow-up efforts."

—*Teacher Leader, Middle School, Florida*

Since reading and math are the foundation of all learning and the focus of high-stakes assessments, effective schools throw out the traditional school schedule and reinvent the school day and school week to provide extra instructional time for basic skills as well as time during the school day for remediation and enrichment (Jerald, 2001; Goodwin, 2000; U.S. Department of Education, 2001). A growing number of schools that have experienced success with low-socioeconomic-status students report that they have accomplished this growth through extending instructional time and expanding the resources for reading and mathematics. Many elementary schools double the amount of time each day for reading and mathematics instruction.

In the Lapwai School District in Idaho, the elementary school requires a minimum of 90 minutes of reading each day, and the middle school has, with the agreement of all parents, postponed all electives until underperforming students achieve reading proficiency. Brazosport, Texas, may have been the first school district in the United States that completely reworked its academic schedule to create an entirely new hour-long academic period from 2:30 until 3:30 to provide immediate, intensive remediation and enrichment during the school day. Students already performing at proficiency use this time for educational enrichment and special projects. The goal is to have all students achieve proficiency as soon as possible so they can experience this enrichment.

Today, large numbers of Texas school districts have created a similar remediation or enrichment period. Other school districts, like Pocano Beach, Florida, have reorganized their middle school academic program into a 4-day block program. This leaves each Friday for remediation, individual tutoring, and teacher collaboration. Students who achieve appropriate levels of proficiency use Fridays for career experiences, job shadowing, community service, or special projects. Many alternative schools, such as Meridian Academy in Idaho, have adopted the extended 4-day academic week with remarkable success.

**Secrets of Success
in High-Performing, High-Poverty Schools**
Four-Day Academic Week

Many high-performing schools have been reorganized into a 4-day academic week. This means that Fridays become a full day for remediation, enrichment, and reteaching. And while this change can be extremely difficult in a large school, it is remarkably easy in small learning communities or alternative schools. Effective schools realize they must have adequate schedule time during the school day or week to focus on students who have not achieved curriculum benchmarks. Without this remediation and reteaching, students fall too far behind to catch up. The full day for such remediation has proven to be a remarkably effective approach. Students who achieve proficiency participate in a variety of enrichment activities.

Extend the School Day

"Well, we realized right away that there was just not enough time in the traditional school day to accomplish all we needed to do. The next step in our thinking was so logical. We simply 'stretched' the school day. We started school earlier and stayed later with after-school programs."

—*Principal, Oklahoma*

Perhaps the easiest way to provide extra instructional time is to use before- and after-school programs that extend the school day. Some schools stagger teachers' instructional day, with part of the school faculty starting as early as 7:00 a.m. and completing their work in the early afternoon. Other teachers begin at 10:00 a.m. or later, and then continue their work into the late afternoon or early evening. Some effective alternative schools offer classes from 7:00 a.m. to 10:30 p.m. each day. This extra time is used for remediation and enrichment or for completing homework with technology, library resources, and individual teacher assistance. Parents support these programs because it ensures that their children are in a safe, supportive, and educational environment until they can arrive home after work. Many successful schools use adult volunteers, mentors, older peer tutors, and university students to staff these programs.

Extend the School Year

"If you're focused on increasing achievement for the long haul, how could you ignore kids for three months every summer?"

—*Elementary Principal, Michigan*

Since poor children and youth experience a significant loss of achievement during the summer months, effective schools develop a variety of approaches designed to provide nutrition, recreation, and academic remediation and enrichment during the summer months. Some schools adopt a year-round school schedule; others, like many Texas schools, extend the school year into the summer months, reallocating the old 3-month summer vacation into several shorter breaks. Other schools establish part-time summer programs on a few days each week in cooperation with public libraries, parks and recreation departments, local businesses, and universities. Others implement year-round schedules that significantly reduce the time spent away from school. Once again, the goal is to provide free nutritious meals during the summer as well as recreation and academic enrichment—even on a part-time basis. Few strategies are as important to the children of poverty as programs that give them the opportunity to catch up academically, accelerate, and obtain nutritious meals during the summer months.

The Education Trust has encouraged schools to review the entire year-long calendar. The Trust maintains that most schools are left with only 15 to 18 8-hour days per academic course per year after subtracting the summer months and weekends, professional development days, testing days, religious and public holidays, early releases for activities, and sports and school assemblies (Jerald, 2004). Many effective schools eliminate some of these unnecessary days off, early release days, and other non-critical interruptions from their schedules.

Create Small, Supportive Learning Communities

"High schools should break into units of no more than 600 students."
—*National Association of Secondary School Principals (1996, p. 5)*

The magnitude of the problems that surround the children of poverty in their home and community all but overwhelm their academic interest and performance. No student can learn effectively and achieve high academic proficiency if he or she is hungry, scared, worried, abused, taunted, bullied, or isolated and humiliated. Students need to feel safe, secure, cared for, and supported before they can seriously focus on academic achievement.

In the article, "The Influence of Scale: Small Schools Make a Big Difference for Children From Poor Families," researchers Craig Howley and Robert Bickel studied the effects of school and district size on student achievement and found that the achievement of economically disadvantaged students decreases as enrollment or size increases. Their study of data from 13,600 schools in 2,300 districts from four states (Georgia, Montana, Ohio, and Texas) confirmed similar findings from previous studies in Alaska, California, and West Virginia: "As size goes up, school and district-level student achievement go down" (Howley & Bickel, 2002, p. 28).

The authors suggest that district enrollment in affluent communities be limited to 3,000 students and 750 in impoverished communities to offset the negative effect of large institutions on the achievement of poor students. These limitations would "generate the smaller elementary, middle, and high schools needed to support the achievement gains of students of poverty" (Howley & Bickel, 2002, p. 28).

For low-socioeconomic-status children and youth, a supportive educational atmosphere has an overwhelmingly positive effect. It can improve their attitudes, help them learn more effectively, and transform their lives. For the children and youth of poverty, many of whom have had negative school experiences and may lack a supportive, caring family, the small school atmosphere can have an immediate, positive impact. Effective schools and programs for poor students often create an "all-for-one, one-for-all" camaraderie among teachers, parents, and students similar to that found in elite military organizations, superior athletic teams, cohesive private schools, and successful companies. Students in such programs become committed to their school and peers, creating an environment of positive pressure to succeed. A positive, supportive atmosphere contributes directly to a student's improvement in school attendance, academic achievement, and a positive attitude toward school and life.

Effective schools seek to address the needs of the entire child through free- and reduced-priced breakfast and lunch programs; a wide variety of community services including health, dental, and vision programs; extra instructional time; and highly trained, experienced teachers. Schools that have been especially effective with low-performing students have gone even further by attempting to reorganize large, impersonal schools into small communities of support. These educational communities enable a small group of teachers and students to work almost exclusively together (DuFour, DuFour, Eaker, & Karhanek, 2004). This enables teachers and students to know each other personally and work to care for and support one another (see chapter 5).

Effective communities of support take on the characteristics of a supportive family or, more correctly, a surrogate family—a place where students feel safe, cared for, respected, challenged, and supported. For the children of poverty, such a community of support may fill a void in their lives and is critical to academic success.

The school as a community of support is a broad concept that intertwines school membership and educational engagement. Productive school membership is the result of a sense of belonging and social bonding among all members of the school community. Positive educational engagement focuses on school activities, but especially blends classroom academic work and extracurricular activities. For a school to develop a family atmosphere and serve as a community of support, teachers must be morally committed to educating at-risk youth and possess sufficient autonomy and resources to develop the effective programs required to help these students.

Many schools create these communities of support as voluntary educational options or alternative schools. When teachers choose to work with certain types of students, and students choose to work in particular educational programs, the positive influence on achievement as well as behavior is magnified.

Establish Small Learning Environments and Alternative Schools

"Do our kids appreciate this school? Let me describe a recent event. It was late Friday. I was on the way out when the phone rang. The last thing I wanted was another call, another problem. Everyone else was gone. I thought about letting the answering machine take it, but I answered; and was I glad I did. One of our seniors, who had left during the year to live on the East Coast in a more stable family situation, was on the line. He was graduating on schedule and had just been hired in an electrician training program. He was calling to ask if he could list our school as the beneficiary of his newly acquired life insurance policy. Can you believe that? I cried."

—Principal, Alternative School, Idaho

"No one knew my name, no one called on me. I was the invisible man. But over here, it's like a happy family. I'll never go back."

—Student, Alternative Middle School, Alaska

A growing number of large middle and high schools have significantly reorganized themselves into smaller educational units involving optional, more personalized programs. They have created these small communities as career academies; stand-alone career-theme programs; "families, houses, or tribes"; and magnet or alternative schools. Over 30 years of research have documented the positive benefits of small schools: better achievement, better student attitudes and behavior, better attendance, and less violence (Barr & Parrett, 2003). The reverse is also true; for every additional 600 students, there is a corresponding increase in student disruptions (Smith, Gregory, & Pugh, 1981). Students, teachers, and parents all benefit when the small atmosphere of a community of support is enriched with the opportunity to voluntarily participate.

For middle and high school students, the opportunity to attend school in a smaller, more personalized setting is of great value, especially for youth who have been largely disenfranchised by public education (Nathan & Johnson, 2000). Adding a career-themed and personalized instructional program to small schools seems to have dramatic, positive effects. In a national study by Adam Gamoran, students who attended career-themed magnet schools had higher achievement than students in traditional high schools and private parochial schools (Gamoran, 1996). In a classic study of how well students' needs were being met by schools (as measured by Maslow's hierarchy of needs), students in alternative schools felt that their needs were being met more significantly than students in conventional public schools, even with a more diverse student population (Smith, Gregory, & Pugh, 1981).

While the creation of small schools or small alternative schools does not guarantee that students will achieve academic proficiency, there is growing conviction that it is an important prerequisite (Dessoff, 2004).

- A recent study by the New York State Education Department, published by the National Dropout Prevention Center/Network, examined 13 low-performing middle schools in 12 school districts. Six of the schools studied recommended "monitoring and evaluating the effectiveness of intervention programs as well as providing alternatives to retention for students who are failing academically, and providing alternative programs at each grade level to help accommodate students who do not learn well in traditional classrooms" (Duttweiler, 2003, p. 19). The study went on to recommend that "there should be options for alternative schooling ([such as] a school-with-in-school) for students who would benefit from focus on behavioral modification, smaller class size, a more structured environment, and one-to-one tutoring." For high-poverty schools to become high performing, "districts need to look at alternatives, especially new ways to engage students" (Duttweiler, 2003, p. 19).

- Four years ago, West Clermont, Ohio, a Cincinnati suburb, transformed two traditional high schools with a graduation rate of approximately 76% and significant student attendance and behavior problems. The schools were remodeled to create five small schools with between 200 and 400 students with a special theme (world studies, creative arts and design, technology, and so on). As of 2004, the graduation rate had risen to 85%.

- In Benwick, Maine, Noble High School was redesigned to create 15 learning communities of 100 students or less and later built a new building designed around "team-learning pods."

- In New York City, 42 small schools recently opened and 60 more are scheduled to open.

- In the next 6 years, the Chicago Public Schools plans to close 60 large schools and create over 500 new schools with fewer than 500 students each. Only one-third of the new schools will be overseen by the school district; the others will be charter or contract schools operated by independent groups (Paulson, 2004).

- The Bill & Melinda Gates Foundation has dedicated over $100 million to expanding restructuring models to remake the traditional American high school: "Most recently, the Foundation has committed nearly $30 million to create new 'early college' high schools with a plan to triple the availability of these small high schools by 2009. Located on college campuses and elsewhere, the schools target disadvantaged students to help them earn up to 2 years of college credit along with their high school degrees" (Hendrie, 2005, p. 9).

- For over 3 decades, alternative schools have been rescuing high-risk youth: getting them off the streets, off drugs and alcohol, and re-engaging them in learning. The National Dropout Prevention Center/Network has identified alternative public schools as the most effective intervention in preventing students from dropping out of school (Duttweiler, 2003).

Provide Effective and Successful Transitions

For the past century, K–12 public education in the United States has been divided into districts composed of kindergartens, elementary, middle (or junior high), and high schools that for the most part have each developed and grown independently. Leadership organizations at the district, state, and national level have emerged to support our model. Universities prepare student teachers and states certify and license teachers for different levels; state, regional, and national organizations accredit our schools based on standards developed for each level. We keep our age-segregated students separated by these levels. We like it this way and show little intention of changing our institution.

But what about the transition between these levels in the system? Do we provide for the developmental, social, and learning needs of our diverse children as they enter and progress through our schools? For underachieving children of poverty, these transitions can range from lifesaving to brutal.

Earlier sections of this chapter and book have addressed the importance of starting early; providing additional instructional time; holding high expectations; engaging parents, families, and the community; and targeting low-performing students and schools. Each of these priorities has a continual impact on an underachieving student as he or she transitions within our schools. Yet far too few of our schools today place their attention, energy, or resources on ensuring that all of our students successfully transition to and between our levels of schooling.

The following transition practices should be considered in any district enrolling underachieving poor students:

- **Provide full-day kindergarten.** Districts should make full-day kindergarten available to all students with demonstrated needs.

- **Provide effective preschool programs.** Districts should work with their communities to ensure the availability of Head Start, Even Start, and other proven models of pre-kindergarten intervention to disadvantaged children.

- **Plan home visits.** Elementary teachers should visit the homes of their students. While particularly important in kindergarten and the early grades, home visits can dramatically enhance the relationship between home and school.

- **Provide transition visits and orientations.** All grade levels should provide incoming students and their families with an orientation and visit prior to entry. These experiences should include school tours; opportunities to meet and discuss expectations with faculty, staff, and school leaders; and time to review recommendations for remediation or acceleration.

- **Communicate and study student data.** Educators and school leaders at the departing and entry grades should develop specific activities to engage and communicate with each other regarding student progress and needs.

- **Develop summer catch-up programs and opportunities.** Districts should work closely with their communities to develop and provide summer interventions to address the learning and acceleration needs of underachieving poor students.

- **Develop academies at the middle and high school levels.** Since the transition to middle and high schools has been identified as a particularly critical time for students who are underachieving or uneasy with new environments, many schools have launched highly successful academies. These single-grade programs are often self-contained in a separate wing or area of the school with a dedicated team of teachers and staff.

- **Develop a senior project or require community service.** Many high schools (and a growing number of middle and elementary schools) require all students to complete a culminating project. Projects are often the outgrowth of ongoing community service efforts in which students have participated.

- **Prepare for postsecondary education and work.** Schools should augment traditional career counseling with career pathways programs and curriculum as well as opportunities to explore the workplace through internships, apprenticeships, and job shadowing.

- **Coordinate transition support.** Every school should ensure that the responsibility for successful transition support is appropriately assigned and distributed among school staff. Accurate data should be maintained and made available to teachers and parents. Many secondary schools now employ a transition specialist to coordinate this important work.

While this section concludes the chapter, by no means should the implementation of effective transitions be considered an afterthought or alternative strategy. Providing underachieving students with effective transitions to and within school levels will dramatically affect their achievement and success in school.

**Secrets of Success
in High-Performing, High-Poverty Schools**

Smoothing the Transition From the Middle Grades to High School

Nine High Schools That Work (HSTW) schools were recently recognized for a variety of successful transitions that enabled their students to dramatically improve both achievement and graduation rates in high school (Bottoms & Anthony, 2005, pp. 4–5). The practices included:

- Careful evaluation of eighth-grade achievement data and targeted supports based on individual needs

- Immediate tutoring for students struggling upon entry

- Double-dosing in mathematics and English/language arts instruction

- Double-blocked classes of English I and II and algebra I required for all ESL students

- Freshmen academies that keep ninth graders with the same teachers and counselors all day

- Pairing incoming ninth graders with community members for mentoring and tutoring

- Examining curriculum from grades five to eight to determine areas of frequent difficulty for incoming ninth graders

---

The Power of Reorganizing Time, Space, and Transitions

Reorganizing schools and transforming daily school schedules can be an almost insurmountable job, but it is essential to ensure that all students learn effectively. Schools in which children of poverty learn effectively have demonstrated in the most dramatic manner that even modest investments in changing the school culture can result in huge dividends. School reorganization—including schedule changes, calendar changes, the provision of effective transitions, and the creation of small learning communities—has universal, positive power to help us teach our most needy and challenging students.

Next Steps

Complete and Discuss the Self-Evaluation

District and school leadership teams should begin or continue their work by completing the Self-Evaluation Rubric (page 220), comparing their perceptions as a group, and discussing the appropriate next steps.

Provide Additional Instructional Time

To be effective with low-socioeconomic-status students, schools must provide opportunities for additional time for instruction, remediation, and enrichment. Schools must start early, extend the school day, reorganize the school day, and add Saturday and summer academic opportunities.

Restructure Large Schools

Large schools should be restructured into smaller educational environments of 400 or fewer students where a group of teachers and students work exclusively together for much of the day. These smaller educational environments, sometimes called "houses," may be structured as teacher/student teams, educational families, schools-within-schools, or alternative programs. Such programs ensure that teachers and students know each other well and that no student feels isolated, overlooked, or alienated.

Create and Support Small Learning Environments and Schools

Small learning environments should be created and supported at all levels of the K–12 system as alternative public schools, magnet schools, or, where possible, charter schools. These schools should be available to students, parents, and teachers through choice, and instructional programs should be customized to meet the specialized needs of underachieving, high-poverty students.

Provide Successful Transitions

Every district and its schools should develop a comprehensive plan of providing transitional support for students as they transition from school to school, grade level to grade level, and from school to work. Collect data on transitioning students, and use this data to guide the development of programs and procedures.

Reorganize Time, Space, and Transitions
Self-Evaluation Rubric

What is my school's or district's progress?	BEGINNING			EMBEDDING			SUSTAINING		
	No Action Has Been Taken	Efforts Are Limited	Results Are Being Gained	Efforts and Results Are Being Enhanced			Practices Are Widespread, Policies Are in Place, and Results Are Increasing		
Does my school or district . . .	1	2	3	4	5	6	7	8	9
Provide additional instructional time?									
Provide effective preschool programs and all-day kindergarten?									
Extend the school week?									
Reorganize and extend the school day?									
Extend the school year?									
Create small, supportive learning environments and communities?									
Provide and support alternative schools?									
Provide effective transition support to preschool?									
Provide effective transition support to kindergarten?									
Provide effective transition support to elementary school?									
Provide effective transition support to middle school?									
Provide effective transition support to high school?									
Provide effective transition support to post-secondary education?									
Provide effective transition support for suspended and expelled students?									

The Kids Left Behind © 2007 Solution Tree Press • www.solution-tree.com

Chapter 12

Educating the Kids Left Behind: A Matter of Personal Conscience

"I have never been so hopeful for our students . . . for every one of them. The changes we have put in place over the past couple of years have changed not just the lives of our students, but their futures. These kids are breaking the cycle. . . . They'll get out!"

—Principal, High-Performing and High-Poverty School, California

The new American revolution that has swept across the political, social, and educational landscape of our country brings the promise of personal civil rights and economic justice to an ever-growing number of American children and youth. Its impact has left no community untouched and no parent, educator, or student unaffected. Yet for all the drama surrounding No Child Left Behind, the most significant policy change ever to occur in public education is progressing in a surprisingly quiet and business-like manner. While concerns continue regarding No Child Left Behind policies, classrooms all across the country are posting remarkable gains. Many schools enrolling poor and minority students are achieving high levels of academic proficiency. But while more schools in every community and state are meeting adequate yearly progress, others are still failing and continue to need significant improvement.

As the new American revolution in education moves forward—one classroom, one school, and one district at a time—more underachieving poor and minority students are catching up. In this sense, the revolution has become an extremely personal matter of conscience. It is a revolution of individual teachers, principals, superintendents, and school board members—each wrestling with the demands of competing forces attempting to influence their work and moving ahead more determined than ever to succeed.

The new American revolution is all about individuals dealing with intense moral and ethical issues—essential civil rights issues. Each person associated with public education must make a highly personal decision about whether to work to teach all students effectively or whether to resist this idealistic goal and continue the programs, policies, and practices of the old world of education that have their foundation in indifference, ignorance, or race and class prejudice. Such practices have doomed previous generations of poor children and youth to a second-class education, second-class citizenship, second-class jobs, and second-class lives.

The goal of the new revolution reflects a truly noble aspiration, perhaps the most challenging to ever be articulated toward fulfilling the promise of civil rights for all our citizens: educating all students regardless of race, income, language, disability, or educational background. The goal is not just couched in educational jargon; it has been widely discussed in terms of basic human rights. Education is now being considered by many as the most fundamental of all civil rights. No society, anywhere or at anytime in the history of the world, has ever mandated and attempted to meet the challenge of universal educational proficiency. Yet early returns have been more than promising. A growing number of studies document that the dream is attainable and, in fact, being fulfilled in schools and classrooms throughout the country.

The accomplishments of the revolution have not come easily. As with any fundamental shift in policy, progress toward the goal of universal proficiency continues to be fraught with seemingly overwhelming challenges, miscues, and unintended consequences. It has also not been without prolonged and often bitter conflicts and controversies. Yet more underachieving students of poverty are catching up every day.

The revolution has touched everyone even marginally connected to public education: from the classroom to the boardroom to our nation's homes. State legislators, superintendents, school board members, school administrators, community leaders, students, and parents have all faced the need to assume new and difficult roles, learn sophisticated new skills, and function in a more demanding and complex manner. Throughout it all, there is strict accountability that begins with the requirement of testing all students, public disclosure of schools' successes and failures, and pressure to achieve yearly student growth toward proficiency through improved teaching performance in every classroom. Old excuses no longer work. Past strategies of obfuscation and deceit have been rendered impotent, although unfortunately, the revolution has led some to think of new, creative efforts to manipulate policies. The world of American education is being transformed.

The educational revolution has led to remarkable successes. There have also been tragic failures. It has brought out the very best in so many educators, and simultaneously, seemed to elicit the worst in others. Thousands of high-poverty, high-performing schools have emerged while in other districts, many students continue to be assigned to low-performing schools, retained, encouraged to drop out, or even systematically pushed away. The revolution has led to teachers becoming assessment-literate, the creation of professional learning communities, and dramatic improvement of student performance. The pressures of this revolution have led other schools to "hide" dropout rates and falsify test results. There have been significant achievements and heartbreaking failures. There have also been serious, significant philosophical debates over the negative effects of a single-test assessment approach, the amount of required testing, and the idea of high-stakes assessment.

Several of the nation's leading educators, including Deborah Meier, Linda Darling-Hammond, and Ted Sizer, voice concern that the No Child Left Behind policies actually damage the public schools' most needy and fragile students, driving them to give up educationally and leave school. They warn that we cannot allow this to continue. Many others like Kati Haycock, joined by a hundred African-American and Latino superintendents, have urged Congress not to "turn back" the accountability provisions of Title I, which directly target and support the underachieving children of poverty. Throughout it all, yet another generation of students continues to move slowly through the grades and classes of public education as educators seek to implement effective interventions, address problems and challenges, work on sustaining successes, and scramble to learn the complex skills of this changed world of teaching and learning.

With only a few years of experience with the new policy, we have had little time to create and perfect national, state, and local systems to accurately monitor progress and improve practices. Yet an emerging body of educational research has begun to document the developments of new hope for the underachieving poor and minority children of America. And while a recent *New York Times* editorial called for significant changes and improvement in the No Child Left Behind law, it insisted that the essential elements of the legislation that requires states to close the achievement gap between white and minority students must remain intact, "must remain sacrosanct" ("Fixing 'No Child Left Behind,'" 2005).

Fulfilling the Revolution: Civil Rights for All

After only a few years of this dramatic new policy, the educational landscape has been permanently altered. Compared with any other period in American history, this educational reform has occurred almost overnight. Suddenly, the nation has begun to focus on the underachieving students who have almost always been ignored and even discouraged from continuing in school. More American teachers now recognize that a high-quality education is necessary for providing all students with the skills and knowledge they must have to obtain economic justice and personal civil rights.

223

The Kids Left Behind

The challenge is not yet over. Efforts to meet the challenge have hardly begun, although important milestones have been met: Poor and minority students are learning effectively, and a growing number of high-poverty and high-performing schools is a tribute to the efforts of schools, communities, and educators throughout the United States. The door of opportunity is being opened for many more of our students, and their future now holds a greater promise of freedom and justice. Finally, as a nation, we are positioned to ensure that no child is left behind.

Educating the kids left behind is truly a matter of personal conscience. When we choose to do so, we can. Thousands of schools and classrooms have proven this by using the strategies in this book. National and state policies support this reality. All that remains is the continuing work. In this new world of education, the public schools of America are indeed up to the challenge of successfully catching up our underachieving children of poverty.

Eight Components of High-Performing, High-Poverty Schools Self-Evaluation Rubric

What is my school's or district's progress?	BEGINNING			EMBEDDING			SUSTAINING		
	No Action Has Been Taken	Efforts Are Limited	Results Are Being Gained	Efforts and Results Are Being Enhanced			Practices Are Widespread, Policies Are in Place, and Results Are Increasing		
Does my school or district . . .	1	2	3	4	5	6	7	8	9
Ensure effective district and school leadership?									
Engage parents, communities, and schools to work as partners?									
Understand and hold high expectations for poor and culturally diverse students?									
Target low-performing students and schools, starting with reading?									
Align, monitor, and manage the curriculum?									
Create a culture of data and assessment literacy?									
Build and sustain instructional capacity?									
Reorganize time, space, and transitions?									

Appendix A

The Professional Learning Community Continuum*

By Robert Eaker, Richard DuFour, and Rebecca DuFour

When school personnel attempt to assess their ability to function as a learning community, they are likely to create a simple dichotomy—the school either functions as a professional learning community or it does not. The complex process of school improvement cannot, however, be reduced to such a simple "either/or" statement. It is more helpful to view the development of a PLC along a continuum: Pre-initiation, Initiation, Developing, and Sustaining. Each element of a PLC, as shown in the following pages, can be assessed during the four stages of the continuum:

Pre-initiation   The school has not yet begun to address a particular principle of a PLC.

Initiation   An effort has been made to address the principle, but the effort has not yet begun to impact a "critical mass."

Developing   A critical mass has endorsed the principle. Members are beginning to modify their thinking and practice as they attempt to implement the principle. Structural changes are being made to align with the principle.

Sustaining   The principle is deeply embedded in the school's culture. It represents a driving force in the daily work of the school. It is so internalized that it can survive changes in key personnel.

Assess the position of your school on each area of the continuum. Identify examples and illustrations to support your placement.

Shared Values: How Must We Behave to Advance Our Vision?

Pre-initiation   Staff members have not yet articulated the attitudes, behaviors, or commitments they are prepared to demonstrate in order to advance the mission of learning for all and the vision of what the school might become. If they discuss school improvement, they focus on what *other* groups must do.

The Kids Left Behind	Initiation	Staff members have articulated statements of beliefs or philosophy for their school; however, these value statements have not yet impacted their day-to-day work or the operation of the school.
	Developing	Staff members have made a conscious effort to articulate and promote the attitudes, behaviors, and commitments that will advance their vision of the school. Examples of the core values at work are shared in stories and celebrations. People are confronted when they behave in ways that are inconsistent with the core values.
	Sustaining	The values of the school are embedded in the school culture. These shared values are evident to new staff and to those outside of the school. They influence policies, procedures, and daily practices of the school as well as day-to-day decisions of individual staff members.

Goals: What Are Our Priorities?

	Pre-initiation	No effort has been made to engage the staff in setting and defining school improvement goals related to student learning. If goals exist, they have been developed by the administration.
	Initiation	Staff members have participated in a process to establish goals, but the goals are typically stated as projects to be accomplished, or are written so broadly that they are impossible to measure. The goals do not yet influence instructional decisions in a meaningful way.
	Developing	Staff members have worked together to establish long- and short-term improvement goals for their school. The goals are clearly communicated. Assessment tools and strategies have been developed and implemented to measure progress toward the goals.
	Sustaining	All staff pursue measurable performance goals as part of their routine responsibilities. Goals are clearly linked to the school's shared vision. Goal attainment is celebrated and staff members demonstrate willingness to identify and pursue challenging stretch goals.

Collaborative Culture: Administrator/Teacher Relations

Pre-initiation Questions of power are a continuing source of controversy and friction. Relationships between teachers and administrators are often adversarial.

Initiation Efforts have been made to reduce friction by clarifying "management rights" and "teacher rights." Both parties are protective of intrusion onto their turf.

Developing Administrators solicit and value teacher input as improvement initiatives are developed and considered, but administrators are regarded as having primary responsibility for school improvement.

Sustaining Staff are fully involved in the decision-making processes of the school. Administrators pose questions, delegate authority, create collaborative decision-making processes, and provide staff with the information, training, and parameters they need to make good decisions. School improvement is viewed as a collective responsibility.

Collaborative Culture: Teachers Working Together

Pre-initiation Teachers work in isolation. There is little awareness of what or how colleagues are teaching.

Initiation Teachers recognize a common curriculum that they are responsible for teaching, but there is little exchange of ideas regarding instructional materials, teaching strategies, or methods of assessment.

Developing Teachers function in work groups that meet periodically to complete certain tasks such as reviewing intended outcomes and coordinating calendars.

Sustaining Teachers function as a team. They work collaboratively to identify collective goals, develop strategies to achieve those goals, gather relevant data, and learn from one another. Unlike a work group, they are characterized by common goals and their interdependent efforts to achieve those goals.

Parent Partnerships

Pre-initiation   There is little or no effort made to cultivate a partnership with parents. Parents are either ignored or viewed as adversaries.

Initiation   An effort is made to keep parents informed of events and situations at school in order to secure parental support for the school's efforts.

Developing   Structures and processes for two-way communication with parents are developed. The parental perspective is solicited on both schoolwide issues and matters related directly to their own children.

Sustaining   The school-parent partnership moves beyond open communication. The school provides parents with information and materials that enable parents to assist their children in learning. Parents are welcomed in the school and there is an active volunteer program. Parents are full partners in the educational decisions that affect their children. Community resources are used to strengthen the school and student learning.

Action Research

Action research is investigation carried out by teachers and practitioners in real-work settings to answer a question or assess the impact of a practice or method on improving student learning.

Pre-initiation   While individual teachers may try experiments in their own classrooms, no structures to support, assess, or share their findings are in place. Many staff members have no knowledge of or involvement in action research.

Initiation   Some staff members participate in pilot action projects. The sharing of findings is largely informal.

Developing   Staff members have been trained in action research methods and conduct action research to improve their professional practice. Findings generated by this research are beginning to influence classroom practices.

Sustaining   Topics for action research arise from the shared vision and goals of the school. Staff members regard action research as an important component of their professional responsibilities. There are frequent discussions regarding the implications of findings as teachers attempt to learn from the research of their colleagues.

Continuous Improvement

Pre-initiation   Little attention is devoted to creating systems that enable either the school or individual teachers to track improvement. The school would have a difficult time answering the question, "Are we becoming more effective in achieving our shared vision?"

Initiation   A few people in the school are tracking general indicators of achievement, such as mean scores on state and national tests. Positive trends are celebrated. Negative trends are dismissed or suppressed.

Developing   Individual teachers and teaching teams gather information that enables them to identify and monitor individual and team goals.

Sustaining   Everyone in the school participates in an ongoing cycle of systematic gathering and analysis of data to identify discrepancies between actual and desired results, goal setting to reduce the discrepancies, developing strategies to achieve the goals, and tracking improvement indicators.

Focus on Results

Pre-initiation   The results the school seeks for each student have not been identified.

Initiation   Results have been identified, but are stated in such broad and esoteric terms that they are impossible to measure. Improvement initiatives focus on inputs—projects or tasks to be completed—rather than on student achievements.

Developing   Desired results have been identified in terms of student outcomes and student achievement indicators have been identified. Data are being collected and monitored within the school or district. Results of the analysis are shared with teachers.

| The Kids Left Behind | Sustaining | Teams of teachers are hungry for information on results. They gather relevant data and use these data to identify improvement goals and to monitor progress toward the goals. |

Appendix B

NSDC Standards for Staff Development (Revised, 2001)*

Context Standards

Staff development that improves the learning of all students:

- Organizes adults into learning communities whose goals are aligned with those of the school and district. (Learning Communities)
- Requires skillful school and district leaders who guide continuous instructional improvement. (Leadership)
- Requires resources to support adult learning and collaboration. (Resources)

Process Standards

Staff development that improves the learning of all students:

- Uses disaggregated student data to determine adult learning priorities, monitor progress, and help sustain continuous improvement. (Data-Driven)
- Uses multiple sources of information to guide improvement and demonstrate its impact. (Evaluation)
- Prepares educators to apply research to decision making. (Research-Based)
- Uses learning strategies appropriate to the intended goal. (Design)
- Applies knowledge about human learning and change. (Learning)
- Provides educators with the knowledge and skills to collaborate. (Collaboration)

Content Standards

Staff development that improves the learning of all students:

- Prepares educators to understand and appreciate all students, create safe, orderly and supportive learning environments, and hold high expectations for their academic achievement. (Equity)
- Deepens educators' content knowledge, provides them with research-based instructional strategies to assist students in meeting rigorous academic standards, and prepares them to use various types of classroom assessments appropriately. (Quality Teaching)
- Provides educators with knowledge and skills to involve families and other stakeholders appropriately. (Family Involvement)

References

American Association of School Administrators. (AASA). (2004, September 30). Understanding public school accountability [PowerPoint presentation e-mailed to AASA members]. Arlington, VA: Author.

Amundson, K. J. (1991). *101 ways parents can help students achieve*. Arlington, VA: American Association of School Administrators.

Anne Arundel County Public Schools. (2006). *Goals of the Anne Arundel County Schools: The standard by which success will be measured*. Retrieved June 29, 2006, from www.aacps.org/aacps/boe/news/goals.asp

Ansary, T. (2004, November/December). The muddle machine: Confessions of a textbook editor. *Edutopia*, 31–35.

APCO Associates. (1999). *Perceptions: Understanding and responding to what people think about service-learning*. Battle Creek, MI: W. K. Kellogg Foundation. Retrieved June 21, 2006, from www.learningindeed.org/tools/other/Perception.pdf

Archer, J. (2006, January 25). Houston marketing its K–12 curriculum nationwide. *Education Week*, 10.

Asimov, N. (2004, August 12). Big win for run-down schools brings hope. *San Francisco Chronicle*, B1.

Associated Press. (2004, December 19). *Neediest kids often get least-qualified teachers*.

Austin, L. (2004, September 7). Houston downsizes to tackle dropout rate. *Boston Globe*. Retrieved June 20, 2006, from www.boston.com/news/nation/articles/2004/09/07/houston_downsizes_to_tackle_dropout_rate/?rss_id=Boston%20Globe%20--%20National%20News

Bailey, J. M., & Guskey, T. R. (2001). *Implementing student-led conferences*. Thousand Oaks, CA: Corwin.

Balfanz, R., & Legters, N. (2004). *Locating the dropout crisis: Which high schools produce the nation's dropouts? Where are they located? Who attends them?* Baltimore, MD: Johns Hopkins University.

Barksdale, M. L., & Davenport, P. W. (2003). *8 Steps to success: An educator's guide to implementing continuous improvement*. Baton Rouge, LA: American Productivity & Quality Center.

Barnett, W. S. (1996). *Lives in the balance: Age-27 benefit-cost analysis of the High/Scope Perry Preschool Program* [Monograph]. Ypsilanti, MI: High/Scope.

Barr, R. D., Joyner, S., Parrett, W., & Willison, S. (2004). *Idaho reading initiative: Focus on minority and low socioeconomic students*, 2004 Legislative Session. Boise, ID: Boise State University, Center for School Improvement and Policy Studies, College of Education.

Barr, R., & Parrett, W. (1995). *Hope at last for at-risk youth*. Needham Heights, MA: Allyn & Bacon.

Barr, R. D., & Parrett, W. H. (1997). *How to create alternative, magnet, and charter schools.* Bloomington, IN: Solution Tree (formerly National Educational Service).

Barr, R. D., & Parrett, W. H. (2001). *Hope fulfilled for at-risk and violent youth: K-12 programs that work* (2nd ed.). Needham Heights, MA: Allyn & Bacon.

Barr, R. D., & Parrett, W. H. (2003). *Saving our students, saving our schools: 50 proven strategies for revitalizing at-risk students and low-performing schools.* Thousand Oaks, CA: Corwin.

Barth, P., Haycock, K., Jackson, H., Mora, K., Ruiz, P., Robinson, S., & Wilkins, A. (Eds.). (1999). *Dispelling the myth: High poverty schools exceeding expectations* [Report]. Washington, DC: Education Trust.

Benard, B. (1991). *Fostering resiliency in kids: Protective factors in the family, school, and community.* Portland, OR: Northwest Regional Educational Laboratory, Western Center for Drug-Free Schools and Communities.

Benson, B., & Barnett, S. (1998). *Student-led conferencing using showcase portfolios.* Thousand Oaks, CA: Corwin.

Benson, P. L., Galbraith, J., & Espeland, P. (1998). *What kids need to succeed.* Minneapolis, MN: Free Spirit.

Bernhardt, V. (2005, February). Data tools for school improvement. *Educational Leadership, 62*(5), 66–69.

Black, P., & William, D. (1998). Inside the black box: Raising standards through classroom assessment. *Phi Delta Kappan, 79*(8), 139–148.

Books, S. (Ed.). (1998). *Invisible children in the society and its schools.* Mahwah, NJ: Lawrence Erlbaum.

Borman, G., Hewes, G. M., Overman, L. T., & Brown, S. (2002, November). *Comprehensive school reform and student achievement: A meta-analysis* [Report no. 59]. Baltimore, MD: Johns Hopkins University, Center for Research on the Education of Students Placed at Risk.

Bottoms, G. & Anthony, K. (2005). *Raising achievement and improving graduation rates: How nine high schools that work sites are doing it.* Atlanta, GA: Southern Regional Education Board.

Bracey, G. W. (2002a, February). Raising achievement of at-risk students—or not. *Phi Delta Kappan, 83*(6), 431–432.

Bracey, G. W. (2002b). What students do in the summer. *Phi Delta Kappan, 83*(7), 497–498.

Bridgeland, J. M., Dilulio, J. J., Jr., & Morison, K. B. (2006, March). *The silent epidemic: Perspectives of high school dropouts.* Washington, DC: Civic Enterprises.

Brookover, W. B., & Lezotte, L. W. (1979). *Changes in school characteristics coincident with changes in student achievement.* East Lansing: Michigan State University, Institute for Research on Teaching and Learning.

Brown, J., D'Emidio-Caston, M., & Benard, B. (2001). *Resilience education.* Thousand Oaks, CA: Corwin.

Calderón, M. (1999). School reform and alignment of standards. In Mid-continent Research for Education and Learning (Ed.), *Including culturally and linguistically diverse students in standards-based reform: A report on McREL's diversity roundtable I* (pp. 23–46). Aurora, CO: Author.

Carey, K. (2003). *The funding gap: Low-income and minority students still receive fewer dollars in many states.* Washington, DC: Education Trust.

Carter, S. C. (2001). *No excuses: Lessons from 21 high-performing, high-poverty schools.* Washington, DC: Heritage Foundation.

Cauthen, N. K. (2006, June). *When work doesn't pay: What every policymaker should know.* Columbia University: National Center for Children in Poverty.

Cawelti, G., & Protheroe, N. (2001). *High student achievement: How six school districts changed into high-performance systems.* Arlington, VA: Education Research Service.

Center for Human Resources. (1999). *National evaluation of Learn and Serve America school and community based programs* [Summary report]. Waltham, MA: Brandeis University and ABT Associates. Retrieved June 29, 2006, from www.learnandserve.org/about/role_impact/index.asp

Center for the Study of Reading. (1989). *Ten ways to help your children become better readers.* Champaign: University of Illinois. (ERIC Document Reproduction Service No. ED347496)

Chaddock, G. R. (2004, July 15). How school reform is altering classrooms. *Christian Science Monitor, 96*(161), 2.

Chadwick, K. G. (2004). *Improving schools through community engagement: A practical guide for educators.* Thousand Oaks, CA: Corwin.

Chappuis, J., & Chappuis, S. (2002). *Understanding school assessment: A parent and community guide to helping students learn.* Portland, OR: ETS Assessment Training Institute.

Chavkin, N. F. (1989). Debunking the myth about minority parents. *Educational Horizons, 67*(4), 119–123.

Chubb, J. E., & Loveless, T. (2002). *Bridging the achievement gap.* Washington, DC: Brookings Institute.

Class focus: It's not just poor students who need attention. (2005, November 13). *Washington Post,* B1.

Clinchy, E. (2000). *Creating small schools: How small schools are changing American education.* New York: Teachers College.

Cohen, J. S., & Banchero, S. (2004, August 18). Top suburb schools hit by "No Child" sanctions. *Chicago Tribune.*

Coleman, J. S., Campbell, E. Q., Hobson, C. J., McPartland, J., Mood, A. M., Weinfeld, F. D., et al. (1966). *Equality of educational opportunities* [Survey]. Washington, DC: U.S. Department of Health, Education, and Welfare.

Colorado Foundation for Families and Children. (1995). *School expulsions: A cross-system problem.* Report to Colorado Juvenile Justice Delinquency Prevention Council.

Comer, J. P. (1980). *School power: Implications of an intervention project.* New York: Free Press.

Comer, J. P. (2004). *Leave no child behind.* New Haven, CT: Yale University.

Comer, J. P., Ben-Avie, M., Haynes, N. M., & Joyner, E. T. (1999). *Child by child: The Comer Process for change in education.* New York: Teachers College.

Comer, J., Haynes, N., Joyner, E., & Ben Avie, M. (Eds.). (1996). *Rallying the whole village: The Comer Process for reforming education.* New York: Teachers College.

Comprehensive Center—Region IV. (2001, Spring). Using data for educational decision-making [Special issue]. *Newsletter of the Comprehensive Center—Region IV, 6*(1).

Conrath, J. (1988). A new deal for at-risk students. *NASSP Bulletin, 72*(504), 36–40.

Conrath, J. (2001). Changing the odds for young people: Next steps for alternative education. *Phi Delta Kappan, 82*(8), 585–587.

Corron, K. (2000). *The schooling practices that matter most.* Portland, OR: Northwest Regional Educational Laboratory.

Council of Chief State School Officers. (2006). *What are the Surveys of Enacted Curriculum?* Retrieved July 21, 2006, from www.ccsso.org/projects/Surveys_of_Enacted_Curriculum/

Davis, D. (1998). *Easy ways for families to help children learn.* Portland, OR: Northwest Regional Educational Laboratory.

Davis, J., & Farbman, D. (2004, December 1). Rethinking time: The next frontier of educational reform. *Education Week, 24*(14), 52.

Delpit, L. (1995). *Other people's children: Cultural conflict in the classroom.* New York: New Press.

Despeignes, P. (2004, August 27). Consensus: Poverty rose by million. Uninsured rate also escalates. *USA Today,* p. A1.

Dessoff, A. (2004, September 14). Think small. *District Administration: The Magazine for K–12 Educators.* Retrieved June 21, 2006, from www.districtadministration.com/page.cfm?p=856

Dewey, J. (1916). *Democracy and education.* New York: McMillan.

Downey, C. J., Steffy, B. E., English, F. W., Frase, L. E., & Poston, W. K. (2004). *The three-minute classroom walk-through: Changing school supervisory practice one teacher at a time.* Thousand Oaks, CA: Corwin.

Dryfoos, J. G. (1994). *Full-service schools: A revolution in health and social service for children, youth and families.* San Francisco: Jossey-Bass.

DuFour, R., & Eaker, R. (1998). *Professional learning communities at work: Best practices for enhancing student achievement.* Bloomington, IN: Solution Tree (formerly National Educational Service).

Dufour, R., Dufour, R., Eaker, R., & Karhanek, G. (2004). *Whatever it takes.* Bloomington, IN: Solution Tree (formerly National Educational Service).

Duttweiler, P. C. (2003). *Comprehensive school reform: Common issues and lessons learned for improving low-performing schools.* Clemson, SC: National Dropout Prevention Center.

Eaker, R., DuFour, R., & DuFour, R. (2002). *Getting started: Reculturing schools to become professional learning communities.* Bloomington, IN: Solution Tree (formerly National Educational Service).

Echevarria, J., Vogt, M., Short, D. J., & Short, D. (2004). *Making content comprehensible for English-language learners: The SIOP model.* Boston, MA: Allyn & Bacon.

Edmonds, R. R. (1979a). Effective schools for the urban poor. *Educational Leadership, 37*(1), 15–27.

Edmonds, R. R. (1979b). Some schools work and more can. *Social Policy, 9*(2), 28–32.

Edmonds, R. R. (1981). Making public schools effective. *Social Policy, 12*(2), 56–60.

Edmonds, R. R. (1982). Programs of school improvement: An overview. *Educational Leadership, 40*(3), 4–11.

Education Commission of the States. (1998). *The progress of education reform 1998.* Denver, CO: Author.

Education Commission of the States. (2004). *Report to the nation: State implementation of the No Child Left Behind Act.* Denver, CO: Author.

Education Trust. (2001, December 12). *First-of-its-kind report identifies thousands of high-poverty and high-minority schools across the U.S. performing among top schools in their states.* Retrieved December 16, 2001, from www.edtrust.org/news/12_12_01_dtm.asp

Education Trust. (2002, May). *Dispelling the myth . . . over time* [Report]. Washington, DC: Author.

Education Trust. (2003a, November 18). *Don't turn back the clock! Over 100 African American and Latino superintendents voice their support for the accountability provisions in Title I (NCLB).* Retrieved July 7, 2006, from www2.edtrust.org/EdTrust/Press+Room/archives.htm

Education Trust. (2003b, Winter). A new core curriculum for all: Aiming high for other people's children [Special issue]. *Thinking K–16, 7*(1).

Education Trust. (2003c, March). Presentation on Houston public schools at the Closing the Gap Conference, Houston, Texas.

Education Trust. (2003d, December). *Telling the whole truth (or not) about high school graduation: New state data.* Retrieved June 21, 2006, from www2.edtrust.org/NR/rdonlyres/4DE8F2E0-4D08-4640-B3B0-013F6DC3865D/0/tellingthetruthgradrates.pdf

Education Trust. (2004, Winter). The real value of teachers: If good teachers matter, why don't we act like it? [Special issue]. *Thinking K–16, 8*(1).

Edwards, V. B. (Ed.). (2005, January 6). Quality counts 2005: No small change, targeting money toward student performance [Special issue]. *Education Week, 24*(17).

Elmore, R. F. (2006). What (so called) low-performing schools can teach (so-called) high performing schools. *Journal of Staff Development, 27*(2), 43–45.

English, F. W. (2000). *Deciding what to teach and test: Developing, aligning and auditing the curriculum.* Thousand Oaks, CA: Corwin.

English, F. W., & Steffy, B. E. (2001). *Deep curriculum alignment: Creating a level playing field for all children on high-stakes tests of educational accountability.* Lanham, MD: Scarecrow.

Epstein, J. L. (1995). School/family/community partnerships: Caring for the children we share. *Phi Delta Kappan, 76*(9), 701–712.

Epstein, J. L. (2001). *School, family, and community partnerships: Preparing educators and improving schools.* Boulder, CO: Westview.

Epstein, J. L., Sanders, M. G., Simon, B. S., Salinas, K., Clark, J., Rodriguez, N., & Van Voorhis, F. L. (2002). *School, family, and community partnerships: Your handbook for action* (2nd ed.). Thousand Oaks, CA: Corwin.

Fager, J., & Richen, R. (1999). *When students don't succeed: Shedding light on grade retention.* Portland, OR: Northwest Regional Educational Laboratory.

Farris, A. (2005). *Sheltered Instruction Observation Protocol: An inclusive framework.* Boise, ID: Boise Independent School District.

Fenwick, L. T. (2001). *Patterns of excellence: Policy perspectives on diversity in teaching and school leadership.* Atlanta, GA: Southern Education Foundation. (ERIC Document Reproduction Service No. ED472206)

Fielding, L., Kerr, N., & Rosier, P. (1998). *The 90 percent reading goal.* Kennewick, WA: New Foundation.

Fixing "No Child Left Behind." [Editorial.] (2005, April 5). *New York Times.*

Fogarty, R. (1997). *Problem-based learning and other curriculum models for the multiple intelligences classroom.* Glenview, IL: Skylight.

Fredericks, L., Kaplan, E., & Zeisler, J. (2001). *Learning In Deed: Integrating youth voice in service-learning* [Issue paper]. Denver, CO: Education Commission of the States.

Freedman, S. G. (2004, September 29). Politics aside, a school's real success. *New York Times.* Retrieved June 27, 2006, from www.gcssk12.net/news/news_74.htm

Fullan, M. (2003). *The moral imperative of school leadership.* Thousand Oaks, CA: Corwin.

Fullan, M. (2005). *Leadership and sustainability: System thinkers in action.* Thousand Oaks, CA: Corwin.

Gamoran, A. (1996). Student achievement in public magnet, public comprehensive, and private city high schools. *Educational Evaluation and Policy Analysis, 18*(1), 1–18.

Gardner, H. (1991). *The unschooled mind.* New York: Basic Books.

Gathercoal, F. (1999). *Judicious discipline* (4th ed.). Ann Arbor, MI: Caddo Gap.

Gehring, J. (2004, August 11). To stem dropouts, urban districts switch strategies. *Education Week, 23*(44), 1–19.

Gewertz, C. (2005). One subject at a time. *Education Week, 24*(21), 34–37.

Glasser, W. (1998). *Choice theory: A new psychology of personal freedom.* New York: HarperCollins.

Godfrey, R. (1980). *Outward Bound: Schools of the possible.* Garden City, NY: Anchor Books.

Goldberg, M., & Cross, C. T. (2005, September). Time out. *Edutopia,* 35–37.

Goldenberg, C. (2004). *Successful school change: Creating settings to improve teaching and learning.* New York: Teachers College.

Good, T. L., & Brophy, J. E. (1986). School effects. In M.C. Wittrock (Ed.), *Handbook of research on teaching* (3rd ed., pp. 570–602). New York: MacMillan.

Goodwin, B. (2000, May). *Raising the achievement of low-performing students* [Policy brief]. Aurora, CO: Mid-continent Research for Education and Learning. Retrieved June 21, 2006, from www.mcrel.org/topics/policyBrief.asp

Greene, J. P., & Forster, G. (2004, September). The teachability index: Can disadvantaged students learn? *Education Working Paper,* 6. Retrieved June 20, 2006, from www.manhattan-institute.org/html/ewp_06.htm

Greene, J. P., & Winters, M. A. (2004, May). Pushed out or pulled up? Exit exams and dropout rates in public high schools. *Education Working Paper,* 5. Retrieved June 22, 2006, from www.manhattan-institute.org/html/ewp_05.htm

Gregory, G. H, & Parry, T. (2003). *Designing brain-compatible learning* (2nd ed.). Thousand Oaks, CA: Corwin.

Haberman, M. (1991). Pedagogy of poverty versus good teaching. *Phi Delta Kappan, 73*(4), 290–294.

Hall, D., Wiener, R., & Carey, K. (2003). *What new "AYP" information tells us about schools, states, and public education.* Washington, DC: Education Trust. Retrieved July 2, 2006, from www2.edtrust.org/NR/rdonlyres/4B9BF8DE-987A-4063-B750-6D67607E7205/0/NewAYP.pdf

Haycock, K. (2001, March). Closing the achievement gap: Helping all students achieve. *Educational Leadership, 58*(60), 6–11.

Haycock, K. (2003, Winter). A new core curriculum for all: Aiming high for other people's children. *Thinking K–16, 7*(1), 1–2.

Haycock, K. (2004). Statement on the Harvard Civil Rights Project and Urban Institute Report on high school graduation rates and NCLB. Retrieved June 21, 2006, from www2.edtrust. org/EDTrust/Press+Room/harvard+project.htm

Haycock, K. (2005, January 25). Presentation to Joint Session of Idaho Senate and House Education Committees, Boise, ID.

Haycock, K., & Chenoweth, K. (2005). Choosing to make a difference. *American School Board Journal, 191*(4), 28–31.

Hecker, D. E. (2005, November). Employment outlook: 2004–14. *Monthly Labor Review, 128*(11), 70–101.

Henderson, A., & Mapp, K. (2002). *A new wave of evidence: The impact of school, family, and community connections on student achievement.* Austin, TX: Southwest Educational Development Laboratory.

Hendrie, C. (2005, January 5). Gates foundation expands support for early college high schools. *Education Week, 24*(16), 9.

Herman, R. [Project director.]. (1999). *An educator's guide to schoolwide reform* [Prepared by the American Institutes for Research]. Arlington, VA: Educational Research Service.

Hershberg, F. (2005, January). Presentation at the Boise Independent School District on value-added assessment, Boise, ID.

Hershberg, T., Simon, V. A., & Lea-Kruger, B. (2004, December). The revelations of value-added: An assessment model that measures student growth in ways that NCLB fails to do. *School Administrator, 61*(11), 10–13.

Hilliard, A. III. (1991, September). Do we have the will to educate all children? *Educational Leadership, 49*(1), 31–36.

Hoff, D. J. (2005, November 9). NY schools chief unveils achievement-gap agenda. *Education Week, 25*(11), 23.

Holcomb, E. L. (1999). *Getting excited about data: How to combine people, passion, and proof.* Thousand Oaks, CA: Corwin.

Howley, C., & Bickel, R. (2002, March). The influence of scale: Small schools make a big difference for children from poor families. *American School Board Journal, 189*(3), 28–30.

Idaho Department of Education. (2004). *Idaho reading indicator (IRI).* Retrieved June 21, 2006, from www.sde.state.id.us/IRI/default.asp

Improved access to rising tide of data is urged [Reporter's Notebook]. (2005, December 14). *Education Week, 14.*

Iowa Association of School Boards. (2000). IASB's Lighthouse study: School boards and student achievement. *Iowa School Board Compass, 5*(2). Retrieved July 5, 2006, from www.ia-sb.org/ studentachievement/Technicalreport2.pdf

J. A. and Kathryn Albertson Foundation. (2005, spring). *Idaho parent resource.* Boise, ID: Author.

Jackson, B., & Cooper, B. (1993). Involving parents in urban high schools. *Education Digest, 58*(8), 27–31.

Jacobs, H. H. (2004). *Getting results with curriculum mapping.* Alexandria, VA: ASCD.

Jagers, R. J., & Carroll, G. (2002). Issues in educating African American children and youth. In S. Stringfield and D. Land (Eds.), *Educating at-risk students* [Yearbook of National Society for the Study of Education, vol. 101, part 2] (pp. 49–65). Chicago: University of Chicago.

Jencks, C. (1972). *Inequality: A reassessment of the effect of family and schooling in America.* New York: Basic Books.

Jerald, C. D. (2001). *Dispelling the myth revisited: Preliminary findings from a nationwide analysis of "high-flying" schools* [Report]. Washington, DC: Education Trust.

Jerald, C. D. (2003, November). Keynote at the National Education Trust conference, Washington, DC.

Jerald, C. D. (2004, December). Creating high-performing schools [PowerPoint presentation]. Boise, ID.

Jones, R. (2001). How parents can support learning. *American School Board Journal 188*(9), 18–22.

Just for the Kids. (2006). Web site text. Retrieved July 7, 2006, from www.just4kids.org/jtfk/ index.cfm?st=US&loc=Educators

Kannapel, P. J., & Clements, S. K. (2005, February). *Inside the black box of high-performing, high-poverty schools: A report from the Prichard Committee for Academic Excellence.* Lexington, KY: Prichard Committee for Academic Excellence.

Karoly, L. A., Greenwood, P. W., Everingham, S. S., Hoube, J., Kilburn, M. R., Rydell, C. P., et al. (1998). *Investing in our children: What we know and don't know about the costs and benefits of early childhood interventions.* Santa Monica, CA: RAND.

Kelly, P. P. (2006). *Educational neglect and compulsory schooling in Idaho.* Boise, ID: Boise State University, Center for School Improvement and Policy Studies, College of Education.

King, J. (2004, February 23). Paige calls NEA "terrorist organization." *CNN Washington Bureau.* Retrieved July 6, 2006, from www.cnn.com/2004/EDUCATION/02/23/paige.terrorist.nea

Kitchen, R., DePree, J., Celedón-Pattichis, S., & Brinkerhoff, J. (2004). *High achieving schools initiative final report.* Albuquerque: University of New Mexico. Retrieved June 20, 2006, from www.unm.edu/~jbrink/HASchools/hp_final_report2.pdf

Klein, D. (2000, August). High achievement in mathematics: Lessons from three Los Angeles Elementary Schools. [Paper commissioned by the Brookings Institution.] Retrieved July 21, 2006, from www.csun.edu/~vcmth00m/brookings.pdf

Klopfenstein, K. (2004, December 12). The Advanced Placement expansion of the 1990s: How did traditionally underserved students fare? *Education Policy Analysis Archives, 12*(68). Retrieved June 21, 2006, from epaa.asu.edu/epaa/v12n68

Kohl, H. (1994). *"I won't learn from you" and other thoughts on creative maladjustment*. New York: New Press.

Kohn, A. (2000). *The case against standardized testing: Raising the scores, ruining the schools*. Portsmouth, NH: Heinemann.

Kozol, J. (1967). *Death at an early age: The destruction of the hearts and minds of Negro children in the Boston public schools*. Boston: Houghton Mifflin.

Kozol, J. (1991). *Savage inequalities: Children in America's schools*. New York: Crown.

Kozol, J. (2005). *The shame of the nation: The restoration of apartheid schooling in America*. New York: Crown.

Krovetz, M. L. (1999). *Fostering resiliency: Expecting all students to use their minds and hearts well*. Thousand Oaks, CA: Corwin.

Kuykendall, C. (1992). *From rage to hope: Strategies for reclaiming Black and Hispanic students*. Bloomington, IN: Solution Tree (formerly National Educational Service).

Ladson-Billings, G. (1994). *The dreamkeepers: Successful teachers of African-American children*. San Francisco: Jossey-Bass.

Land, D., & Legters, N. (2002). The extent and consequences of risk in U.S. education. In S. Stringfield & D. Land (Eds.), *Educating at-risk students* [Yearbook of National Society for the Study of Education, vol. 101, part 2] (pp. 1–28). Chicago: University of Chicago.

Latinos in schools: Some facts and findings. (2001). Washington, DC: White House Initiative on Educational Excellence for Hispanic Americans. (ERIC Document Reproduction Service No. ED449288)

Learning In Deed. (2006). Frequently asked questions about Learning In Deed and service learning. Retrieved June 29, 2006, from www.learningindeed.org/news/faq.html

Learning Point Associates. (2004). *All students reaching the top: Strategies for closing academic achievement gaps*. Naperville, IL: North Central Regional Educational Laboratory.

Levin, M. (2005, December). *Disciplinary alternative education programs: What is and what should be* [Policy brief]. Austin, TX: Texas Public Policy Foundation. Retrieved July 6, 2006, from www.texaspolicy.com/pdf/2005-12-DAEPs-pb.pdf

Levin, M. (2006, March) *Schooling a new class of criminals? Better disciplinary alternatives for Texas students* [Policy perspective]. Austin, TX: Texas Public Policy Foundation. Retrieved July 6, 2006, from www.texaspolicy.com/pdf/2006-03-PP-DAEP-ml.pdf

Levine, D. U., & Lezotte, L. W. (1990). *Unusually effective schools: A review and analysis of research and practice*. Madison, WI: National Center for Effective Schools Research and Development. (ERIC Document Reproduction Service No. ED330032)

Lewis, B. A. (1995). *The kid's guide to service projects: Over 500 service ideas for young people who want to make a difference*. Minneapolis, MN: Free Spirit.

Lewis, C. (2002). *Lesson study: A handbook for teacher-led improvement of instruction*. Philadelphia, PA: Research for Better Schools.

Loveless, T. (1998). The tracking and ability grouping debate. *Fordham Report, 2*(8). Washington, DC: Thomas B. Fordham Foundation. Retrieved June 21, 2006, from www.edexcellence.net/library/track.html

MacIver, D., & Balfanz, R. (2000). The school district's role in helping high-poverty schools become high performing. In Mid-continent Research for Education and Learning (Ed.), *Including at-risk students in standards-based reform: A report on McREL's diversity roundtable II* (pp. 35–69). Aurora, CO: Author.

Makkonen, R. (2004). Teaching migrant students: Lessons from successful districts. In M. Sadowski (Ed.), *Teaching immigrant and second-language students: Strategies for success* (pp.77–84). Cambridge, MA: Harvard University.

Manset, G., St. John, E., Simmons, A., Musoba, G., Gordon, D., & Chung, C. (2000). *Wisconsin's High Performing, High Poverty Schools.* Napierville, IL: North Central Regional Educational Laboratory.

Marzano, R. J., Pickering, D. J., & Pollock, J. E. (2001). *Classroom instruction that works: Researched-based strategies for increasing student achievement.* Alexandria, VA: Association for Supervision and Curriculum Development.

Marzano, R. J., Waters, T., & McNulty, B. A. (2005). *School leadership that works: From research to results.* Alexandria, VA: Association for Supervision and Curriculum Development.

Massell, D. (2000, September). *The district role in building capacity: Four strategies* [Policy brief RB-32]. Philadelphia: University of Pennsylvania, Consortium for Policy Research in Education.

McCombs, J. S., Kirby, S. N., Barney, H., Darilek, H., & Magee, S. J. (2004). *Achieving state and national literacy goals, a long uphill road: A report to Carnegie Corporation of New York.* Santa Monica, CA: RAND.

McGee, G. W. (2004). Closing the achievement gap: Lessons from Illinois' Golden Spike high-poverty high-performing schools. *Journal of Education for Students Placed at Risk, 9*(2), 97–125.

Meier, D., & Wood, G. (2004). *Many children left behind.* Boston: Beacon.

Meyerson, A. (2000). *Low-income schools that work.* Retrieved June 21, 2006, from www.heritage.org/Press/Commentary/ED042700.cfm

Monroe, L. (1997). *Nothing's impossible.* New York: Random House.

Morley, R. (2004, November). Breakout session: Iowa Lighthouse Study, Sioux Center School District. First in the Nation in Education Foundation annual conference, Des Moines, IA.

Murphy, C. and Lick, D. (2001). *Whole-faculty study groups: Creating student-based professional development* (2nd ed.). Thousand Oaks, CA: Corwin.

Nathan, J. (1989, July). Before adopting school choice, review what works and what fails. *American School Board Journal, 176*(7), 28–30.

Nathan, J. (1996). *Charter schools: Creating hope and opportunity for American education.* San Francisco: Jossey-Bass.

Nathan, J., & Johnson, N. (2000, December). *What should we do? A practical guide to assessment and accountability in schools.* Minneapolis: University of Minnesota, Hubert H. Humphrey Institute of Public Affairs.

National Association of Secondary School Principals. (NASSP). (1996). Breaking ranks: Changing an American institution. A report of the NASSP on the high school of the 21st century. *NASSP Bulletin, 80*(578), 55–66.

National Center for Children in Poverty. (2004). *Low-income children in the United States.* Retrieved June 21, 2006, from www.nccp.org/pub_cpf04.html

National Center for Education Statistics. (2002). *Yearly income based on educational level.* Washington, DC: U.S. Department of Education, Office of Educational Research and Improvement.

National Center for Educational Accountability. (2006). *School improvement service 1.0: Benchmark practices to high-performing school systems [Step 2, Inspire].* Denver, CO: Author.

National Commission on the High School Senior Year. (2001, January). *The lost opportunity of senior year: Finding a better way* [Preliminary report]. Washington, DC: Author. Retrieved July 6, 2006, from www.nps.k12.va.us/aaa/CIA/lostop/Senior_Year_Report_Final.pdf

National Education Association. (2006). *Special education and the Individuals With Disabilities Education Act.* Washington, DC: Author. Retrieved June 29, 2006, from www.nea.org/specialed/index.html

National Parent Teacher Association. (1998). *National standards for parent/family involvement programs.* Chicago, IL: Author.

Newmann, F. M., Smith, B., Allensworth, E., & Bryk, A. (2001). *School instructional coherence: Benefits and challenges.* Chicago, IL: Consortium on Chicago School Research.

No Child Left Behind Act, 20 U. S. C. § 6301 (2002).

Northwest Regional Educational Laboratory. (1998). *Easy ways for families to help children learn.* Portland, OR: Author.

Ogbu, J. U. (1992). Understanding cultural diversity and learning. *Educational Researcher, 21*(8), 5–14, 24.

Olsen, L. (2005). Sleuths seek secrets of high-flying schools. *Education Week, 24*(34), 24–25.

Olson, A. (2002, December). PowerPoint presentation at the Creating High-Performance Schools Conference, Boise, ID.

Padrón, Y. N., Waxman, H. C., & Rivera, H. H. (2002, August). *Educating Hispanic students: Effective instructional practices (Practioner Brief #5).* Santa Cruz: University of California, Center for Research on Education, Diversity, & Excellence. Retrieved June 21, 2006, from www.cal.org/crede/Pubs/PracBrief5.htm

Parnell, D. (1985). *The neglected majority.* Washington, DC: Community College Press.

Parrett, W. H. (2005, January). Against all odds: Reversing low achievement of one school's Native American students. *School Administrator, 62*(1), 26–29.

Paulson, A. (2004, September 21). Chicago hope: "Maybe *this* will work." *Christian Science Monitor.* Retrieved July 18, 2006, from www.csmonitor.com/2004/0921/p11s01-legn.html

Payne, R. K. (2001). *A framework for understanding poverty.* Highland, TX: aha! Process.

Perkins-Gough, D. (2006, February). Accelerating the learning of low achievers. *Educational Leadership, 63*(5), 88–89.

Peters, T. (1987). *Thriving on chaos: Handbook for a management revolution.* New York: Knopf.

Public Education Network. (2004). *The status of state implementation of NCLB requirements.* Retrieved July 6, 2006, from www.ecs.org/html/Special/NCLB/ReportToTheNation/docs/Appendix_B.pdf

Ray-Taylor, R. (2005, January). Lessons learned about the achievement gap. *School Administrator, 62*(1), 12–13.

Reeves, D. B. (2003). *High performance in high poverty schools: 90/90/90 and beyond.* Englewood, CO: Center for Performance Assessment.

Rice, R., et al. (2000, October). *The Lighthouse Inquiry: School board/superintendent team behaviors in school districts with extreme differences in student achievement.* Atlanta, GA: National Faculty of Education.

Richards, A. (2005, January 5). Passions high as S.C. finance case comes to a close. *Education Week, 24*(16), 19, 22.

Richardson, J. (2003, February). The secrets of 'can-do' schools: Louisiana team uncovers traits of high-poverty, high-performing schools. *Results.* Retrieved June 20, 2006, from www.nsdc. org/library/publications/results

Richardson, J. (2005, December/January). Study groups lift Missouri districts' teachers, principals, and students. *Results.* Retrieved June 21, 2006, from www.nsdc.org/library/ publications/results/res12–04rich.cfm

Rogers, M. (1994). *Resolving conflict through mediation.* Clemson, SC: National Dropout Prevention Center.

Rose, L., and Gallup, A. M. (2004, September). 36th annual Phi Delta Kappan/Gallup poll of the public's attitude toward the public schools. *Phi Delta Kappan,* 41–56. Retrieved June 29, 200,6 from www.pdkintl.org/kappan/k0409pol.htm

Sadowski, M. (Ed.). (2004). *Teaching immigrant and second-language students.* Cambridge, MA: Harvard University.

Sagor, R. (2005). *The action research guidebook: A four-step process for educators and school teams.* Thousand Oaks, CA: Corwin.

Sanders, M. G. (1996). *School-family-community partnerships and the academic achievement of African American, urban adolescents* (Report #7). Baltimore, MD: Center for Research on the Education of Students Placed At-Risk. (ERIC Document Reproduction Service No. ED402404)

Sanders, W. L., & Rivers, J. C. (1996). *Cumulative and residual effects of teachers on future student academic achievement.* Knoxville: University of Tennessee, Value-Added Research and Assessment Center.

Santos, M. G. (2004). Raising the achievement of English-language learners: How principals can make a difference. In M. Sadowski (Ed.), *Teaching immigrant and second-language students* (pp. 85–94). Cambridge, MA: Harvard University.

Sarason, S. B. (1971). *The culture of the school and the problem of change.* Boston: Allyn & Bacon.

Schargel, F., & Smink, J. (2001). *Strategies to help solve our school dropout problem.* Larchmont, NY: Eye on Education.

Schiller, E., Fritts, J., Bobronnikov, E., Fiore, T., O'Reilly, F., & St. Pierre, R. (2006, April). *Volume I: The SLIIDEA Sourcebook Report (1999–2000, 2002–2003, 2003–2004, and 2004–2005 School Years).* Bethesda, MD: ABT Associates.

Schmoker, M. (1999). *Results: The key to continuous improvement.* Alexandria, VA: Association for Supervision and Curriculum Development.

Schmoker, M. (2004, November). Start here for improving teaching and learning. *School Administrator, 11*(60), 48–49.

Search Institute. (1999). *Pass it on.* Minneapolis, MN: Author.

Shepard, L. A., & Smith, M. L. (1990). Synthesis of research on grade retention. *Educational Leadership, 47*(8), 84–88.

Shields, C. J. (2004). District profile: Dropping the dropout rate. *District Administration.* Retrieved June 21, 2006, from http://www.districtadministration.com/page.cfm?p=866

Shorr, L. B. (with Schorr, D.). (1989). *Within our reach: Breaking the cycle of disadvantage.* New York: Anchor Books.

Silberman, C. E. (1970). *Crisis in the classroom.* New York: Random House.

Simon Youth Foundation. (2001). *Simon Youth Foundation 2001 Annual Report.* Indianapolis, IN: Author.

Slavin, R. E. (1995). Detracking and its detractors: Flawed evidence, flawed values. *Phi Delta Kappan, 77*(3), 220–221.

Slavin, R. E. and Madden, N. A. (1989). What works for students at risk: A research synthesis. *Educational Leadership, 46*(5), 4–13.

Smith, E. (2003, November). Keynote speech "Leadership for Excellence," Education Trust annual conference, Washington, DC.

Smith, G. R., Gregory, T. B, & Pugh, R. C. (1981). Meeting student needs: Evidence for the superiority of alternative schools. *Phi Delta Kappan, 62*(8), 561–564.

Smith, R. (2005, January). Saving black boys. *School Administrator, 62*(1), 16–25.

Sparks, D. (2000, Summer). Low incomes, high hurdles: An interview with Kati Haycock. *Journal of Staff Development, 21*(3) 37–40.

Spellings, M. (2005, September 29). Statement at the hearing on "Closing the Achievement Gap in American Schools: The No Child Left Behind Act." Retrieved June 29, 2006, from edworkforce.house.gov/hearings/109th/fc/spellingsnclb092905/spellings.htm

Squires, D. A. (2005). *Aligning and balancing the standards-based curriculum.* Thousand Oaks, CA: Corwin.

Stiggins, R. L. (1999). Teams. *Journal of Staff Development, 20*(3), 17–19.

Stiggins, R. L. (2001). *Student-involved classroom assessment.* Upper Saddle River, NJ: Prentice Hall.

Stiggins, R., Arter, J., Chappuis, S., & Chappuis, J. (2004). *Classroom assessment* for *student learning: Doing it right—using it well.* Portland, OR: ETS Assessment Training Institute.

Stiggins, R., & Chappuis, J. (2006, Winter). What a difference a word makes. *Journal of Staff Development, 27*(1) 10–14.

Stigler, J. W., and Hiebert, J. (1999). *The teaching gap: Best ideas from the world's teachers for improving education in the classroom.* New York: Free Press.

Swanson, C. B. (2004, July 28). The new math on graduation rates. *Education Week, 24*(43), 30–31.

Taylor, B. O. (2002, January). The effective schools process: Alive and well. *Phi Delta Kappan, 83*(5), 375.

Teddlie, C., & Stringfield, S. (1993). *Schools make a difference: Lessons learned from a ten-year study of school effects.* New York: Teachers College.

Thernstrom, A. M., & Thernstrom, S. (2003). *No excuses: Closing the racial gap in learning.* New York: Simon and Schuster.

Togneri, W., & Anderson, S. E. (2003). *Beyond islands of excellence: What districts can do to improve instruction and achievement in all schools.* Alexandria, VA: Association for Supervision and Curriculum Development. Retrieved June 20, 2006 from www.learningfirst.org/publications/districts

Tomlinson, C. (1999). *The differentiated classroom: Responding to the needs of all learners.* Alexandria, VA: Association for Supervision and Curriculum Development.

Tomlinson, C. (2001). *How to differentiate instruction in mixed-ability classrooms.* Alexandria, VA: Association for Supervision and Curriculum Development.

U. S. Census Bureau. (2005). *2004 American community survey.* Washington, DC: Author.

U. S. Department of Commerce. (1999). *Statistical abstract of the United States 1998.* Pittsburgh, PA: U. S. Census Bureau.

U. S. Department of Education. (2001). *The longitudinal evaluation of school change and performance (LESCP) in Title I schools.* Washington, DC: Author.

U. S. Department of Labor. (2000). *New jobs require greater education and skills.* Washington, DC: Author.

Ulichny, P. (2000). *Academic achievement in two Expeditionary Learning Outward Bound Demonstration schools.* Retrieved June 21, 2006, from /www.elschools.org/results/success/Ulichny.pdf

Veale, J. R., Morley, R. E., Erickson, C. L., & Dryfoos, J. (2001). *Practical evaluation for collaborative services: Goals, processes, tools and reporting-systems for school-based programs.* Thousand Oaks, CA: Corwin.

Viadero, D. (2004, January 21). Achievement-gap study emphasizes better use of data. *Education Week, 23*(19), 9.

Wagner, T. (2002). *Making the grade: Reinventing America's schools.* New York: RoutledgeFalmer.

Wasik, B., & Slavin, R. E. (1993). Preventing early reading failure with one-to-one tutoring: A review of five programs. *Reading Research Quarterly, 28*(2), 179–200.

Waters, J. T., Marzano, R. J., & McNulty, B. A. (2003). *Balanced leadership: What 30 years of research tells us about the effect of leadership on student achievement.* Aurora, CO: Mid-continent Research for Education and Learning.

Wayman, J. C. (2005). Guest editor's introduction. *Journal of Education for Students Placed at Risk, 10,* 235–239.

Wehlage, G., Rutter, R., Smith, G., Lesko, N., & Fernandez, R. (1989). *Reducing the risk: Schools as community support.* New York: Falmer.

Weinstein, R. S. (2002). *Reaching higher: The power of expectations in schooling.* Cambridge, MA: Harvard University.

Weston, S. P. (1999). *Performance and poverty 1999* [Report]. Lexington, KY: Prichard Committee for Academic Excellence.

Wheelock, A. (1992). *Crossing the tracks: How "untracking" can save America's schools.* New York: New Press.

White, K. A. (1999, May). High poverty schools score big on Kentucky assessment. *Education Week, 18*(34), 18.

Williams, T., Kirst, M., & Haertel, E., et al. (2005). *Similar students, different results: Why do some schools do better? A large-scale survey of California elementary schools serving low-income students.* Mountain View, CA: EdSource.

Wright, S. P., Horn, S. P., & Sanders, W. L. (1997). Teacher and classroom context effects on student achievement: Implications for teacher evaluation. *Journal of Personnel Evaluation in Education, 11*(1), 57–67.

Yap, K. O., & Enoki, D. Y. (1995). In search of the elusive magic bullet: Parental involvement and student outcomes. *School Community Journal, 5*(2), 97–106.

Electronic Resources

Accelerated Schools PLUS (AS PLUS), www.acceleratedschools.net

Alaska Council on Economic Education (ACEE), www.cee.alaska.edu/acee.asp

American Association of School Administrators (AASA), www.aasa.org

American Federation of Teachers (AFT), www.aft.org

Association for Supervision and Curriculum Development (ASCD), www.ascd.org

Bill & Melinda Gates Foundation, www.gatesfoundation.org

Breakthrough to Literacy, www.breakthroughtoliteracy.com

California Education Alliance (CEA), www.unitedpurpose.org

Center for Civic Innovation at the Manhattan Institute (CCI), www.manhattan- institute.org/
    html/cci.htm

Center for Performance Assessment, www.makingstandardswork.com

Center for Policy Research (CPR), www-cpr.maxwell.syr.edu

Center for Research on the Education of Students Placed At Risk (CRESPAR), www.csos.jhu.
    edu/crespar

Center for School Improvement and Policy Studies (CSI & PS), csi.boisestate.edu

Center for the Study of Reading (CSR), csr.ed.uiuc.edu

Center on Education Policy (CEP), www.cep-dc.org

Center on School, Family, and Community Partnerships, www.csos.jhu.edu/p2000/center.htm

Children's Defense Fund (CDF), www.childrensdefense.org

Coalition of Essential Schools (CES), www.essentialschools.org

Comer School Development Program (Comer SDP), www.med.yale.edu/comer

Consortium for Policy Research in Education (CPRE), www.cpre.org

Council of Chief State School Officers (CCSSO), www.ccsso.org

EdSource, www.edsource.org

Education Commission of the States (ECS), www.ecs.org

Education Resources Information Center (ERIC), www.eric.ed.gov

Education Trust, www2.edtrust.org

ETS Assessment Training Institute, www.ets.org/ati

Expeditionary Learning Schools Outward Bound (ELS), www.elob.org

GreatSchools.net, www.greatschools.net

Heritage Foundation, www.heritage.org

High Schools That Work (HSTW), www.sreb.org/Programs/hstw/hstwindex.asp

High/Scope Educational Research Foundation, www.highscope.org

HOSTS Learning, www.hosts.com

Houston Public Schools, www.houston-texas-online.com/htoeducation.html

Idaho Association of Commerce and Industry (IACI), www.iaci.org

Illinois State Board of Education (ISBE), www.isbe.state.il.us

International Reading Association (IRA), www.reading.org/association/index.html

Iowa Association of School Boards (IASB), www.ia-sb.org

J.A. and Kathryn Albertson Foundation, www.jkaf.org

Jefferson County Public Schools, Louisville, Kentucky, www.jefferson.k12.ky.us

Just for the Kids/National Center for Educational Accountability, www.just4kids.org

Learning First Alliance, www.learningfirst.org

LessonLab, www.lessonlab.com

Louisiana Staff Development Council, www.lsdc.org

Mercatus Center at George Mason University, www.mercatus.org

Mid-continent Research for Education and Learning (McREL), www.mcrel.org

National Association of Secondary School Principals (NASSP), www.principals.org

National Board for Professional Teaching Standards (NBPTS), www.nbpts.org

National Center for Children in Poverty (NCCP), www.nccp.org

National Center for Education Statistics (NCES), nces.ed.gov

National Center for Educational Accountability (NCEA), www.nc4ea.org

National Dropout Prevention Center/Network (NDPC/N), www.dropoutprevention.org/ndpcdefault.htm

National Education Association (NEA), www.nea.org

National Institute for Direct Instruction (NIFDI), www.nifdi.org

National Network of Partnership Schools (NNPS), www.partnershipschools.org

National Parent Teacher Association (National PTA), www.pta.org

National School Boards Association (NSBA), www.nsba.org

National Staff Development Council (NSDC), www.nsdc.org

North Central Regional Educational Laboratory (NCREL), www.ncrel.org

Northern Illinois University Regional Development Institute (RDI), www.cgsniu.org

Phi Delta Kappa International (PDK International), www.pdkintl.org

Prichard Committee for Academic Excellence, www.prichardcommittee.org

QuickReads, www.quickreads.org

Read Naturally, www.readnaturally.com

Reading First, www.ed.gov/programs/readingfirst

Reading Recovery Council of North America (RRCNA), www.readingrecovery.org

Schools to Watch, www.schoolstowatch.org

Science Research Associates (SRA), www.sraonline.com

Search Institute, www.search-institute.org

Sheltered Instruction Observation Protocol (SIOP), www.siopinstitute.net

Simon Youth Foundation (SYF), syf.simon.com

Sopris West Educational Services, www.sopriswest.com

Southern Regional Education Board (SREB), www.sreb.org

Southwest Educational Development Laboratory (SEDL), www.sedl.org

Success for All Foundation (SFAF), www.successforall.net

Teachscape, www.teachscape.com

Texas Public Policy Foundation (TPPF), www.texaspolicy.com

Urban Institute, www.urban.org

U.S. Department of Education (ED), www.ed.gov

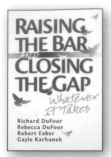

Raising the Bar and Closing the Gap
Whatever It Takes
Richard DuFour, Rebecca DuFour, Robert Eaker, and Gayle Karhanek
This sequel to the best-selling *Whatever It Takes: How Professional Learning Communities Respond When Kids Don't Learn* expands on original ideas and presses further with new insights. Foundational concepts combine with real-life examples of schools throughout North America that have gone from traditional cultures to PLCs. **BKF378**

Learning by Doing
A Handbook for Professional Learning Communities at Work™
Richard DuFour, Rebecca DuFour, Robert Eaker, and Thomas Many
The second edition of *Learning by Doing* is an action guide for closing the knowing-doing gap and transforming schools into PLCs. It also includes seven major additions that equip educators with essential tools for confronting challenges. **BKF416**

The Handbook for SMART School Teams
Anne Conzemius and Jan O'Neill
Learn what makes a school team SMART and how you can collaborate to achieve positive results. This practical, engaging handbook shares best practices essential to building a solid network of support. **BKF115**

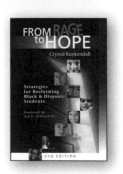

Reclaiming Youth at Risk: Our Hope for the Future
Larry K. Brendtro, Martin Brokenleg, and Steve Van Bockern
This set of three 20-minute DVDs plus a facilitator's guide illustrates effective ways to improve interaction with youth at risk and their families by exploring real schools and residential treatment centers. Learn strategies based on a compelling combination of Native American philosophies and Western psychology. **DVF011**

From Rage to Hope: Strategies for Reclaiming Black & Hispanic Students
Crystal Kuykendall
Foreword by Asa G. Hilliard III
Now in its second edition, this book provides an authentic view of academic underachievement, apathy, and rage among America's Black and Hispanic youth. Become an empowered Merchant of Hope armed with positive strategies for reaching these students and sparking motivation toward achievement. **BKF157**

Solution Tree | Press

a division of
Solution Tree

Visit solution-tree.com or call 800.733.6786 to order.